TRUMPET RHAPSODIES

TRUMPET RHAPSODIES
Collected Nonfiction 1954-1981

§

*A Set of Inventions and Revisions
Based on Magazine Articles
First Published in the Sixties and Seventies
and Now Every Word Improved
in a Self-Portrait
Showing the Author's Recovery
from the Illness of Youth
and Meant to Be Read
from First Page to Last as
an Autobiographical Novel*

§

DONALD NEWLOVE

TOUGH POETS PRESS
ARLINGTON, MASSACHUSETTS

Copyright © 1966, 1969, 1970, 1971, 1973, 1974, 1975, 1977, 1981, 2014 by Donald Newlove.

Copyright © 2024 by Tough Poets Press.

Acknowledgment is made to the following publications in which the works included in this volume first appeared: *Esquire, Evergreen Review, New York Magazine, The Realist, The Village Voice, Viva,* and *WIN Magazine.*

ISBN 979-8-218-50979-8
Tough Poets Press
Arlington, Massachusetts 02476
U.S.A.

www.toughpoets.com

Author's Note

This is a kind of autobiography of my early days as a writer and of my search for a language that trumpeted my youth. All texts have been revamped with inventions and variations that amount to rhapsodies on the original versions to show with improved art my life as a magazine writer in the Sixties and Seventies. The story "Taps," written sixty years ago, has never before seen print.

—DN, 2014

For Nancy
Ageless Starlight

Contents

Taps 9
Prothalamion for Wet Harmonica and Johnny Stompanato . . 26
The GLP Arrives! 53
Dinner With the Lowells 81
Trumpet. 120
The Black Eye 151
Princes of the Switchblade: Trembling on the Street 170
Getting Unpickled 175
Two Lines a Day 184
I've Got a Right to Fish the Blues 188
Those Havana-Chinatown Blues 200
Review of *Dog Soldiers* 207
A Fantastic Journey Into the Psychic Frontier 211
The Beast in the Strand Book Store 231
Rhapsody for Drunkspeare 245

Acknowledgments 253

Taps
Previously unpublished, 1954

The public information officer in charge of the base newspaper barges into my office, his blue eyes marbled with bad news.

"Sheldon Katz bought the farm."

First Lieutenant Sheldon Katz, a Jewish jet pilot, has just plastered his brains against a fence on a frozen New Jersey pasture. In sunlight of brightest steel.

I stiffen over my typewriter. This story will not lead my next issue of *Fighter Scope*. We don't print downers in the base newspaper. No photograph of the crash site, or of the honor guard at Katz's funeral—or of Katz himself. Sheldon Katz has sped off the planet. I sit shocked and stifled as horror fills my office with a terrible light. But the heart soldiers on—if on thin ice.

I soon find that Sheldon Katz comes from nearby Philadelphia and—going by Jewish custom—his funeral will be held tomorrow in the dead of winter at a Philadelphia cemetery. What's more, the bandmaster of the base band picks me to play Taps at the funeral. It's not a duty I can get out of. Our band has four trumpets and the other three—who work on the flight line—can't be spared for a day off in a Philadelphia graveyard. Next morning I find myself on a base bus bound for funeral duty with the honor guard.

On the bus I'm calm. No worries, my trumpet case beside me, the countryside frozen sunlight. An icy morning Sheldon Katz will never see. I'll not get a chance to warm up my lip at the cemetery, so I keep my mouthpiece in a pants pocket for body heat. And I can't stand around those mourners and play scales or even practice with my mute. I have to hit that first note dead on and let the blood fill my lip and turn the notes to cat fur—to silver—to sorrow. I gather my spirit. I must be fearless.

But how can it be that an amateur—a less-than-amateur—is sent out to do a real musician's job? Or a real bugler's? Only because the base commander got a bug in his brain about a base band. But why should airmen even be out marching? We're not infantry. Pointless! I light a cigarette and open the gospels as shorn of miracle and translated by Tolstoy—from the Greek into Russian, and then into English by his close friends Louise and Aylmer Maude. Jesus, the revolutionary. Turn thy cheek—I die for your sins—and later, you shall be washed in the blood of the lamb—that's not Jewish. But through cigarette smoke, Tolstoy's Christ moves me. I'm a humanist Christian like Tolstoy but still see Christians as bland and lily-livered, narrow-minded sectarians. How did sexless Christianity stem from a ballsy Judaism? From Solomon with 700 wives and 300 concubines and writing Thy two breasts are like two young roes that are twins, which feed among the lilies?

I've never had a horn lesson worth talking about and can barely read more than "Star Dust" or my Louis Armstrong transcriptions. I stumble on scales in four flats or sharps. That I'm even in the base band is a fluke. One day the base commander orders all 201 files combed for musicians and my little note under hobbies—"play the trumpet"—lands me in the declared-from-God base band along with a bunch of musical goofs much like me. All must attend rehearsals and play—no exceptions. Three afternoons a week we rehearse "The Washington Post March" and other Sousa specials in the base theater, much to the agony of our gay bandmaster, a staff sergeant who reads music better than the rest of us. Saturday mornings we lead a base parade on the flight line. Pennants whipping, we sound like a Scottish regiment—more bagpipes than brass and reeds—and as I march my mouthpiece beats my lips fat as beestings. Now I'm to play at an Air Force funeral. I'm trusting but this is my virgin Taps for the dead. Be it in Philadelphia or at Arlington National Cemetery on Armistice Day, be my heart strong and spirit a tall ship, I fear an uncertain sound. No falling snow, only brilliant glare on the icy countryside. This two-hour ride goes direct to the gravesite where we will drape the coffin and perform our duties. The bus chokes us with stuffy heat and my blues smell sweaty. Through brain-tightening nicotine I read Tolstoy for strength.

So, First Lieutenant Sheldon Katz, twenty-two, Jewish. What is a Jew? I know they worship in a temple and believe in the Old Testament. Fine by me. Back home in Jamestown, I know only Jews like the beautiful Lasser twins who differ from Lutherans or Catholics simply by a Sephardic smoothness of face. Although they do have the Holocaust and a kind of secret history one never mentions. Nearby Buffalo had 500,000 people and I would sit in the James Prendergast Library thinking of the people of twelve cities big as Buffalo being murdered by Hitler and plowed into mass graves or burned to ash. Hard to imagine! Having read Laura Z. Hobson's best-seller about anti-Semitism, I know that being a Jew also means rising above defaming prejudices about Jews and money and Jews and movies, and means as well those gentlemen's agreements that bar Jews from certain resort hotels and from buying certain property. All very un-American—which raises my ire. So Jews are clannish. What's wrong with that? And, yes, many Jews are wealthy, but even more live in hovels on New York's Lower East Side and slave at sewing machines in sweatshops and were but lately bottom dogs among the immigrants. My strongest feelings about Jews spring from the Constitution and the Bill of Rights. America's Jews deserve to pursue happiness as much as do its Swedes or Irish. My jaw clenches thinking about it.

But everything leading up to this funeral duty underscores

a lack of passion—a coolness on my part. Even in marriage, all I know about passion comes from books. Packed into my footlocker is my carry-around college while in the Air Force: 22 hardcover and pocket-size India-paper volumes of *The Oxford World Classics Complete Works of Leo Tolstoy*—which I've been reading for four years. All my passion comes from Tolstoy—my sense of God, art, family, morality, and the ties that bind. I'm secondhand, my spirit a ragbag of feelings from his family novels and tales of peasants in agony and horses having their throats cut by the knacker. My wife says she never knows what I'm thinking. How could she? I edit my every thought for writerliness. I'm not human. I'm a ribbon of ink.

I close my Tolstoy. See Sheldon Katz's still milk-fed cheeks.

All right, the Jews believe in Jehovah, an ever-thundering and angry Old Testament God who has plenty of time amid the trillions of stars and planets to part the Red Sea and promise his Chosen a Messiah. If that isn't self-delusion and a con game. Does he tyrannize all life in the universe as he does the Jews? Does he give the fish-people of some far, far Venus the Ten Commandments and smack their fins for idolatry—thrash them for the big fish-people eating the little fish-people—and warn that they'll go to Gehenna for their fish-sins and fish-incest? Is their Jehovah a fish-Jehovah in their own image? Do their cold seawater hearts burst into flame on Holy Days? And does he demand that each fish-man always see himself as a sinner and ashamed? *Guilt! Guilt!* Jehovah's lifeblood thrives on guilt. This devil feeds on his followers' guilt. Then he sends to Venus a fish-Christ to make every finny guilt doubly clear and intense. *Sinners! Vipers! Whoremongers! Curse all moneychangers in my fish-father's temple!* And you liars, murderers and fornicators, shape up and curb your foul desires. Yes, even on Venus, does a passion for higher being lead the spirit into the paths of righteousness while I, Staff Sergeant Newlove, here at McGuire Air Force Base, have become a voluptuary of the chow line, a libertine of the NCO Club—and flourish among the wicked and foul-mouthed.

But time betrays me and each man into hunger for a higher belief—a state beyond the bitter aftertaste of pleasure and wantonness—something above absence of belief and the empty echo when I say God. The cynic and the skeptic are incomplete men, while the agnostic stifles on his half-breath of hollow disbelief. No tiny sips for me! I want the full glass! So I renounce all banal beliefs, but replace them only with a feast of great prose—a spiritual life as revealed by Tolstoy and Shaw, bolstered by a queer longing for vegetarianism like theirs as a form of religion—some regimen past butchery and animal slaughter. Perhaps Buddhism is the way—but which of the four paths of Buddhism? And must I still wear cowhide on my feet? The Air Force frowns on rubber flip-flops and wooden clogs. Will my Lutheran wife even go along with my rebirth as family-abandoning Siddhartha in her house and bed? Will she love her Buddha over the cornflakes? Or over cottage cheese and blueberries—dimly a more spiritual breakfast than cereal? In her own way, whether she knows it or not, she lives in a world founded on bloodshed—and will defend it! Should I, like Gandhi—another Tolstoyan vegetarian—espouse passive resistance to wickedness and deplore animal slaughter, all that frying and sizzling and baking of carcasses? Christ and Gandhi aren't mere poets, they're martyrs. There's something weirdly attractive about martyrdom, something antisocial but communal, like becoming a spiritual Leftist—a Commie waving a Red flag for God. Half of me shouts about religion, *"None of it! none of it!"*—and half cries for a structure of spiritual action. I hunger for a holy place within me, a place to keep bright and clean and where God will be happy to visit. I hunger for a Sabbath, not the listless Sunday-morning cigarette-befouled barracks I've known for years. I hunger for an altar on which to sacrifice and purify—sacrifice *what* I don't know. But I do know the hunger that leads me to this swept and raised place, a place within where I might replenish my spirit, give over my sins and misdeeds and find refreshment, and where *Parsifal*'s Good Friday music can cast its spell, or Wagnerian church chords speed Lohengrin to his destiny on a white swan. As I think these things, do I see them someday mine? Can I strip my heart naked and wander the world as a holy fool? *Wake, wake, Staff Sergeant Newlove.* Turn this corner and find some small loaf and a few fishes to feed on forever, your portion of grace, and let your clouds be cleared by the sun. Let the Absolute shine through you, heat and stroke you, teach you the right path. Surrender! Greet without alcohol whatever angel may come. Wash your hands of falsehood. Prepare the way of the Lord into your being. Trust in the Divine Presence.

I have long fugues on stuff like this. Not on sex but on a whole-body hunger to break through gray-mindedness and the terrible materiality of the earth about me.

I slip the gospels according to Tolstoy into my trumpet case and take out his *A Confession*, where he tells of the passionate, even suicidal battle in him between reason and faith:

> My position was terrible. I knew I could find nothing along the path of reasonable knowledge except a denial of life; and there—in faith—was nothing but a denial of reason, which was yet more impossible for me than a denial of life. From rational knowledge it appeared that life is an evil, people know this and it is in their power to end life; yet they lived and still live, and I myself live, though I have long known that life is senseless and an evil. By faith it appears that in order to understand the meaning of life I must renounce my reason, the very thing for which alone a meaning is required.

Yes, these spiritual battles and contrivances—these Gods and Jehovahs—had their use in focusing men's energies and at times kept men from making messes of each other's flesh. But no matter how I tried to make sense of religion, I always failed to make sense of the Crusades, the Inquisition, the Salem witch trials, and now the Holocaust. Men made God evil. If there were a Judeo-Christian God he'd long since abandoned this planet. And yet, some higher nature kept sway, a demanding and indwelling voice sparkling in the blood. No matter how I cast him out, I could still be surprised by enough pain or joy to ask, Is he still here? As it was, I had to stay on base some nights and, although falling somewhere between an agnostic and an atheist, even in winter might stagger at midnight over crusted ice, from the NCO Club to the base chapel, and sip bottled beer in a rear pew, stare at the softly lighted altar, lust after Tolstoy's moral muscle, his *The Kingdom of God Is Within You*, and would even kneel for a prayer—that ever unimpeachable and rationally acceptable Twenty-third Psalm—then cock my ear, eyes wide and mouth open, and catch the seashell of God's silence.

I open my trumpet case, unscrew each piston and wipe it with spit until the valves dance under my fingers, then lock the horn up again. Sheldon Katz defended our rights—first in Korea, now in New Jersey—and died doing it. I'll give him the best sendoff in me.

Yes, I can play Taps, a child bugler can play Taps. I can't play as well as James Jones's Private Robert E. Lee Prewitt in *From Here To Eternity*, who once played Taps at the Tomb of the Unknown Soldier at Arlington National Cemetery on Memorial Day—but I have the musical and literary mind for a glorious Taps—for notes ever hovering and clear but never played the same way twice, a tempo all up to the player, as with Louis Armstrong. I have a sense of the song's history of the night on US bases around the globe. I hear haunting ice-blue notes quiver over barracks at lights out and catch the ears of young airmen in their sacks, notes long-drawn on loudspeakers and spreading over the small lights of the flight line between the roars of the afterburners. Such notes linger for a lifetime but come first as a kiss on the heart, a pinch, and a sadness that has its own heavenly ache—its restraint just as thrilling as "The Stars and Stripes Forever" when its last big bars stir hearts to dizzy flag-waving and dancing—though Taps is only a sorrowful epitaph for the day. This is me whenever I hear or play it:

> *Dayyyyyyyyyy is donnnnnnnnne*
> *Gonnnnne the Sunnnnnnnnn*
> *Frommmm the laaaaake*
> *Frommmm the hilllllll*
> *Frommmm the skyyyyyyyyyyyyyyyyyyyy*
> *Rest in peeeeeeeaaaaaaacccccce*
> *Sooooooollllllldier braaaaaavvvve*
> *God-oo-ooo-ooo-ood*
> *Is*
> *Niiiiiiighhhhhhhhhh*

Will I do the repeat? Is my lip up to it? Nobody else at this funeral, not even the honor guard, knows whether I should play a half-volume repeat—that breathtaking echo from far hills—God's whisper from heaven, piercing the breastbone and lifting out the heart. I'm up to it! I will be Prewitt. I'm ready to grab their throats and leave them stung and choking. Not death but a sunrise! As long-held glassy notes shape themselves in my mind, my dream of virtuosic playing—my rapture—lifts me above my life as wretched editor of *Fighter Scope*'s juiceless hype and above the drug of the chow line with its piggish second and third helpings, and above the fumes and pasteboard life of the NCO Club bar—as I level all mourners with one from the heart, my first public solo, which will choke up even the honor guard and lure Jehovah himself down for Sheldon's battered brain and body. Oh, for God's sake, yes—I will do the repeat.

So before chow last night I went into the empty base theater, where we rehearse, warmed up on Louis's "Cornet Chop Suey," then laid out Taps in the hollow theater that lets cat fur rub up against the stone walls and linger on the serviceman's night-song. Tried the repeat with the mute—but nobody will want to hear a mute unless I blow with sheer genius. Maybe just with my hand in the bell? More tone control? I played scales to strengthen my lip, even four flats and sharps. Scales never really do build my lip—you need heart, not rote—but I make believe and show myself I'm serious. Make-believe is my deepest self and demands constant realism in daily life. Four flats and sharps lend a cutting-edge to fantasy and my growing sense of skill. The trouble is that I always forget which note is the fourth flat or sharp because I avoid pieces in those keys.

I live off-base with my wife in New Egypt. We row about her Swedish moodiness and my flightiness and hidden thoughts—those parts of my character overblown by alcohol—and our fights rise to a great pitch. I smash my fist through the bedroom wall, then we have sex. Senseless? Her body is my best drink and I cannot stay my hand or lust. What my wife's flaws are I no longer remember—her greatest is breaking down and marrying me. Her worst anger.

Her woe toward me arises from having borne our son at the base hospital, not in Philadelphia or Manhattan where better treatment might be had. At the base hospital her milk goes sour or turns blue, I don't know, and she can't breastfeed. I've been at the NCO Club downing brews all through the birthing, and don't even know she's called the base ambulance to come for her. At last I hear she's given birth and I show up smelling of beer and barren of flowers—a knife through her heart. "*Where are my flowers?*" she asks. Through the nursery window I see a rising and falling large blood-drop pooled in my son's navel. When I tell her of this, her look says that divorce papers will be served at the door. My little worried smile—my reserved glow of joy—mean nothing. Sadly, I've become overweight in the Air Force and am not the handsome, muscular ex-Marine she'd married but rather am a large muffin swathed in Air Force blue. I am driven by an unbending need to be self-directed, self-empowered and by an Emersonian creed of Self-reliance—or call it self-concern boosted by drink. A blue flame of Bill-of-Rights self-regard—the spirit absolute at my heart's core—overheats me and my writer's honesty becomes a gruesome gyroscope standing me upright, fists clenched. After a fight we lie abed and suck common sense from the darkness, and in their way these clear-minded peace talks replenish us more than sex. For her these moments are never passionate—reason grips her too strongly. Mine are Russian and seek the heart of things. We scrabble after ideas about hormones and getting a grip on our adrenals. It's heartening to see through these stupid glandular eruptions. And that's the full scope of my passion. Emotionally, in my dark pride I might be a Finn or a Dane—some Arctic character—with this post-battle fresh self-understanding an icy cherry-flavored vodka spreading cool brilliance up and down my arteries. We lay naked and read the ceiling. I call on my power to break things down and enter a rapture of Socratic genius. My keen mind races through Hemingway and D. H. Lawrence. Depths of understanding shift about in me. I stalk the marital bedroom like Tolstoy.

Off-duty I write a never completed first novel about Lindbergh and his dead son Charles. The great hero suffers the worst loss, the kidnapping and murder of his son, a babe snatched from its cradle. Secretly, I plan never to become famous so that I will not have to bear such a loss. The novel exorcises my fears about my own son—though at the time I don't know this. But I think it smart to block my Lindbergh-like fame, ward off something dark and overwhelming, the full life-size depression waiting to roll in. There's no way to reclaim the five years drained from my life by service in the Marine Corps in World War Two and now in the Air Force. As my mother often says, You've got to grin and bear it—and *this* is the easy part, my son. My son's heart thump and my beaver work researching Lindbergh are twin pumps priming my spirit. Something about me evades *her* understanding—how spinal my devotion to writing is, the urge that blows aside all that stands between me and the sunstorm in language. My wife, brighter than I, has a degree in languages, knows English, Latin, French, Swedish—and later Russian and Chinese. My goal: to write a book that I will enjoy years later, a book created for me and strives to lift my being. Most great books do not grip me enough for a second read—become too prosy, with only set-pieces or high-flown passages that rise above my later skim. I set out to write a book whose every page burns with originality and stirs without letup. No prosiness dulls a page. At best I can't make much of this clear even to myself, much less to her. I know only that I want to feel every word on the finished page. Are my feelings a cancer on our marriage? For God's sake, why don't novels have the heady heldentenor glow of *Lohengrin*, or the great shout of Beethoven's *Ninth*—heroic works with each page from the heart of a lion. *War and Peace* may match the *Ninth* but even that I've only read once. The trouble probably is that at nineteen—my brain still dropsy with adolescence—I read a rhapsodic novel that begins . . . *a stone, a leaf, an unfound door; of a stone, a leaf, a door. And of all the forgotten faces. . . . O waste of loss, in the hot mazes, lost, among bright stars on this most weary unbright cinder, lost! Remembering speechlessly we seek the great forgotten language, the lost lane-end into heaven, a stone, a leaf, an unfound door. Where? When?* Or as Milton put it, *Look homeward Angel now and melt with ruth.*

Driving home from the base by day, I pass through billiard-cloth green Jersey flatlands and hillocks with fat dairy cows that look lifted from the Isle of Guernsey and that console and drug me with a thick, rich, green-golden peace. God's peace, I wonder, that Tolstoy saw on Yasnaya Polyana, his country home? Then comes our tiny upstairs kitchen and bedroom in our New Egypt farm house where from a window I watch as the barn cat deguts a mouse, swallows it headfirst and whole, without chewing, but leaves a small pile of blue mouse guts. Where is God's peace in this? And every one of those pasturing cows will be slaughtered when its age demands it—and sawn in half, hacked into joints, ribs, loins, and dozens of special cuts, then fried, baked, or broiled in fat-sizzle and eaten. All with God's blessing invoked about the table by my Christian landlord? Does that Fiend Above really care? Although my barracks buddies call me Leo Stovepipe and my deepest faith in life springs from Tolstoy, all my elective spirituality emerges from thoughts about the Life Force. How can you eat a cow, or a creature as beautiful as a deer, and believe in God? Tolstoy gave up meat much to his wife's disgust, and I was torn between his regard for Jesus—his translation of the four gospels, as I said, leaves out the miracles, which he found false—and Shaw's regard for Henri Bergson's *Creative Evolution* and the Life Force and Nature as a spiritual biosphere—and toss in Emerson's "The Oversoul." I sense nature's intelligence using man as an eye for looking down into its own structure and out at the universe. But nature also has darkness raging where blood spills in endless waves. Somehow cows standing in pastures filled with golden photons marry nature's glory to horror. Me, someday, gone forever? Ha, foolish thought. Death and life will somehow merge into a third state, just as film actors live on in light through celluloid—or as the bliss of God shines through the human frame and creates an immediate being both eternal and transcendent. I see death deliver a promise of peace everlasting, even to cows, cats, mice, and beasts of field and woodland. A passion for life overrides depression and death and keeps both at bay—a passion that the very organs of the body depend on for full health, whatever blackness lurks in the sunlight. Even an arthritic old black Lab that's no longer taken along on duck hunts, needs love and attention when his master returns smelling of the bay and the duck blind—the hunger for love rises and begs from the dog's eyes, the dog that served so faithfully in the past but can go out into the cold waters no more or thrill to a heavy mouthful of fresh-stinking duck feathers in his jaws as he splashes ashore, his heart racing—and though the hunt is over, that old dog still needs to keep his organs fed with passion for life, love from his master's hand and eye. God's own blood races through us as a passion for life, and yips from our dog's throat. The dog that looks at us so yearningly mirrors our own yearning to look into the eyes of God. He—like us—is not always a fiend without mercy—a beautiful, cruel fiend, lavish in his passions, but merciless about the cycles of life and suffering.

All this I struggle with at twenty-five, unbaptized and churchless and free to choose my beliefs. Like the Knight's Squire in Ingmar Bergman's *The Seventh Seal*, I protest the blackness of life, the plagues, and wholesale slaughter at all levels of the animal kingdom—but as does the Knight, I lift to my mouth the daylight shimmering on a bowl of milk and drink the light.

I chew over this cold passion or darkness built into me along with my wolf lust for language and worry over its spiritual signs whenever I have a free moment, as on this death trip to Philadelphia. Now we pull onto the road winding into the cemetery, find the grave, and step out of the heated bus into sunlight shocking the snow. A woolen sweatchill from my uniform shakes my bones and my breath shudders in the cold air.

The honor guard sergeant takes charge, arranges the Air Police rifle squad some ways off, and with a corporal spreads a flag on the coffin as the mourners arrive in cars. Among the mourners I see a frail woman in a black veil support a lame man in a long black overcoat and black snap-brim hat who limps but has no cane.

Clearly Sheldon's parents. But for some strange reason Mr. Katz wears no tie and keeps his collar unbuttoned. Is he deranged? She lets him outdoors like this? I note a small tumor on his neck. His maimed eyes look ready to burst.

The cemetery lies in a frozen light-flash of stones and trees a minute before just slammed to earth. No metal seats wait—far too cold to sit out here. I stand off from the honor guard and mourners, near a fresh snowy hillock, my shoes half-buried. After a while a rabbi says something rather melodious. Is he singing? Groaning? It isn't English. Hebrew? Yiddish? I can't tell, though my wife could. Mr. Katz savors every word and gulps it down—his pale dark face fallen taffy. His eyes fly up as he mumbles and mutters, his mouth torn at the edges: he answers a phone call from the bright heavens where his son died.

Now the rabbi speaks in English and says words I catch only parts of, "Owe everything to God . . . purify, better, finer . . . lift ourselves up . . . no barrier between man and God . . . He that chastises also consoles . . . and so we offer up this soul to Thee . . . Take him into the Upper World, Lord . . ." The rabbi steps back into the mourners. I chill and sweat in heavy wool.

The sergeant of the honor guard alerts me to get ready. I bend and open my trumpet case. The six-man rifle squad raises its arms at heaven and fires six rounds of blanks giving a weak spit unlike the solid crack of live rounds. Mr. Katz jumps, shocked. He twitches and trembles. His lips bobble, eyes soaked in delirium. Legs weave as his soul now far underground sucks ashes and mud. Pain cramps him as misery bloats his face. His open-mouthed groans shock me as unmanly grief, yet his thick lips spasm and his jaw draws wide with loud shouts to God. Has he seen Sheldon's body? That would kill any father. He clutches his chest. Heart attack? Stomach cancer? Bathed in blackness, he staggers in a Gehenna I've seen only in artworks. Not just has a shattering accident rent his son, but Mr.

Katz now stumbles on the rock-bed of his stony religion. He is that fear-wracked figure with his palm hiding one eye in Michelangelo's *Last Judgment*. This is religion. Judaism without mercy. No more rosy days, breakfasts in the Catskills, and leisurely endearments over fine linen cloths. For Satan has swum up and his arms welcome Mr. Katz. *Enjoy, enjoy!*

The honor guard sergeant removes the flag from the coffin and with his corporal folds it precisely into thirds and hands it to Mr. Katz who cannot lift his arms. Mrs. Katz—her arms a shelf—steps up and accepts the flag. The honor guard sergeant nods at me and the coffin begins to lower.

I stand at attention, my horn locked under my arm and—bound by my heavy blue greatcoat and woolen dress blues—feel sweat drain down my back despite my frost-fountain breath. Oh God, I smell my sweat and wool and long to be home in the tub with my wife scrubbing my back raw with her Swiss loufa just as she scrubs herself harsh pink with it each time she bathes. I want to feel balls of dead skin leave my back and leave me as polished as my beloved gold-plated brass horn. I want to be clean and new. I want to be fearless and hit my note dead on.

I rub my lips with balm and focus on the quickly cooling mouthpiece only half-warmed by my body heat. The coffin lowers. Turning, I lift my horn at an angle away from the mourners. My fingers plunge and race the valves to slick them up. My God, the valves freeze more or less halfway down, or rather in steps—the first valve sticks three-quarters of the way, the second half-way, the third a third of the way. The pistons fuse to their shafts and will not move up or down—not with a hammer even had I one. I should have used glycerin, not spit, in this frigid air. *You shithead!* This frozen horn is unplayable. There's no way I can blow air through these blocked pipes, nor even imitate a bugle. The blood drains from my head. My lungs die. I stare in shame and fear at the honor guard sergeant and at Mr. and Mrs. Katz and the lowering coffin.

My bare fingers in the bell, I play Taps—*the echo*. It is a new Taps. Much like the old Taps—but oddly different, in a strange new key that is almost no key. The stopped air barely moves through the pipes or past my fingers in the bell. This Taps does not ring from the gravestones and hillocks, but lies upon the ear in more muffled tones—muted notes fainter than mourner ever heard, although I blow myself blind as Samson in the blaze of noon.

An agonized shout from Mr. Katz rips through my Taps. He doesn't like my playing? The coffin lowers below the snow. Mr. Katz tears his coat and shirt open, rips through his undershirt and—shouting and shouting—tears at the heart beneath his bare hairy chest. His wife grabs his coat. His black hat falls back. The coffin drops from sight. Mr. Katz howls upward and throws himself flat onto the coffin below, as I try to keep playing above deep screams from the grave, *Sheldon, don't leave me! Oh God, bury me too! Sheldon! Sheldon!*

Fat snow crystals spiral into drops on my bell. Day is done in the midmorning.

> *Gone the sun.*
> *From the lake, from the hill. From the sky.*
> *Rest in peace, soldier brave. God is nigh.*

That night I lie abed with my sleeping wife and through the fall of ice tinkling on the bedroom windows play the Taps repeat I failed to play in the right key. I go too far in my rapture—my jaw drops open, my mind eclipses and my soul shudders. I am down in the coffin with Sheldon and as all the valves of my body freeze his absence of breath is my absence of breath. I am Socrates stiffened by the great forgotten language in the shadow of a plane tree. I listen for my son's breathing. At last his silence becomes unbearable. I slip out of bed and go to his cradle in the kitchen. I stand listening for the seashell of his breath as I have listened for God's whisper in the midnight chapel. All is silence. Great fear shoots through me. I lean my ear toward him, my breath held tight. All is still silence. As in a bad dream, my jaw chatters. My hand quakes sliding his shirt up and under his breastbone a steady thump, gurgle, thump lifts up through my fingers and brings me to the lost lane end into heaven.

Snow falls on the farms of New Egypt and sweeps the black flats of the flight line while a recorded Taps cuts through the darkness and flurries settle in crusts on the stones and black tree limbs of a Philadelphia cemetery as my notes linger in the night and I hear Mr. Katz howl from the soles of his feet to heaven. I watch his shirt rip and his knotted fingers dig for his heart or to grip and pull out his guts and gizzard. Again he throws himself into Gehenna and his passion bolts at me as again I bungle Taps. Sheldon, wherever you are, did you hear any of this song and uproar? My brain sends out radio waves seeking Sheldon in the unsearchable darkness beyond our biosphere. I lay shaken and listen to my heart and the winter silence broken only by my wife's breath. I grope among my own organs for God.

A star-blue see-through hand forms behind my closed lids—its each finger joint long as my body—and reaches down from a night-heaven white with flurries and presses its tips against Sheldon Katz's hard-frosted breastbone, and lifts upward his head now healed and spirit beating, upward, upward through the crust of his grave.

Then I drift from a dock onto a dark river and glide on the flow.

Maguire Air Force Base, 1954
Greenwich Village, 2014

Prothalamion for Wet Harmonica and Johnny Stompanato
The Realist, Number 68, August 1966

I arise from a drunkard's bed and go into the city to witness the birth of Andy Warhol's first musical venture, *Mr. Stompanato*, a tuney love saga—in drag *and* in reverse drag—about the unfortunate death by butcher knife of Lana Turner's paramour, John Stompanato.

By reverse drag I mean that a small graying boy with silver hairs by Clairol plays Lana's 14-year-old daughter Cheryl—who did the dirty work on Johnny—while the towering Queen of Underground Movies Mario Montez plays Lana. Also in reverse: Cheryl is played as a boy—Lana's sonny/girl—named Cheryl. Cheryl and leading lady Lana are in love and damn that nasty Johnny for trying to seduce Cheryl. So-o, call Andy soapy and sentimental—if you must.

Warhol's studio loft on East 47th has a steel-plated street door. I've been invited by the leading lady's lover Larry Bucetti, who unforewarned will today become the leading man. I arrive on time at 2 p.m.—across from Grand Central YMCA—to find a knobless metal door sprayed bright silver. I see my vague figure on the door as in a misty mirror—a drunken jumbled jagged double without features—no reassuring shadow—just a half-fiction in a world of surface.

I am about to phone upstairs and have the mirror opened when four uptownies—I'm from the Lower Russias of the East

Side—mince out and as they trip away leave the door open. I check my breast pocket for its pint of Gordon's gin and fully armed go through the mirror.

I climb three flights through space and time to the bedrock of the Underground: The Warhol Factory! Unsure of my credentials I choose not to knock at this silver-sprayed door—and just walk through my second mirror. I feel unfixed and gin-free and all stirred up in a left-handed body. My bones wear a flesh fabric. I should not have bought this backup pint today. Far down a huge space a shirtless muscular man washes his hair at a sink. He dries it as I glide toward him on rubber flip-flops. Once his hair dries he gives it a good mussing up and speaks. Yes, a friend of Mario's—I can stay, don't worry. Yes, they're shooting today—at 1:30. It's now 2:00. We're alone.

He's cameraman Dan Williams and has a white shoestring tied around his head for his glasses to hang them from when he looks through his camera lens. I've never seen a shoestring of any color knotted to a frame's earpieces. But it's a little pro touch I'll remember—I tell him I'm going to make a movie myself in about two months when the money comes through.

What about? he asks.

Well, it's modest, in 8-millimeter, color. I'm going to buy about 15 reels and give these two talented actor friends of mine a $50 bill which one of them supposedly will have received in the mail from a phantom donor with the message DRINK ME. Then I'll just follow them from bar to bar on the Lower East Side as they blow their windfall. They start with five shots apiece lined up on the bar at Stanley's.

These two actors really have personal magnetism, Dan, so plot doesn't matter. One carries a shopping bag filled with cans of spray paints—*ahh!* We descend into the subway and surreptitiously blot out all the James Bond posters and spray the letters F—U—C—

(I pause)—S—C—H—I—A everywhere to drive people mad and then climax the story with a 3-minute gilding job on the Alice in Wonderland statue in Central Park. Turn it gold or copper. Then we run like hell. I'm going to make this movie. But it may be overly literary.

Jesus, it sounds great, Dan Williams says. And the publicity, you already got it.

We're still alone. It's a variation on a story by Dickens, I say. Called "Making a Night of It" in *Sketches by Boz*. Here in the States we'd call it "Getting Pickled" or "Tying One On." It'll be handheld. I follow their night out down to the last detail—until our revels end. It just may be too literary—but Chaplin did it once as a two-reeler called "A Night Out." Maybe I'll learn something from Andy.

Dickens is very modern, Dan says. Where is everybody? A phone answers in the astral. He goes to muffled ringing from a long heavy wall phone—detached from a wall and placed on a desk—with the coin return and the rest of the phone surgically swollen with duct-tape and the whole taped phone sprayed silver—to drive people mad? But—it *is* a pay phone laid out in place of a private line: not an official pay phone—it has simply been hijacked and turned into a home or office phone. What's more it only receives calls. When you put coins into it, it doesn't work and what's more the coin return slot is taped over. The very attractive silver spray and taped slot make loot for Andy's minions—they can tell by weight when the coin box is stuffed and the duct-tape worth removing and respraying. Now I see myself in a fractured silver mirror against a proto-glam of silver. The Factory is world capital of silver spray-paint culture—with nothing ragged or ramshackle. Only here, as in Alice's looking-glass, when you read a sign all the words and letters go the wrong way. Mentally. I sense a journey into the sublime.

Men drift in—fags who walk about as if they own the place. I find they've never been here before. They not only jam some rock 'n roll on the stereo but also ask to have special tapes of *"Andy's"* played. Williams fails to serve them.

Barbells lay by a standing exercise bike which I take to be Dan's—he looks kept up. I start to think about just going home and cracking a gallon. My income features lower priced Sherries boosted to forty-proof. I go into a silver bathroom and rebuild myself on Gordon's.

On a worktable lie several great sheets of aluminum foil with signs saying *Do Not Touch*. Andy hot-irons these sheets together and fills them with gas so they float—as do two big puffed up aluminum foil pillows at rest against the ceiling. This Dionysian loft stretches 150' by 60'—with every foot of ceiling stapled with silver foil. One entire 150' brick wall shines with silver paint—talk about a fantasy factory. All overhead pipes gleam with silver foil wrap. And not only does the giant silver bar wall phone lie on the desk—the blocky desk itself stands aglow with silver paint. And silver foil coats the bathroom walls as well and the porcelain commode rises sprayed in royal silver and within has silver spray down to the waterline. File cabinets, work cabinets, all chairs, a travelers theater trunk—the very sink where Williams shaved—and two 24-bottle cases of unopened Cokes join a dream-world of—no, a civilization of silver.

Now Warhol arrives. He is silver. He wears shades and an inhuman platinum wig, false down to the nap. In high-heeled cowboy boots, puce corduroy pants and a brown leather jacket over a blue sweater lettered Wagner College he looks about 39. Veins split on his nose. His cowboy boots demand delicate steps and behind his dark shades he is gentle. As with most others in the loft he has slimness to spare—perhaps because he dines on giant dark-chocolate Hershey bars like that now stuck in his jacket pocket. Andy's giant

Hershey bars stamp him as Superman of the Underground.

Near the lunar telephone three battered silver couches form a tiny living room area. To everyone's annoyance a young lad with a crown of nitty hair walks about and without stop blows a harmonica while the rock n' roll blasts. Four or five faded but raven-haired teenyboppers in black hosiery and cheesy black mica-embossed skirts sparkle themselves about the silver couches and—yawning—aspire for stardom. The skinniest keeps her skirt hiked up to a black rayon crotch that tells Andy, Do with me as you will. She wants fame whatever the cost or danger.

Now Mario walks in.

Spanish, 30, looks 20. Personable, small, with startled deer's-eyes. He speaks everything with sibilant soft edges of wonder. I introduce myself as Larry Bucetti's friend.

But—don't you write or something? You write novels, Larry tol' me.

Yes. Well—they're unpublished. I'm going to make a movie.

Great! There, you see!

Mario introduces me to Andy. Andy, this is Don. He is a writer and he's going to make a movie.

I'd like to write something about this afternoon as a kind of event.

Would you? Andy says softly. I'm so glad.

Mario goes back to the sink to dress. It will take me an hour just to make up.

It takes ninety minutes.

Larry materializes. His facial muscles ripple. I've brought some wine. Bottle for you, bottle for Mario. Christ, I stood out front for a half hour trying to get in. Oh, this is that fortified Marsala you like. Where's Warhol?

That's him. In the silver hairpiece.

A guy named Arnold comes over. Arnold and Larry star in

Flaming Creatures, a masterpiece about an orgy on a rooftop. It features some twenty or so naked mixed couples locked in sexy embraces and enjoying foreplay and mutual masturbation. It's pretty frank and the police chose to lock it up.

Larry's rough deep voice speaks: Aside from the orgy it's a very lousy movie.

I never saw it, Arnold says. He's a jeweler and weightlifter—!— And had a heart attack about six months ago while waiting for a subway.

Who were you with? Arnold asks Larry.

I was with Sheilah. [Sheilah is a false name here.] She was jerking me off and I was groping her and Jack [*Flaming Creatures* is by Jack Smith] kept saying, Keep that up, keep it going—I'll get to you in a minute. So finally he gets to us and down comes Jack with the camera right onto Sheilah's hand and me. I have the most famous cock in underground movies. I mean, it's famous. People buy movie tickets just to see it.

Did you see that twat that I was with?

No, who was she?

Arnold names her. And do you know, a half hour after the take, I brushed her hand accidentally and she jumped like I'd electrocuted her.

Broads, Larry says. Same with me, Arnold. After the movie Sheilah wouldn't talk to me. You'd think I'd done something wrong.

I've heard that story five times now, I tell Larry. What I want to know is did you come?

Dya know, the whole situation was so embarrassing I could hardly get a hard-on. A pure fantasy situation but the reality was too much.

Well, Larry, Arnold says, that's why she wouldn't talk with you.

Arnold tells us about his subway heart attack. It was like someone using the dull side of a meat cleaver to get out of my chest. Nobody would help me. I asked the guy in the cage to call a doctor and he just looked at me like a nut. I just went in and sat down and finally two guys went out to get a cop for me. Two cops came and some guys with a stretcher. But I wouldn't let them put me on it. I'll walk out, I said.

So I want to pass out but I stay awake until they get me on the table—then whoosh. They kept me in this Intensive Care Ward for a week. Men, women—sex made no difference there, because half these people died. I'd lay there and watch them wheel out these corpses.

And age!—age made no difference. One 16-year-old boy, I asked him, What's wrong with you? I had a heart attack, he says. There were two 20-year-old girls there with heart attacks. I don't write well but I'm gonna learn to type and I'll write a book called *Intensive Care Ward*. I can write as well as Jack Kerouac at least. I was with Jack in the merchant marine. He's sitting there with this tall pile of paper. I says, What's that, Jack? It's a story, Jack says. Wow, Jack, you're gonna have to trim that down a bit, aren't you? My ghostwriter will do that, Jack says.

You mean editor? I say.

It's now 4:30. Talk of last week's rushes being shown proves empty. A tall lanky blond guy in black sweatshirt and black pants loads the film case with a 33-minute reel. About twenty people mill about—some few very well dressed and horsey. Larry comes back from shy Mario who has a girl helping with his lashes while he holds a sweater over his bra.

Mario wants to know if you'd like a role, Larry tells me. You could play the movie director in the second reel.

Great!

Dan Williams comes by. I say, Andy isn't doing much painting anymore, is he?

Oh, yes, he's painting some more Campbell Soup cans to make some money to make some movies. He had a Hollywood deal set up but it fell through.

I ask Larry, But this is all for money, isn't it? The movies and the paintings both, they're all just for gullible people?

Of course, Larry says.

Arnold at the silver block of desk reads a nudist magazine. Larry and I walk over to get seconds.

This belongs in that bottom drawer and put it back, Arnold says. Just a minute, I want to copy some addresses.

Arnold's concern for the magazine becomes justified when we see that it has no price on it. An advertisement within tells that this particular magazine costs a stiff ten bucks, while others are $20, $30, $40 and even $50 an issue. In color and unretouched. All the nudists are in their teens or early twenties. Many men look very well built, even half-hard, and the girls shine with lovely curves. It's one of those rare times in life when the word exciting in concert with a published work means just that. Even the guys begin to be exciting.

I can't look at this anymore, I say just as a teenybopper passing leans over and points a fingernail at a wet lad's half-swollen dick and says, He's built.

He's cheating, I say. You can see he just came out of the shower.

We go over to Mario.

Mario calls Arnold for help.

Did he mean Andy Warhol?

Beats me, Larry says.

Andy wants me to sing for the whole movie, Mario/Lana says. Everything I say I have to sing. I can carry a tune, but making up everything I'm going to say and singing it too, that's very hard. How do you like my new red wig? I just got it. Isn't it dear? I can't wait to see it in the rushes.

'S gorgeous, Larry says. Very nice.

At this moment Mario's the best-looking broad in the house. Really rather exciting, a cross between Maria Montez and Lupe Velez. Lana Turner in a red wig? No.

Mario has his personal makeup kit and wardrobe and prides himself on his ease at passing as a girl. He now wears a purple dress with sleeve flounces—high heels, long lashes, carmine lipstick, falsies, feminine underwear and, let's be frank, is an interesting proposition—if you dig deep—smoldering guys dolled up as girls with mournful, downcast eyes. Just now Mario's piqued and pettish. When he complains about what he thinks Andy will ask him to do, his startled mascara eyes unnerve you. You want to pet her. Give her *tendresse* and care. Her eyes fill with wet pearly glossy calfskin and tempt you. Her lips . . .

She pouts, I don't know what I'm supposed to do. How do you say it now, Larry? Johnny Stefano?

Stompanato, René, Larry says, using Mario's real name. Deep-voiced Larry, by the way, has hard deep muscles and could run around the room with Dan Williams over his shoulder.

Stompanato! she cries and stamps both heels in fiery Spanish. With all this whorish makeup, René looks a spent 25, not his real 30, while his eyes—though adrift with illusions—bear a weary knowledge and beleaguered feminine witness to our wicked world—rather as if the late Cobra Woman and Mario's namesake Maria Montez has been streetwalking for a year and feels used to a frazzle—*For It Is Written that Cobra Woman Must Dance Forever or Die.*

Andy walks up and says, We're having a script conference downstairs.

Child Mario says, I'm ready. Oh, I haven't got my nail polish on! He reaches in distress into his purse on the floor and plucks out his polish. You have to come too, Don, she says. Her teeth grit through a lousy job with her polish. You're my movie director. And you're my lover in the movie, Larry.

Is there really a script? I ask.

I'm so mad at Andy, she says. He just *puts* you out there and makes you do everything. And here I am the only one who is supposed to speak for an hour and ten minutes. Oh, *what* am I going to sing?

Remember Warhol's *Empire*? Eight solid hours of the Empire State Building at night stationary. *Sleep*, six solid hours of a man sleeping, and in this the merest turn of the head or swallow becomes earthshaking action to be applauded. More recently he also filmed *Blowjob*, a 35-minute shot of a man's face while being sucked off off-camera: the big moment comes when the man reaches for and lights a cigarette. The house goes wild.

Warhol fans lately find him toying with the fashionable zoom lens and even tilting the camera a trifle. His earliest technique looks back to cinema's Stone Age and his films can run to Tolstoyan length while swelling a story-gnat into a basketball and exhausting all possible interest in staying awake. Curiously at times a sense of intentional art wells up.

No matter what their techniques, implicit social comment arises from *Harlot* (Mario plays Jean Harlow), *The Life of Juanita Castro* (Fidel's sister), and *Arthur*, about Sybil Burton Christopher's jet set discotheque of that name. One thinks about *Blowjob*, after the first shock, "It happens—it's a legitimate subject—and who is to say the man isn't in bed with his wife?" *Mr. Stompanato* must by default say something about Hollywood, much as a Warhol canvas crowded with dozens of cans of Campbell's many soups speaks about our culture. All Warhol films drive forward through inertia and tedium to arrive at some statement hovering over their vacuums. Think of Andy lettering soup cans with 48 different soups—the boredom! His Brillo Box sculptures simply remain more stationary statements. And why must an artist say what he means? The more mystery the more urgency to seek out intent.

Are all these people faggots?

They sure look it, Larry says. Arnold isn't. I don't know about Andy. But he sure surrounds himself with types I personally would avoid trying to meet. It takes place in a bare wing of a warehouse. The camera stands primed for action—flood lamps burn—a small mike hangs over the playing area. Andy restricts this area to about five square feet.

We all go down to the script conference.

Mario may move a yard and a half either sideways or toward the camera. With no props but a hamburger and a Coke, a container of milk, a single goblet and an off-camera wardrobe of sweaters and skirts, Mario's singing must transform bare space into a nameless room in Lana's mansion—into her studio—into a sound-stage where she films a movie—and back into the first room where Lana not only eats lunch but changes clothes—with the camera frozen on a five-foot-square playing area.

The script conference consists of Mario asking, Where do I set the Coke bottle? I can't set it on the floor.

Set it on the floor, Andy says.

Andy, I can't do that! I just won't do it. I wouldn't set a Coke bottle on the floor.

Then have the maid take it away.

Oh, all right—but I really do wish I had a table or a chair, something to work with.

Since it doesn't exist yet, the story never arises during the conference. Andy holds this powwow simply to help Mario convince himself of the reality of whatever takes place. Not only does Mario have to carry the film with the lone speaking role, his commitment must blind him to the hard juiceless chew of performing without a script while film runs at full-tilt boogie. He must be heart and soul for Warhol and surrender to Andy as Auteur Hero.

At this moment Mario has no inkling that light years part him from looking like Lana Turner. The Underground's greatest female star can be any woman he says he is just by saying so. With the same voice and gestures he can be Rita Hayworth or Sophia Loren. His reviews attest to his serious artistry. His face adorns highbrow magazines. With a peculiar Spanish dreaminess he slinks catlike into fantasy and curls up as a pussy.

The annoying young lad on the harmonica walks about playing so loud in this echoing wing that the technicians—Andy and the actors—must shout to be heard above him. No one wants to tell him to shut up. A woman here named Vyvian—who plays Lana's maid—stares at him with deep anger. Vyvian has dark hair and middle-age spread and horn rims and fills a solid fuchsia dress. She's ready to kill. He keeps blowing blues with sucking and kissing sounds, and sneaks up behind people to blow in their ear.

Have you any idea what's going to happen?

Not the slightest, Larry says.

How are *you* going to have a love scene without saying a word to her?

Mystifies me.

And I wonder what kind of movie director never speaks? Only Warhol?

Delays and setting up take an hour while Mario grows more fretful. She stares daggers at Andy who has now taken off his shades and returns her looks with the big batting eyes of a night-feeding lemur. Warhol has outlandish strange eyes. They almost never show feeling—only a gentleness.

At times the way a scene goes allows a fast-lifting mist of happiness to grace his lips. He never disapproves of an ongoing scene but sometimes whispers a direction. He steels himself to the merciless camera: switched on, it never stops until the reel change. No editing will follow. Foolish commercial directors say that the heart of filmmaking lies in editing. Warhol stays unmoved by those old farts. Oh sure, some acting troupes pride themselves on playing without props and relish their skill at make-believe on a bare stage. They'd love to try this on film. With *Mr. Stompanato* a few props do get handled but the sets must be made up. The audience must blot out the queer truth before its eyes—or rather enter into the queerness and let it startle—and crawl all over your back. We can't even see the silver pipes just beyond this "set" where Lana Turner's swank digs and huge studio clearly will go unbuilt, unseen, and even unimagined. Andy grants his audience a limitless editing budget—for the audience must "edit" between parallel dimensions: the unbearable emptiness of what they do see and the bizarre magnitudes that glimmer beyond that unbearableness. I sense that this love saga may hit a brave new low among Andy's masterpieces— just. *Andy! Andy!* Mario cries over the damned harmonica. Should I wear my bolero for my entrance, or the jacket?

Wear the bolero!

He smiles, almost, and knows his decision makes no difference about anything.

Stefanito! she repeats. Stefanito.

Stompanato, René, Larry says.

She stamps her heels and cries, *Stompanato!*

Warhol never cries *Places* but at last the actors take position, with mike level set for Mario's singing and backup by harmonica. The harmonica backup stares into the camera and blows smoke rings at the lens. Mario stands off-stage—or off-postage stamp.

Graying in a black sweater and black pants little Cheryl leans against a white stanchion—silent, smoking, stiff with stupor.

Mario hangs strengthless and bitchy—bites his lips—rolls his eyes amid mascara—he is feminine impatience poised against colossal misfortune. Getting in character? Has he, in fact, ever seen a Lana Turner movie? Not going by his looks but as he hopes.

Vyvian the maid hides behind Cheryl's stanchion which looks more like the bridge in *Winterset* than Lana Turner's kitchen.

Andy pushes the camera switch. *Mr. Stompanato* rolls.

Paul of the Harmonica waits for a few feet of leader to pass through the camera. His finger punctures a smoke ring as he sucks another smoke ring back into his mouth. He lifts his mouth organ and blows a harsh blues straight into the camera. He fades back and off to one side. Ah, Brecht's Streetsinger from *The Threepenny Opera*, how brilliant of Andy! Upstage, Mario enters—slow and stilted—singing:

My name is Lana Turner
And I've just come from the studio
Where I'm making a picture
And I'm going home
To see my son Cheryl (Cheryl is spoken)
    And my lover
Johnny (Stomp! Stomp!) *Stompanato!*

The harmonica drifts in. Wonderful! The stage shifts in dreams from the Factory to Beverly Hills.

SINGSPIEL:

Oh, there you are, Cheryl!
Tell me, darling, have you seen Johnny?

(Little Cheryl, withdrawn past all awakening, drags on his/her cigarette butt.)

Johnny, darling, Johnny Stompanato . . .
Haven't you seen him?

(Mario really seems desperate for Cheryl to say something and help with the scene.)

Darling, you haven't done anything to him, have you?
Did you kill him?
Did you shoot him?

(Cheryl drags on his/her fag.)
Oh, you shot him!
Why did you do it, darling?
Did he try to seduce you?
I know he did.
Is lunch ready?

The real and heavy-fisted Stompanato died under a butcher knife wielded by Cheryl in Lana's bedroom. But one must admire Mario's leap into the heart of the scene. He knows that it turns on lunch and he doesn't clutter the action with talk of the body, the pistol or knife, the police, a lawyer.

A grateful sigh of good feeling passes from the technicians to Mario on the word "seduce" that ties Cherylboy to Johnny and jerks the plot into the Genêt and Pirandello spaces of triple-think.

The movie rolls on in two parts at 35 minutes each. I will shorten the action—or rather the pauses.

Vyvian! Is lunch ready?

Vyvian off-stage speeds a cutting whisper: *Vyyvian!* And breaking the film's esthetique speaks: Yes, it is!

A not unsettled Mario welcomes another human voice to play against. He drops his singing. Vyvian, will you help me change my sweater. I want to wear my bolero.

Vyvian flowing in fuchsia wafts on with a sweater. She's been recruited from the hangers-on, even as have I—but she has zip sense of play or fantasy. Whatever Lana asks her to do she takes as stark realism.

Gaga with star power Mario says, Unbutton this jacket.

Unbutton it yourself, Vyvian says, not acting.

Vyvian, unbutton this!

Oh for—Christ's sake. Vyvian unbuttons the jacket. Ya wanna wear this cardigan?

Help me on with it.

Vyvian's eyes roll. The new sweater and its buttons take two minutes barren of mirth or drama. You look great, Vyvian says at last.

This changing of sweaters spells a strong drop in the flow of the picture as Lana in her undergarments breathes in and out and stares droopily and dopily and bats her eyes at a daydream just above the camera. Deep soul moods collect and jell for the highbrow press.

Thank you, Vyvian.

You're welcome. Vyvian walks off—sour, not acting.

Lana tra-las, *Vyvian!* I want to change my shoes.

Vyvian returns, jaw agape. I'm not going to do it. I won't help you change your shoes.

Darling, you've got to help me change my shoes. I can't do it myself.

I'd like to know why not.

Please, change my shoes.

Oh, my God.

Vyvian takes off Lana's shoes. Lana holds out a foot to be adorned by a new shoe.

Whattaya want! Vyvian cries. Just put your foot into it!

Put it on my foot, Lana/Mario says.

Vyvian stands—fuchsia billows—and behind a Coldstream Guard's tight jaw fights murdering Lana.

Put it on yourself.

I *can't* put it on myself.

Lana's femininity bores through Vyvian's manly don't-shit-me. Vyvian puts one shoe on. You can do the other yourself.

No, I can't. Put it on.

Why the hell should I put your shoe on?

Put it on.

Vyvian puts it on, insulted, not acting.

Lana says, Now let's have lunch.

During these scenes Harmonica Paul passes about the stage and gives a sullen stare into actors' faces. Jumps them behind the ear with his mouth organ—sucking and kissing it—and blows smoke rings through the acting area as climaxes, such as they are, rise. While Mario/Lana may have no real idea of the original drama of Stompanato's death by ripped aorta, Paul hadn't even been born when Cheryl cut up Johnny in Lana's bedroom. But he girds for make-believe at whatever job Andy assigns him.

Vyvian leaves and serves lunch from off-camera. A hamburger floats to Lana on an ethereal hand.

Lana asks, Can't we have some ketchup?

Sure.

Vyvian's hand holds a plastic bottle of Heinz ketchup over the open burger in Mario's hand and tries to squirt it. It won't squirt. At last she hands the bottle to Cherylboy. He squirts ketchup onto meat with abandon. The burger ready, he and Lana study each other at hearts' depth, then hold up the sandwich between them. They know just what they're doing. Lana's mouth comes down on the burger. Cheryl's mouth comes down. They chew into each other's eyes and out into the camera, still chewing—existence is a cud of meat and ketchup. Their cheeks fill with family feeling. They chew—faces locked—mother and son/daughter together—in love.

Not a word rises as they chew. Their cheeks bunch with curds of burger. Their faces bunch cheek-to-cheek in the frame. Cheryl chews with the far-seeing intensity of an assassin. Lana's eyes droop with the desperations of life. She turns to her son/daughter who still chews hard as a Turk whirling headstrong for heaven. Or has Johnny's death chilled sonny-girl's eyes? Lana chews on, drinking in her son's queer nature. Their faces on the sandwich munch ever closer.

As they eat and join closer and closer, the idea's brilliance spreads. Mother and son will soon be licking burger crumbs from each other's lips. And necking? We behind the camera glitter with eagerness for a bright kissing scene. The two actors chew toward their ketchup honeymoon. Lana deepens into her mellowest depths of acting. Her concern for Cheryl can be aborted only by suicide. She must give all of herself physically to her foreshortened son.

The last nibble and crumbs hang on their lips. And now Mario—his sensibility for highlighting the act perfect for this climax—cuts the incest short and cries, Vyvian! Let's have a Coke!

Vyvian's arm unfolds off-camera and hands her a Coke.

Thank you, Vyvian.

Now mother & son/daughter swig the Coke. Pass it back and forth, joined almost mouth to mouth. By accident she caresses his face. He lapses into his only interest: stiff staring withdrawal.

Vyvian!

Oh Christ. What?

Take this Coke bottle.

Set it down on the floor.

Vyvian, you must. Take it.

Ohhh . . . A hand takes the bottle as Paul Harmonica blows a razz into her ear and, himself breaking the esthetique, says, Tha' mussa been goo' food.

Nobody answers him. He shoulda stayed shut up.

I say that mussa been goo' food!

No reply and since no one will talk with him he bangs out some sounds on his mouth organ. He walks up and down behind the actors and gooses them with sucking harmonics.

An Andy minion creeps toward the playing area and whispers to Mario, *Sing!*

I say that must have been good food! Paul says.

Cheryl hands him an apple to shut him up. He crunches into the apple—a jealous Othello biting into his big handkerchief speech. Another Andy minion creeps by Paul and tells him to play lower. Paul gnashes into his apple like Godzilla.

Mario's lips purse as he sings downstage and shows off his slim figure and full bust. He searches for lyrics and more or less sings an old Harry James hit from *Carousel*.

If I loved you
Round in a whirl I would go,
Wanting to tell you
I know . . .
If I loved you . . .
Words would not come in an easy way . . .

And so on as Mario glows and breathes deep, his eyes torchlight. The story wavers.

At 35 minutes the film runs out with nothing happening, aside from film flapping in the camera. I follow the film changer upstairs where he switches reels under a coat. I ask, How long will this break last?

Just as long as it takes to change this film.

I go back down. Mario and Larry huddle.

What the hell are we going to do in the second reel? I ask.

I'm the lover, Larry says.

And you are the movie director? Mario says as if I have lines.

Since no plot exists for reel two, I try to help mock up a semblance of action. Look, René, how many people are there? There's you, your lover, Cheryl, and the movie director—Vyvian's gone now. Brush her out. I think I'll be Orson Welles.

Yes? René says, struggling.

There are four of us. We have to lift this reel onto our backs. We can do it! One of us is your lover, one your director, one your son. What are you going to do with these men?

Kiss them, René says.

Well—I . . . do I want to kiss René?

Look, in the middle of the plot, Larry says, I'll bring you in a bottle of wine and we'll drink it. I brought it for you anyway.

Oh thank you, Mario says. He looks about at his three actors, then takes Larry aside. They hash over what turns out later to be the film's highlight. Larry nods and comes back. Andy switches on the second reel. It hums in its case and zips open Andy's illustrious bohemian universe.

Mario swings his hips into camera. He tosses a throwaway line at Vyvian as she wilts forever from the viewer's mind. From here on in, Cheryl, Larry and I change her sweaters and blouses for her. She sings against the camera in a dream. As the singing ends I watch Larry waiting to enter. I'm to carry on a sweater, button it—then unbutton it quite a ways, as we have decided sans Warhol. The idea of lining out a plot against the director makes me sad, and of course it may sink the esthetique. But I'm damned if I'll stand naked before a lens with no action.

We choose to open the bottle of Marsala during this scene to give us something to do. I can open a bottle as well as anyone—certainly better than Lana.

Paul works his harmonica about the stage and wonders what's up. Cheryl buttresses the stanchion. Mario steps into camera range and sings insipid lyrics I can't quite catch. I feel drunk as his eyes flaunt their mascara with flood-lamp glow. As his gibberish winds down I am drunk. His lips drip paint—he's sold himself on his Lana. Jesus, the heavens of invention he's in.

Larry turns to me off-stage and asks, What did you think of the first reel?

Fearless stuff! The poverty of imagination overwhelms all criticism.

Andy seemed to like it too.

It's pure Warhol.

Mario sings again, more or less. At song's end he retires to what in the viewer's mind must be Lana's bedroom. He eyes sonny-girl for maid's work. Cheryl, help me change my sweater.

Cheryl quibbles not. Lana pushes her chest at him as he undoes the buttons. Paul blows blues from the stanchion. Lana's lace tits gape wide. She offers her 14-year-old daughter a reserved half-smile about her famous Sweater Girl bosom and in her bra is as close to Lana as Mario will get in this flick. Cheryl slips her into pink cashmere.

Lana walks into the lens and sings, chin high.
Now I'm going to my studio
Where I'm making a movie
And I'm going to be helped
By my movie director.
But since we'd already made up my entrance, this wasn't it yet.

I eye Larry. He looks at me and says, I've got to rehearse.

He plops down to the floor and in three minutes does 50 push-ups to work his beef up to acting level. Alone with the lens for three minutes Lana rises to delirium and shimmers sex and in the starlight of narcissism revels in her talent as she feeds her fans shifty shoulders and pouty lips and wordless moods by the bucket and bouquet.

Postal clerk Larry keeps in shape tossing mail bags. He arises without a sweat. Rubs his palms hard and lets them swell with eagerness to boff Mario. Okay, he winks at me, and walks around to the other side of the playing area. He changes into a ripped T-shirt and flips into Brando Uncaged.

But first Lana asks Cheryl to help her change into something fresh and her bust has got the better of Cheryl who noses his mother's bare shoulder and nibbles her cheek and feels up her falsies. Larry stands off-stage watching this. He shows no fear of Cheryl. I drift over to him but stay silent.

I could bite this little fuck in half, he says.

Well, Cheryl, stop it,
I've got to go to the studio,
My lover is waiting for me.
Paul waltzes through blowing and sucking and Lana sings:
Well, here I am at the studio,
Where is my movie director
And where is my lover?

Larry waits off-stage in his T-shirt. Now his 50 pushups pump sweat.

Darling! she cries, and Larry washes over her in hungry waves. He pats her bush and kicks her ass onto his knee and hoists her like a beanbag. He says not a word. He's made his entrance. She hangs in his arms. They kiss.

I'd wondered how Larry would make his entrance. Now all his boyhood dreams come true. I admire his grip on the action. As her man-of-steel lover in some studio movie he swashes and sweeps her up. She hangs in his arms. Lana's whole ensemble melts into his muscles. Time floods by, kiss follows kiss. My pal Larry kisses Lana Turner, not Mario. It's his big screen test for Andy—grab it and run, Larry! He swallows Lana heart and soul. And I envy him as she sucks away at his wet dream muscles and sweat from pushups. His face runs red with kisses and love smears. Lana, Lana—I want to marry—I mean kiss Lana. Why should Larry have all the fun? Yes, these two make something strong and stirring out of a gay weakness for pretty little guys in pastels. But this is Lana Turner, famed tits and all and I want some.

Oh-h-h! she moans.

I am afire. I rub my pint of Gordon's through my jacket. Like my heart, it's empty and I've no place to throw it.

Let's have a little glass of wine, Mario says and Larry cracks the bottle of Marsala he brought her.

They drink from their lone goblet. Larry and Lana smolder

over the goblet. They lip and tongue the goblet. Suddenly they're hard back on each other's neck, with no chair or table to lean on and Larry a bit shorter than Lana in her high heels. How did Larry become Mario's lover? He sure enjoys it. Hey, for them the glass is full. And even I had one night's luck—the full glass!—some months ago with a blonde dancer who writes and models—maybe half a year ago—or was it longer? Wow, Mario shoves her mug so deep into Larry!—his first action in the movie where he gives out and is not being serviced. And Larry loves it. His fingers dig on fire into her red wig. What passion! I want more beauty in *my* life.

This public slobbering goes on and on. It's the greatest love scene since the Burtons. No kiss, no outpouring like this has ever before been filmed. Impossibly it rises above Cheryl and the hamburger. Larry nips her neck and buries his head under her chin and tongues and tongues the bare pulsing in her defenseless neck. Lana's eyes flap, now volcanic with world-weariness. Once again, she realizes, a man has exploded in her arms. She sucks her lower lip, drags Larry's head into her bosom, then back as her gaze reads Larry's soul back to his spine. The spitfire chews into him. You bastard, she's saying, I love you. I love you, Larry. You've ripped my heart out, you sonofabitch.

Acting? Acting? Who calls this acting? It's the scent of a lioness in heat and her mate's urge to rape and maul. They grope—they spend—turn soft as dolls as their heads fall.

My entrance comes. Mario nods to me through her haze of Marsala and risen heartbeat. Now she, Larry and Cheryl attempt to drink a quart of milk—not Marsala. Larry doesn't want any milk and Mario won't let it go to waste. So she forces it on Cheryl. The boy drinks and drinks but at last passes his glass off to wandering minnesinger Paul. Does that shut Paul up? Not a bit. All during the kisses he sucked away behind the lovers and shoved his head into the shot. They weren't listening.

Now we're at the studio
And my movie director's
Going to tell me what to do.

I walk on from the camera carrying a sweater. Although I'm her director, Lana hardly recognizes me. Well, like Larry, I've rehearsed and pumped up on Gordon's and look forward to my gift bottle of Marsala from him. Lana stands agog, swirling in star power. I look about at my "sound-stage" and gesture my instructions. She nods. I shake my silent head and pull at her and say, You need a fresh sweater. She unbuttons herself. I ask myself, What would Welles do at this moment in a Warhol movie?

Lana all Larryed up and filmy with sweat plunges her face into the blue cardigan I hand her. Larry and I help with buttons off, buttons up. I rap my writing board and point at the camera and, wordlessly, say *Sing!*

Lana walks one and half yards toward the lens and spreads her legs and hands on hips belts out "Night and Day." But from the beat-beat-beat of the tom-tom to the tick-tick-tock of the stately clock, Mario should not be called upon to sing Cole Porter. Even so, the lens and mike drink in his singing and sulky breathing and lay bare his soul moods with twenty times the intimacy of Betty Grable's fresh-faced chirping in the old Fox films.

Then Lana and Larry rush back together while Cheryl props up the stanchion and Paul blurts his organ. I think I'm through but Mario nods to me for another entrance. A guy in a blue boating blazer and yachting cap urges me on. I jump back in and Welles her with, Sweetheart, you've got on the wrong sweater for this scene—and start unbuttoning her.

She smiles, looking thankful. Larry and I put another sweater on her and button her up. When she's buttoned, I study her and undo all the buttons and spread her lace to the world. She sings her last song "It's Delightful, It's De-Lovely" with overflowing coffee décolletage.

Her song done she calls me back, a human prop. I button her sweater. Under the hot lamps her shaved chest glistens. My eyes wander. With a furious blaze of brown onions deep in mascara, she whispers, Don, you're staring at my tits.

Damn, caught again.

We gotta make this flick work, René, I say. What do you want next?

She breathes deep and reads the stars for portents.

Help me change my sweater, she says.

I catch my breath at this stroke of genius.

We've changed this mothering sweater ten times at least. We get her jacket off and she stands bared in lace—her dazzling tits a treasure burning in the starry heavens of Hollywood. I fumble in her crevasse. Am I buttoning up Maria Montez? Lana Turner? Sophia Loren?

You're very nice, she tells me.

I want to make love, not toy around, my rosebud.

You will, she says, the camera rolling. You'll make love.

Should I shave like Larry or go woodsy like this?

You're very nice woodsy.

Again Larry and I button her sweater. She smiles at us both, knowing we forgive her the little things she's too heaven-sent to do for herself. *Mr. Stompanato* is a musical about buttoning sweaters. Andy won't tell you that but you should know it before you lay down cash for a ticket. [Once this shoot wraps, Andy switches *Mr. Stompanato*'s release title to *More Milk, Yvette* and his masterpiece gets a snotty review by *Times* movie critic Bosley Crowther. Nor has this now 33-minute one-reel b&w work of art ever seen release on tape or DVD—though we did see it projected onto a sheet in The Factory. There are no publicity shots.]

The picture wraps. We go upstairs and watch rushes from last weekend. Andy plops down on a sprayed-silver couch. The lights dim. On the makeshift sheet of a screen rises Mario's face. It's a headshot. The film runs on. Mario full-face stares into the camera. It's a still. Why does Andy show this still for so long? Mario blinks.

I get queasy. Ahh, it's a Warhol movie.

The hamburger scene follows.

Mario and Cheryl stand cheek to cheek in the rushes. These rushes prefigure today's shooting. A fake script conference today? Perhaps. But Andy actually did have screen tests and have Mario and Cheryl rehearse the hamburger sequence. Before this came two eleven-minute reels of separate heads of Mario and Cheryl. Cheryl in a headshot stares at us. It's another still. Cheryl stares at us. He's not faggy or bizarre. He simply stares into the camera—into us. A good still! He blinks.

What kind of screwed-up test is this? I ask Larry.

It's a Warhol screen test.

He scoops out your soul, I say as five more minutes pass. I really can't bear to look at Cheryl any longer. It's kind of interesting, Larry says. Andy makes you see everyone's sins.

Anyone's. Man or woman. It's true. Guilt exudes from these human eyes.

Cheryl swallows. Applause rises. Paul still walks about blurting his damned harmonica. You fuck, Larry says to him and he stops playing.

What do you mean?

You're an extrovert.

What do you know about being an extrovert?

Larry plays with mail bags all day and could bite dents in Andy's silver pay phone. So I don't fear for him with young Paul. Paul leans down and gargles a fuck you too on his mouth organ. He scrounges away. He goes up like mist and we see him no more forever.

We sit near Andy and ask him how he liked today's filming.

It was very good, he says—and blinks.

I thought it was lousy, I mutter to Larry. Isn't this the worst picture ever made?

It gets stars for lousiness.

But as the rushes go on and we see what ugliness and beauty can come from inspired stillness, I start to feel that I have been in on one of the most weirdly deep, beautiful and original films ever made. My Gordon's gone—I ask Larry about the Marsala he brought for me.

It's under my jacket he says and gets the bottle and unscrews it.

Our strong and stirring troupe of misfits—Paul, Vyvian, Mario, Larry and myself, not to say Andy as well—only underscores the film's statement about human fallibility. Not that film needs a statement! But Lana cannot be more disinterested in the body of Johnny Stompanato lying upstairs in her bedroom. Johnny lies as dead as Tim Finnegan in *Finnegans Wake* who hovers over Joyce's novel as Johnny's body rides ghostlike over Andy's nonpicture and its scratching at art.

Here's to the movies, I tell Larry and toast Underground filmmaking.

You know, I tell Andy, with the close-ups and everything, this could be a great picture.

There are no close-ups, Andy says.

I'm still moved by the weird screen tests in which Cheryl and then Mario pop all their mental organs inside out. That's how it is in Andy's looking-glass world—everything you hide pops out bare-assed.

What do you think, Larry? Could this be a greater film than *Flaming Creatures*?

Nah, man. I didn't even get my cock out.

The GLP Arrives!
Evergreen Review, Vol. 10, No. 44, December 1966

The Village Voice announces the GLP's arrival for his first visit to the capitalist stronghold of Manhattan. He will read at the YMHA, bolstered by distinguished translators Archibald McLeish and the GLP's current right-hand man in English, Ben Belitt. The GLP flies up from his Chilean homeland's vast Andean shore and deserves about four Nobel Prizes, none of which has hit his door. [No longer true. He won in 1971.] His name: Pablo Neruda, the Greatest Living Poet—aside from Jack McManis of State Park, Pennsylvania, which I say without jest.

When I meet him I know Pablo stands tall in the poetry game since he reminds me of Jack. Spiritual ringer for McManis. Same love of the natural sciences, gift for Keats-Rimbaud richness. Men who hear the blood-flow in the veins.

The big night passes and before sleep tarnishes I'll write what I've seen and heard this day. But I will keep my flaws buried and avoid the banality of full self-exposure.

Asleep in my welfare office at Harlem Hospital but sitting up and working forms, I am struck by a thought: I should interview Neruda as he waltzes through Manhattan and its PEN conference of world-figures in belles-lettres. So I spend three hours tracking and just missing him by phone. Then I grip my welfare worker's gut and gasp—gastro-intestinal disturbance! And check out from work at high noon. To nail Pablo.

As I subway to NYU I wonder just what in hell I can ask such a serious man with a life deepened past any I have or will have. He is poetry's vine leaf. I've never written a memorable four-liner—and though I try, I'll spare you. Easy questions will be political, since the GLP's a known Red even as at *WIN* [*Workshop in Nonviolence*] I am a known political dunce. Ha, The Rapier meets The Pillow! At Loeb Student Lounge I am directed by a cop to the fourth floor. On that floor a smiling secretarial drudge says no poets are in session. Is this not where the World-Famed PEN Conference is being held? Where are the celebrities? Where drifts Saul Bellow? Arthur and Henry Miller? Henry Miller—not invited!? And Señor Neruda rests at his hotel.

I walk toward the Fifth Avenue Hotel on Ninth Street, where I know he stays but seldom seems in—I still wonder what the hell I'll ask. I am heavy fleece from the neck up, my head a woolen turnip. Check him out with the Red bit! Oh, no, Donald you know better. You know zip about Marx and Lenin in South America or Russia. But I'm full up with Henry Miller.

The hotel desk says just go to that wall phone and ring him. I don't have a question in mind other than Are you a Henry Miller fan. A male secretary says Pablo's abroad in the city—checking out The Rockettes' big leg-lift?—but he'll answer any questions I have. What are your questions? I'll write them out and send them up. To be this close even to smelling the GLP numbs my blood with cinnamon.

In the bar—as I sip exotic drinks—I write four pages for Señor Neruda to address. Oh, the exotica?—My surprise afternoon off deserves these high-class lime wedges and Lemon Hart Jamaica Rum with hotsy-totsy little umbrellas and 100-proof Wild Turkey and so on. My inspired note now breathes with questions:

Dear Señor Neruda—
I write for *WIN Magazine* (*Workshop in Nonviolence*) and am

also a great admirer of your poetry. I will be covering your recital tomorrow evening and will write a story about it for *WIN*. Perhaps you would answer a few brief questions for me so that my piece will have a more personal flavor than if I had simply reported on the event of your reading. The questions are:

About poetry:
1. Have you a new book being translated into English?
2. Are you familiar with the work of Robert Lowell and, if so, what do you think of it?
3. Which contemporary American or English poets do you admire?

About politics:
4. What do you think of nonviolence as a philosophy?
5. Where are your sympathies in the war in Vietnam?

Thank you very much.

PS. I have a friend, John McManis, whom I consider a very great poet and I would like to quote you a four-liner of his:

> THE DUSTY MILLER
> After you're gone
> The dusty miller will eat
> The carpet flowers
> In my furnished room.
>   —John McManis

You may leave your answers in an envelope at the front desk, or else perhaps allow me to see you personally. I will phone your secretary to arrange an appointment to see you, if you will allow it. I am completely as your disposal as to time—this afternoon or evening or any time tomorrow or Sunday.

PPS. I do hope you will read "The United Fruit Co." tomorrow.

I seal the letter but then recall two more lines by McManis I wish I'd put into the letter, from his elegy for Big Bill Tilden, the tall gay tennis champion:

> Implacable as Lacoste, death made him fall
> Who lent such measure to a tennis ball.

Of Jack, Pablo, and Louis

Neruda—like S. Z. "Cuddles" Sakal—radiates kindness but without the double chins. "You want me kind? I'm kindness. You're a good boy." Discipline strengthens his tenderness.

I catch him in the bar—just where I wrote my cue sheet for his answers. Lillian Russell and Diamond Jim Brady would think this Fifth Avenue Hotel bar *haute monde*—so beautiful but going to pot—though I sit through a Collins and a Black Russian and a Hair of the Thirsty Dog and a verde cayo writing my questions. I drift out to the lobby phones to call Señor Neruda's secretary and deliver the mail when a man beside me says, Oh, he's in the bar.

Hey, I just came from the bar.

Go back, Louis Armstrong huge in my veins. All the saints march into the Fifth Avenue Hotel bar. Neruda? Nobody here by that name. No sweat, no nada, where's Pablo? Then I see him distinctly and walk to where he sits with a lovely woman and a handsome man. I'm nervous—understandably—approaching a man widely seen by myself and Jack McManis as the Greatest Living Poet. Jack reads him in fancy Spanish, I only in Ben Belitt's crunchy English.

Señor Neruda, I say, laying on my Spanish.

His smile breaks rosy and beaming. Yes, how are you?

I am somehow not who I think I am but rather have wandered in from a world apart from the Fifth Avenue Hotel bar although I have been in this very room through many beverages in florid glasses. But I gird myself against slippery tongue and like mishaps.

I'm Donald Newlove with *WIN Magazine*, I say and give *WIN* the heft and thrust of *The New York Times*. And I'd like to ask you a few questions whenever you feel free.

I'm free, sit down.

He points to a seat, which the handsome man clears, and I sit. Down. Carefully. I—

Is that the magazine you work for? he asks, nodding at my normal stack of books underarm.

No, this is *Selected Poems of Pablo Neruda* and *Doctor Zhivago*. I do not intend to read *Doctor Zhivago*. I carry it only for balance.

What?

This is your own book, sir.

Yes, I recognize the design.

I have been carrying it around for a year as my bible. This is the Grove Press edition.

He smiles. You are a very nice man.

Well, thank you. That reminds me. I'd like to send you my favorite Louis Armstrong record—*Louis Armstrong Plays W. C. Handy*. From Columbia.

Columbia!

The record company? You know, anyone can send you a gift such as the Beecham 1937 *Die Zauberflöte* with Erna Berger as Queen of the Night. But it takes something extra to pick the right Louis from my 65 Louis LPs as a special-special gift for the poet of "The United Fruit Co." and "The Heights of Machu Picchu" and

> The jaguar touches the leaves
> With his phosphorescent absence

What? the GLP says.
His handsome friend says:

> *El jaguar tocaba las hojas*
> *Con su ausencia fosforascente*

Ah! Pablo says.
I'll drop the record off at the desk, I say.
You are so kind! What is this magazine?
It's called *WIN*, an acronym for Workshop In Nonviolence. I've written out my questions. They're very short.

Served, he eats a jelly omelet while his handsome friend and his beautiful friend eat salads and study me. I'm not in top shape as he dives into my questions. I avoid coughing while he reads, and say to his friends, If we had time I would tell you about Jack McManis, who is the world's greatest poet—after yourself, sir. To my knowledge, anyway.

To your knowledge? the handsome friend says.

Well, I've not read every living poet. And you never know when a Lithuanian will come out of the woodwork. Nor do I speak Spanish although I do "compose" translations—even of Señor Neruda.

How wonderful! the beautiful woman says, aglow, and to her friend, Carlos, you should "compose" poems in English.

I watch Neruda—reading me! Scanning my prose rhythms. *What do you think of nonviolence as a philosophy?* And so on. He dances down my questions between forkfuls of jelly omelet. He does not gorge. My bright questions leave him buffaloed? Now, I can tell, he's ready for my McManis quotation. Ah! You think I kid about McManis.

May I quote, I ask Pablo, the first stanza of a thirty-liner Jack McManis wrote after hearing another condescending lecture on Wordsworth?

I am honored, Neruda says.

> Wordsworth, William Wrongwords, Lackwords Willy,
> Old grapplejack of words, you drive us silly
> So out of breath with rainbows and all that!
> Where was the world of flesh and blood and chat
> While you conned stale anthem ions on the wall
> Of never-were gold flowers that could not fall?

Neruda's handsome friend, whose name I pick up as Carlos Cortinez, says, That does not sound like praise for Wordsworth.

I think it does, the beautiful woman says and I see her wedding ring as Carlos pats her hand to silence her.

No, he begins with irony, now that you mention it, I say. But it goes on to praise Wordsworth. Jack's voice may not come through at first—being original—but when he lands he sticks. *Old grapplejack of words*, God, I love that—a jack is someone like a steeplejack who climbs heights. You know, Señor Neruda's poems in this country are for the happy few. As are Jack's still. But *Of never-were gold flowers that could not fall* to describe a fantasy of gold flowers painted on a wall? That's reaching for the heights.

Is very beautiful, the beautiful woman says. Gold flowers is beautiful.

Matilde, her husband Carlos warns her about her English.

Before I went to bed last night, I say, I memorized "The United Fruit Co."—my own version—and it must have carried over into my dreams. I found myself as a revolutionary in a South American capital and I'd overthrown the dictator and I was telling him that I'd changed my mind. He could have the country back. This has been a bloodless revolution, I tell him, but I'm the wrong person to head the government. This banana republic needs a political hack like you to lead it because the people don't know any better. And I hand him my pistol and say, Here is your scepter back. The country's all yours. And as I leave the room I hear click, click behind my back. And I turn to him and say, It was never loaded, sir. Even so, I know I will likely never get out of the country alive. Then I woke up. Wonderful dream, Carlos says. What do you make of it?

Between us? That I'm a political incompetent.

New people arrive at the table. Nervous, I touch up my sobriety. Neruda calms me. Don't be afraid, ask me whatever you wish.

I study him. He looks in good shape, fleshy with life: A brandied skin-tone and calfskin fingers—big spender and consumer of the best things in life, many of them not free. No Whitman he! Square eyes under long sharp bulging lids—the eyes of a bandit living on gravy. Fairly tall, heavy, with spiritual support from things seen—not from faith, although his poetry leaps into the mystical, digs into the elemental, and rises magnificent and rich with half-caught thoughts—bars of gold sunlight glimpsed in a corner of the soul. Plenty of solid aristocratic bonhomie. Jack, too, is a cheerful tragedian.

He lays his fork on the tombstone smear of his omelet and damasks his mouth. I look at the jellied plate. I think of the swelling and surreal jellies of Neruda's *One Hundred Love Sonnets* published when he was twenty.

> All day I saw your flying hand before me,
> Light flooded in, a tree of opening roses
> and from Residencia en la Tierra:
> Come to my heart dressed in white, with a bouquet
> of blood-red roses and goblets of ashes,
> come with an apple and a horse

At heart, I think, Neruda keeps a black island within for his drier tragic and Spanish lines—though he fears in his song no senseless swirl or melted piano, as with Lorca's fearless magnificence when declaring *Not death but a fruit stand!*—a line none too clear and yet wondrous. For the Spanish surrealists, imaginative decision falls from the sun.

Awareness is all, for a poet. Jack thinks D. H. Lawrence the poet of the century, for his great death poems and elemental works on the natural sciences—snakes and pansies and so on. Neruda as well blooms with flowers and fragrances, fondles limestone and lithe jaguars. Most fans at the moment see Lawrence as the master of ecstasy. But Jack tags him as a poet in smoked glasses who sees darkly. But Jack adds, "There is only one living poet who sends me and that's Pablo Neruda—who is so good he transcends the party-line bosh he frequently wallows in. He's some punkins. Reminds me of Lorca so often. Grand love, grand disgust. *No es la muerte,/Es la tienda de las frutas*—Lorca (Not death but a fruit stand) defining the USA on his visit to New York." As does McManis, Neruda reveals the life force to itself—his "Ritual of My Legs" is sixty-eight lines about discovering his legs. Neruda often writes in factual but subliminal shorthand, both surreal and stony. Jack as well can grapple words into golden knots and climb the brow of Prometheus. Neruda suspends himself in running light—a tremendous trout in the transparencies of existence. Both poets can at once draw together stars and our lives and horses, dogs and artichokes. Neruda's famed *Odas Elementales* turns on essences of essences. No one is more atomic or easeful at splitting plant tissue and cells than Neruda, not even the GLP. Neruda tracks the Amazon but Jack is the greater anaconda of language—though still unsung.

Pablo stares at my damp shirt pocket and the umbrella from my bushytailed rum drink. His cognac fingers fold my questions and slip them into his pocket. He lances me with a sharp look. These are very serious and interesting questions, he says. I am a political man.

Good God, he thinks I'm CIA! That Vietnam question.

I would like to write out my answers in my room and then give them to you. Would that be all right?

Wonderful!—I want to cry out that I am *not* with the CIA, I am a Harlem Hospital social worker!—But it doesn't seem the right thing to say.

I stand nerve-bright and shake his hand—again bow to his companions—and blunder outdoors—dazed that I am about to inherit a historical document: a holograph page of Neruda on Robert Lowell! I stagger through the Village art show cluttering the streets and wonder how wide a mat and how big a frame this note will demand. It should fit right over my desk. What'll I give him in return? Of course! *Louis Plays Handy.*

Ah, Jack! Ah, Lorca! Ah, Pablo! I have stumbled onto the pure tongue of poetry.

The Greatest Living Man

Time was when a trumpet decided the heftiest jazz master. Louis'd toss up fifty high C's, a Herculean trumpet hurricane. His phrasing and shadings broke the heart—homecoming pieces like "Cabin in the Cotton" and "That's My Home" and "Sleepy Time Down South." He'd purl high C and trill D, E, F. His greatest glory, in the honky tonks and ballrooms, went unrecorded. Cutting disks in a studio he turns businesslike but caring—artful, often inspired, perhaps afloat on a stick of pot but keeping clean lines to save on studio time—while the gin mills framed his greatest leaps. To me, Louis Armstrong is the greatest living human being—the blue

Albert Schweitzer of Dionysus—the big daddy wine-sprinkler of upper paradise who gives us the raw birth of jazz. More genetic and expressive even than Pablo. Jack states that music is a mug's game and writing music for math majors and takes less intellect or flame-footedness than verse. Poetry pumps sublimity through the veins—music mere delight and dance. I agree, of course, being in the union, but my inmost being admits that I choose the high flights of musical invention to the care and reserve of ink and had I the genius I'd be Louis, not Shakespeare. Jack thinks Louis murdered ensemble music by focusing on soloists "He's the one who let all those madmen out," Jack says. But Louis can't help it—even in ensembles you always catch his brass thoughts spilling out. No one else matches him in shading and spirit.

Okay, let's skip forward. I gather these pages on a weekend during which I've seen Neruda three times aside from his reading at the YMHA and am trying to write the story as it happens.

An Amazing Evening! Yes Yes Yes Yes Yes.

The audience sits rapt as Neruda speaks. After each poem the ovation thrills. Applause rises for the translators as well. As the evening ends, beatitude spreads everywhere. All stand, the whole house, no one leaves. Reporters stand clapping, people shout *Bravo Bravo Bravo!* A pink rock, the GLP stands applauding back at us. Magnificence flows. I was here when even Eliot hadn't drawn such response. The YMHA has never seen anything like this—applause so strong and stinging that the GLP reads three extra unpublished poems. We won't let him go! One new verse tells of a naked mermaid who comes into the company of men. "Her eyes were the color of distant love." For a mermaid, that's a police photo. Fishy green adolescent eyes! Gave me shivers—the shiver-test of poetry. And again all shoot out of their seats with a roar and hard clapping. What a triumphant night for the GLP. I stand in tears amid an alien tongue.

The GLP has arrived. In vine leaves.

As the applause builds over him—yes, I really am crying—the sunless GLP takes it in. Well, perhaps a slight smile lifts into a cheek of this angelic penguin—slowly his palms toll back at us. Will it ever end? I don't want it to. If he'd stand there, I'd clap all night.

I have my own spy in the audience. Dian Suflin, a Portuguese major—and in her opinion the translators miss the relentless anguish and poignancy Neruda brings to each work. Dian and I have an arrangement to see the GLP at the Fifth Avenue Hotel Sunday morning for an interview. Results will show up herein. I write on the run!

No patchwork poet, Neruda reads from an organ on Olympus. A calm throb, not nasal, neither grave nor affected—and yet seemingly without a microphone he reaches poetry folk mobbed against the back wall. The crowd pleases him and doubtless undermines his cool. If Big Bob Lowell's here I've missed him and would've nabbed him for a word to *Evergreen Review*—though for some reason I feel he never reads high lit' like this article down at *Evergreen*-level. [I've decided against *WIN* and am selling out to *Evergreen Review*, a splashier venue.] Many pin Lowell as the American GLP—an understandable but grievous error when Jack publishes so rarely. When he read my copy of Lowell's *Life Studies* and I asked what he thought, he admitted there are two or three poems in it.

At the height of the shouts and rejoicings I am stunned to hear Robert Bly, a translator-reader, call this gathering a tribute to the world's GLP. He says those very words: *greatest living poet*. And carried off into overkill he adds *"on earth!"* I stand and clap but long to correct him. The thought that we do listen to the greatest living poet—*on earth!*—sweeps through the crowd and—through tears—I want to make clear to these deprived folk that the real GLP lives in State Park, Pennsylvania—as I clap away with them.

Pablo Squiffed

Now backtrack.

After sleeping off my Saturday pickle juice, I skip to the Fifth Avenue Hotel at 2:00 A.M. to see if Neruda has left me a letter at the desk. Whom do I meet standing at the elevator but Pablo himself.

I stand beside him.

How are you? he asks, in a booze aura bronzed by angel-wings.

Sober! Slept! Glorious. I fear I was not at my topmost clarity with you and Carlos and Matilde this afternoon. How are you?

You want me to write that letter. I haven't written it yet.

Take your time.

No, no. I want to talk with you personally. You are an interesting young American. Why don't you come back on Saturday morning?

I'd be happy as the devil. May I bring a girl with me? She speaks Spanish and Portuguese.

Oh, yes.

Did you read that four-line poem by my friend McManis? What did you think of it?

It was very rich. I like the carpet flowers.

You can't really tell how beautiful he is from a four-liner. I'd love to show you some of his sonnets and occasional verse. He's richly inventive.

My bare nerves just let me speak this last phrase through my heart thumps—knowing that Pablo has read Jack's classic four-liner. And so I go on, saying, Back in the early forties Jack was the seventh and eighth ranked tennis player in the States. He's in the books. He'd play against the champion, Big Bill Tilden, a very tall guy who sad to say was gay.

I am gay.

Homosexual?

No, I am not that. That is gay?

Yep. Now sometimes Big Bill would play René Lacoste who became champion as well. Lacoste was a mechanic. He never smiled on court. Death perhaps smiles but not Lacoste—unless you think of an alligator as smiling. You couldn't beat him. He won out of sheer mechanical ability. Like Big Bill, Lacoste also wrote books analyzing his style—though Big Bill's books lean toward a Broadway gaiety. He even wrote and backed Broadway musicals. So Lacoste chewed up Bill even as a writer. Then one night in the fifties Big Bill was arrested in Hollywood for trying to pick up a minor—actually a male prostitute—and got hauled off to jail and to a prison term. Some years later Big Bill—whom Jack had played—died and Jack wrote an elequy to him. I asked Jack what an elequy is and he says a queer elegy. We call *maricones* queers up here. My copy of the elequy is now lost but perhaps Jack will remember it and send me a copy. I only remember the first three lines and the final couplet. The opening is

> The Vice Squad
> was helping God
> guard Hollywood

—a richly ironic opening!—leading to Bill's arrest and prison term. The final couplet is

> Implacable as Lacoste, death made him fall
> Who lent such measure to a tennis ball.

—which I think one of the great couplets in the English tongue. Death comes as a tennis player to take Big Bill whose great height and championship skill lent such measure to a tennis ball—a mere tennis ball, raised to glory by Big Bill—who was voted the greatest player of the century's first fifty years. And Death comes not just as any tennis player but as the implacable mechanic, the unbeatable—*Lacoste!* Which is *the cost* Big Bill must pay for his championships and world renown—and maybe for being gay?

We part with an agreement. It's now 3:15 A.M. I'm to meet him at 10:00 A.M. with Dian Suflin, a member of the MBGE—Most Beautiful Girls on Earth and fellow social worker at our hospital. I can't foresee what I will wring out of Señor Neruda. After Jack I want him to know Louis Armstrong. Will jazz be beneath him? Tomorrow we meet, head to head.

I am in your debt, sir.

A Rainbow for the Artists

Now to make this hang together. I run as I write.

From "How Spain Was":

>Dry and taut—day's drumskin,
>a sound shaded, that's how Spain was:
>eagle's nest, flat-landed, a silence
>flogged by the weathers . . .
>All your animal
>loneliness, joined to your wit,
>all things built with your hands
>from a silence abstracted from stones,
>your biting wines, those sweet
>and coarse, your wild
>and delicate vines.
>
>Great sunstone, flawless in
>earth's skin,

> Spain threaded
> by blood and metal, afloat and blue,
> poor offspring of petals and bullets
> alone and living in the world:
> deep-sounding, drowsy, one alone.

This is the man, a master of the Spanish tongue, and his vast strength and tenderness—"All of your animal/loneliness, joined to your wit, all things built with your hands from a silence abstracted from stones"—draw to him all the Spanish Americas and their paparazzi. When I arrive at the Fifth Avenue Hotel his celebrity also attracts a force of Spanish paparazzi. Over the hotel hangs the first rainbow I've ever seen in Manhattan. The paparazzi still talk about the oceanic response to last night's reading. I am infused by the rainbow this pure and uncorrupted morning and sit in the lounge knowing a rainbow rises over the Fifth Avenue Hotel. Did last night's reading feature St. John landing with the bulletin: *In the beginning was the Word* . . . ? Has the Second Coming been announced? Everyone agrees on Neruda's greatness. I too still stand and clap and speed him loud cheers from the night before.

The three paparazzi are genuine and peppy bright gents. They follow Neruda about and film a documentary about him and speak as some the finest young men I've ever met. Arthur Miller has been in and out of the hotel and they expect the American press as well. They are Chileans and their English rises on a delicate shrimp fork. Ambition and wit and eagerness fill them to nab their subject again today. God, they're bright young guys. I dance to stay abreast of their grasp of poetry and film.

I know Neruda by heart and recite to them my version of "The United Fruit Co." as I've scrambled it together:

When the trumpets sounded and all
the universe came forth
Jehovah dealt out the world
to Coca Cola Inc., Anaconda,
Ford Motors and other giant firms:
The Fruit Company Inc.
plucked the ripest for itself,
the juicy coast of my land,
the sweet waist of America.
It christened the lands
"The Banana Republics"
and of our sleeping dead
and restless martyrs
usurped their heroism,
liberty and flags,
and brought forth a comic opera:
it outlawed free wills,
gave Caesar's crowns as gifts,
unleashed jealousy, and planted
the dictatorship of the flies,
Trujillo flies, Tachos flies,
Carias flies, Martinez flies,
Ubico flies, all of them flies, flies sticky
With vassals' blood and marmalade,
drunken flies that crawl and suck
around common graves,
circus flies, clever flies
well-versed in tyranny.

Amid the blood-thirsty flies
The Fruit Company amassed
coffee and fruit in ships and

slid them seaward like trays fat with
treasure from our sunken lands.

Meanwhile, the Indians fall
into the sugary chasms
of the harbors, wrapped
for burial in dawn mist:
a body falls, a nameless
thing, a falling zero,
some tossed bunch of rot
afloat in the garbage.
—(DN, 2008)

The highlight of the reading the night before, this poem alone raised a furor of delight. Delight less from Ben Belitt's mighty rhythms than the trombone gutturals of Neruda's Spanish.

But hearing my maimed lines the paparazzi cry, Why did he say that? Why does he add this? I try to look bilingual and above the universal failings of translation. These bright Chileans bring to mind Carlos and Matilde Cortinez, the aristocratic Chileans I met during Pablo's omelet cornada: beautiful, cigarette-ad people with smoky blue eyes who live on sparrows' tongues and on vast ranches where light leaps from the pampas. Intelligent, informed people!—with whom I feel at a loss of learning. [And even less learned when I find that Chile bears the sky-borne wall of the Andes, not great grasslands.] They look forward to Sunday and the PEN boat-ride around Manhattan. Neruda listens while reading my comments and loads his each word with a spearmint toothpick. He is a man among the elements! A man of the Andes! And since the erotic verses of his twenties, familiar with the earth's varying and attractive bosoms. Too proud for a coffin, he will not die—not while caught up in all his flower-dense and jaguar bursts of life.

[Spanish surrealism is catching.] This poet takes on the color of any nearby animal or object and can mirror the richest hues of any beast or beauty our earth places before him. And here he sits, this king incognito in a banquet of flame.

It's such a paradox, Neruda in New York, says Paparazzi #1, who I learn is named Jaime Barrios. He loves to see antique shops and book shops. And mix with the Puerto Ricans.

The Puerto Ricans! Why? Is he crazy?

Why not?

These damned people sing all the time, dance in church, and pass their wretched lives in a flash of lightning. A year to you or me is a day to them.

It is a different time continuum? Jaime asks.

I'll tell you. By the time you and I just reach the moon in our next life, they'll be unsnapping beers in far Andromeda.

Do you have a rate for the speed of life passing?

No. Not that stands up to a close look.

Glorious brown Andean eyes drill me with Nerudan intensity. Such a paradox, Jaime says—informing me in spangles—that Neruda who is so anti-American has such a special hang-up for New York City. This Tower of heartless and empty-eyed Capitalism!

Thank you.

He is so unbelievable. But give him a lawn chair and he'd be at home on the moon.

I've brought a Louis Armstrong record I intend to give him.

Jaime fills with Chilean rapture.

He digs jazz, man! And Louis Armstrong! He is great on New Orleans!

My heart booms. It may give out.

I'm going to interview him! I say—masking an overflow of pride.

When?

This morning. I'm waiting for my translator.

You are going to interview him! Great! Yesterday we only got Arthur Miller. We'll tape-record you.

Jaime's face fills—the charmed Nerudist, flags aloft.

You know, he says, he's not regarded as highly in Chile as in other South American countries, owing to the hammer and sickle stamped on his forehead. Jaime brushes a hand over his forehead's fallen black raven's wing, and says, He missed the Nobel Prize because such a prize would be an endorsement of his ideas. The masses in Chile don't know him too well. But he rules the rest of South America.

A third Spanish reporter arrives in smoked glasses. I find his name is Luis Prieto, he's Jaime's camera- and sometimes soundman, but his English lacks Jaime's flair. He asks, You work for a magazine?

Yes, for *WIN*, I slur, swallowing the name. It's . . .

I've seen the magazine.

I have too, says Jaime. Everyone has seen *WIN*. Five Beekman Place. *Liberation* is published there too. Luis explains with a heavy accent that he and Jaime, his director, who is twenty, are making a movie about Neruda in New York for which Neruda has promised them both a long interview and a special poem. Luis says, He understands that the middle of the movie will be him. Yesterday he came down and Arthur Miller sat waiting for him. We have our camera set up outside when he decides to go out the other door over there with Miller. So we jump up. 'I'm going to the Century Club,' he says, so that we will know where to find him. He loves us. He sometimes poses. To make it easier for us. We follow him like cats.

I smile bilingually.

He loves us! Jaime agrees. Whenever posterity wants him photographed, we do it. We delight in his every word and gesture.

I smile grandly at Jaime's delight and look about for my translator, Dian.

Jaime grips my shoulder, saying, It's quite funny to see him run around New York City like a Red with his head chopped off going to parties and nightclubs and being applauded. Down in Chile he lives on the beach and loves silence and sailing. He tries to be alone.

That's very grand to know.

With no Dian having arrived, I choose to phone Señor Neruda.

His wife answers in mixed English. We braise some words together in a frying pan and at last Neruda takes the line.

Hi. Remember me? I'm Donald Newlove with whom you spoke two days ago and I gave you some questions you said you'd answer. If you haven't written out your answers, I can take them over the phone.

You are a very nice gentleman and I would like to answer your letter on the phone. Your questions are very short and I am in bed and don't think I would have very much trouble answering them.

That's grand. I'm happy you're in bed. An answer is an answer.

I'm not sure I *can* answer you but ask me.

My speedball pen rises, the phone at my mouth.

Señor Neruda, last night's reading was the most thrilling experience of my life.

Yes. Well, I read well.

Everybody stood up.

Yes, they liked it.

It was the greatest applause any poet has ever received in New York.

I did well.

It was the greatest reading in the history of the United States.

Well, I only read good poems.

I want to congratulate you on a thrilling reading.

Yes, I was successful. He coughs. I read the poem by Jack McManis again that you gave me.

Wonderful. What did you think?

It was even better than before. Much richer.

Yes. He writes well.

He's a very rich poet.

Well, he doesn't like to publish. He feels that the poems turn to rot and why have rot in print although it was once bright and intelligible?

I feel that way!

May I ask you my five questions?

He clears his throat. I would like to answer your questions. Do you remember them?

Yes! Have you a new book coming out?

No. Too bad I haven't.

Are you familiar with the work of Robert Lowell and, if so, what are your feelings about it.

Who?

Robert Lowell. He is the greatest living American poet *who publishes.*

No. I don't know Robert Lowell. You say he is American?

Señor Neruda, you're putting me on. I'm not coming through. What do you think of Robert Lowell? *Roberto Low-ell!*

Oh, the Pulitzer Prize winner!

I think back No. *Yes!* He did win the Pulitzer Prize—almost twenty years back and he's been improving ever since.

What about him?

What do you think of his work? About five years ago he switched to a new style that works tremendously.

What do I think? Nothing clear. "The Quaker Graveyard!" Yes! He's very good. I admire him very much. (I feel that Neruda has just peeked into the Oscar Williams remake of Palgrave's famous anthology of English verse.)

Señor Neruda, "The Quaker Graveyard" was written in 1944.

Are you sure what you feel?

He is astounding.

Astounding?

Very much. I like him.

Which other contemporary American or English poets do you admire?

Well, I have known Archibald McLeish a long time. He's very good, but I don't know the contemporary poets too well. I feel a little lost with them.

Are there some living American poets you like?

Yes! I like Allen Ginsberg's *Howl!* And Ferlinghetti. He coughs. What do you think of Ginsberg?

Ten years ago I thought he was digging his own grave. But now he can turn out a Promethean stanza. He fooled me. What are your sympathies about the war in Vietnam?

Are you writing down my answers?

Señor Neruda, I'm blue with asphyxia writing down answers. Look, first tell me what do you think about nonviolence as a philosophy?

The phone deepens. You see, he says, that applies to some places and some times. I was living in India for four or five years in Ceylon and Burma, when I was twenty-two years old. And I deeply believed in nonviolence then. Now I am in another world. His voice sinks into me so strongly that I can only hobble back to the Vietnam question. What are your sympathies about the war in Vietnam?

You see, I was brought up in Latin countries. All of my life has been a struggle against colonialism. This has been a very great struggle. I am against colonialism. Do you think the Americans are trying to colonize Vietnam?

You mean like West Berlin?

You've been in West Berlin twenty years, he says.

And we'll be in Vietnam for twenty years. We've stoppered a bung hole and can't take the cork out.

Ah, but do the American militarists want to take the cork out?

I don't think so, Señor Neruda. They speak with a forkéd tongue—want to stay and to get out both at once.

I am so defeated thinking about my country that I can't carry on.

This war, I say, isn't even happening in the Pentagon—those guys are eight or ten years into future strategy. Thank you very much for your time.

You are a very nice man and I enjoy talking with you. And about Jack McManis and Lacoste.

Thank you, sir.

His voice runs on in me as we hang up. I see him as a young Chilean of twenty-two drinking in Gandhi in Ceylon and Burma and in the breeding and sprouting miseries of India in 1927. Just now the median life span for an Indian is 25 years and *then* it was less. In 1953 Neruda won the Stalin Prize—the Nobel Prize of the Eastern World—which may be why he veils a jeer at Lowell's Pulitzer. I gossip while Neruda stays a Communist with his jaw set—but on his plate rests a serene jelly omelet. My hand lies on the receiver. I hear the end couplet of *Lear*: "The oldest hath borne most. We that are young/Shall never see so much, nor live so long."

The paparazzi study me. I've done it, I sigh. Had my interview. Ohh, they'd wanted to view me interviewing him. Noon falls hard and I dry up in my quest for the Poet of the Andes. Soon he'll be asleep or on a stage sitting on his grandeur. I've met him four times. The paparazzi live with him. I hear four more lines by McManis that Pablo would adore:

> The rat-chewed Statue of Liberty
> Is turning mildew green.

My, she looks mighty sick!
Is it anemia or gangrene?

A Coda for Pablo and Louis

I start for home to listen to the glorious *Louis Plays Handy* but as I stagger through the Sahara of the Village Art Show without a drink—my pockets plunging with holes after my rum umbrella drinks in the hotel bar—it strikes me that I have not asked Señor Neruda about the Greatest Living Man—Louis Armstrong!

I turn and head back to the Fifth Avenue Hotel. Lift the horn in the lobby. Mrs. Neruda, his second wife, answers. In the background I hear Señor Neruda slapping his body in the shower. *Señor Nuevoamor?* He splashes my name out to his wife. I'd laid on the Spanish. But it's a miss. He doesn't tie Nuevoamor with Newlove. Nor does his wife while the shower gushes and they belch my name about and I writhe. *Señora Neruda, forget it!* I don't speak no English, señor. That's grand, I say, let's hang up.

The paparazzi study me.

Jaime Barrios asks, What did he say?

I fold together many talks and say, He says he and Arthur Miller are going on a boat-ride around Manhattan tonight without Allen Ginsberg.

The Chilean nods, the white sage thick on his twenty-year-old brows. He says, With all those famous people on board I'll be on that boat if I have to sink it.

Luis Prieto says, These famous people are very famous. We need them.

Especially without Allen Ginsberg, Jaime says.

Allen Ginsberg, Luis Prieto says, is starving, hysterical, naked.

But not in public, Jaime makes clear.

Hmm! So Jaime and I go to NYU's Press Center for the PEN ferry ride but the woman in charge tells us that the ride is oversold and that about ninety people will be turned back. And that means men from *Time* and *Newsweek* and the Spanish edition of *Life*. She tells Jaime he hasn't a chance in hell of getting on board.

Jaime smiles. I'll be sailing.

Back in the hotel I again phone Neruda. Now another man, Robert Bly—a reader/translator from YMHA (and originally from Odin House in Madison, Wisconsin)—shows up beside me and picks up the other phone. I'm talking with Señor Neruda, I say.

Oh, Bly says and hangs up. He eyes and hangs over me, Bonaparte with a butterfly on his finger. He has the grim authority of Lowell. So I say, Here, you talk, and hand him the phone. He launches into a beautiful if oversold theme: *That was a thrilling evening last night, Mister Neruda! I can't tell you how thrilled I am. It's like the people of New York had never heard a poem before. I'm still thrilled. Yes, yes, it was great. Thrilling.*

I find myself yawning as I write notes.

Bly hangs up and asks, What are you doing?

Writing notes.

He eyes me with shock. But I can hardly call his chat with Neruda private or confidential—having said the very same words myself.

You're going up to see him? I ask. Perhaps you'd do me a favor and take this record along—for him from me.

He clears his throat. Yes.

Jaime comes over. He asks, What did he say?

He's up but he's bedded down with a raspberry omelet, I say.

Do you know Señor Neruda? Bly asks Jaime.

Yes, sir, I've known him for a long time. I follow him. I'm making a movie about him. Whenever he moves we film it. He likes that.

You must be quite familiar with him, Bly says.

Yes, sir, Jaime says, brushing back his raven's wing. I got about a hundred pictures of you last night on the stage with him.

He's a very great man, Bly says.

Yes, sir. Did you ever hear him improvise?

Bly lights up. No!

Last night, I mean after the reading. He was with the Chilean ambassador. You were on the stage with him earlier.

Yes, but I didn't hear Señor Neruda improvise.

That's when he's best. His stuff isn't so worked over.

I didn't hear it.

When he's really feeling great and loose, he improvises. I have heard him do it on politics. It's one of the great experiences of life to hear Señor Neruda improvise. You've never heard him improvise?

No.

But you were with him on the stage last night.

I've never heard him improvise.

I have heard him several times. He is impossibly glorious when he improvises about elementals and the phosphorescence of jaguars in the forest. It is like nothing else in your life.

Bly cannot speak.

Jaime sighs. You listen with tears in your eyes.

I ask, What does Señor Neruda think about Louis Armstrong?

Jaime turns sunless and serious—his face falls—his hands splay out. He loves him.

He turns his head aside for a deep breath. He turns back to us and fights for a smile. First thing in town he wants to go up to the jazz clubs in Harlem.

Louis lives in the Bronx, I throw in.

Bly says, You listen with tears in your eyes?

These are lines that fall on the soul like dew on the grass, Jaime says. Two nights ago, uh, Neruda is a New Orleans fan—we were at the Dom and Neruda is shelling out the gelt for all of us. Suddenly he throws his head back and says, These nets of music are as wide as the sky! He loves jazz and Louis. Now he wants to hear Miles Davis. You want to know the first thing he said as we landed here? And the whole city lies out there blazing with diamonds?

What? Bly whispers.

What's playing at the Five Spot?

Dinner With the Lowells
Esquire, September 1969

"... *half my lines are not in the original.*"
—Robert Lowell in a note to his
adaptation of *Prometheus Bound*

A happy week for alchemy! *Time*'s Christmas cover shows Bach with his head severed in ecstasy and *Life* has a full-page print of Picasso's ecstatic *The Dream*. Another severed head painting, although with a penis afloat on the girl's dreaming mind. That's about twelve million severed heads in print for Christmas. And an invitation for Sunday-evening dinner with Robert Lowell, who has been severing heads himself in recent work.

It's no matter whether the artist knows he's wetting his fingers in alchemy: a severed head is a severed head—genius at full rapture. Lowell has gone from drawing classical severed heads—Perseus and Medusa, Judith and Holofernes, David and Goliath—to drawing his own beheading in confessions of illness—("My mind's not right"—"Skunk Hour," *For the Union Dead*)—until now in *Near the Ocean* he cuts off his wife's head as well. I think of Yeats's twenty-five years with the hermetic Order of the Golden Dawn, of Graves's *The White Goddess* and of Jung's thirty-year study of alchemy. Has Lowell been reading Jung? I will ask at Sunday dinner. My bliss in severed heads and alchemy runs high. Let us range into clouds of metaphor on this brave island where Lowell governs and prospers with his abundance of verse and magic.

I've heard Lowell read many times, attended his class at the New School some ten years ago, and spoken with him a few times. His readings are often grim—charged—unfathomable bursts ("The Lord survives the rainbow of His will") yet his audiences speak back with sounding applause while Lowell sucks down the full heartthrob with a satyr smile. I like his gritty voice and grinding molars but a new poem of his often goes right over my head—his words a rush of bird shadows circling the room. Some years pass before I catch just the right deathliness or rage or fervor, as if Yeats's "The Second Coming" ("What rough beast slouches toward Bethlehem to be born?") will at last be as easy to grasp as Shelley's "Ozymandias" ("The lone and level sands stretch far away"). In the classroom his readings rend, their slow carnage worrying and troubled, with much hair-rubbing—the poor bare poem laid out spread-legged and nailed to the classroom floor.

In recent years Lowell has made a few trips to South America. So when my friend Carlos Cortinez—at times the companion of the great Chilean poet Pablo Neruda and—this is part of his character—the Director of Cultural Extension Activities at The University of the South in Valdivia, Chile—comes to New York for Christmas week and phones Lowell for an interview, Lowell offers Sunday-evening dinner to Carlos and his wife Matilde—and to his interpreters, my wife Jackie and me. Lowell gives no interviews.

Carlos is writing a book on living American poets, and Lowell, I believe, wants to refresh his own feelings about South America and hash over politics. He has many South American friends whose artistic works hang hamstrung by government whim. And surely he wants to hear how his literary competitors have risen or fallen. He and Neruda stand at a draw for the Nobel Prize.

Sunday Carlos and Matilde show up for a Lowell briefing—as he calls it—at my bottom-rent fifth-floor-walkup Lower East Side pad. Carlos at thirty-four adorns his elegance with tailored silver sharkskin glimmering on his slim figure and with a dark three-month beard he's grown on a scholarship to—this too is part of his character—the University of Iowa International Writing Program. He masks flaws in his stumbling English with square black horn-rims while a suave black lamb Russian astrakhan curls about his skull. Cultural strain tortures his glasses.

Now, Donald, thees Lowell, he ees good poet? Or not? I never read in English nothing he write. Only, what is it, "Quaker Graveyards"? God is rainbow? I no understand. He is complicated poet? Show me a poem! I hope you will write together and type up for me a bunch of question we can ask him for the tape-recorder? Yes, shall we? Then when I get to Iowa I have someone type up his answers from the tape and I translate them into Spanish. Hm?

A fuel strike has hit and we sit around my steamless pad in coats and hats and gloves and spume breath at each other. Jackie serves herb tea. We have only matzoth and margarine to offer them. They find this unleavened Manhattan bread crisp and wonderful and want to take some home with them. Matilde wears a six-dollar leatherette bellbottom suit bought at a five-and-dime—and no coat. She teaches ballet in Valdivia and dwells on going to Moscow for top-grade training rather than back to Iowa with Carlos. [Notebook: She does not go to Moscow. How can I put this? Two years or so after this Lower East Side winter briefing, Neruda divorces his second wife and Matilde divorces Carlos—she goes off to Chile's Isla Negra as Neruda's third wife and is revealed to be the inspiration for many of his earlier most famous love poems! Carlos gets hospitalized for a nervous breakdown. He recovers on lithium but gives up on Neruda and becomes a well-known Borges scholar. Carlos accompanies blind Jorge Luis Borges to a reading at Penn State where he at last meets my mentor and the Greatest Living Poet Jack McManis. Then Borges comes to Manhattan for a reading at the Salmagundi Club and I and my new wife Nancy attend but Carlos fails to appear though I look for him. I write and tell him that we are smelted down over and over in the crucible, Carlos, only to be recast in a stronger mold. But for now—in an *Esquire* of 1969—here we sit in our youth—blue winter wind whistling down Seventh Street—as ice nicks the panes and we chew matzoth and beat our arms for warmth.] Suddenly she punches him.

Hey! What ees that for?

You say *which* for *who*, Carlos!

I never did! I never did do it! *You* are the one who always say *which* for *who*!

They fall over each other on the couch.

I wave my tea as it steams in the ice-light. Come on, Carlos, be serious. This is the Nobel Prize we're wafting about.

Show me one poem! He opens *For the Union Dead*. "The Drinker"—who is this? Is this Lowell? Does he drink? Should I ask him about his drinking? Ees he A.A.? What do you think?

I think manic depressives shouldn't drink.

Crazy people? What does Lowell think of Allen Ginsberg? You said in your Neruda article that Neruda likes Ginsberg very much. Lowell less—maybe Pablo say that to make Lowell nervous? Who is this poem: "The man is killing time—there is nothing else." What is killing time? This is very difficult poem, no? I am fearful I no understand Lowell until he is translated. How about these other poets on my list, will they be easier?—*although* Lowell to me is The Most Important Poet.

Carlos has a list of beat wordwhirlers he wants to interview around the States.

You'll have to use your tape-recorder, Carlos. These wildmen don't even speak English.

Ferlinghetti ees no American?

Sure he is.

What ees "A Coney Island of the Mind"?

It's the poet's mind at play, whirling. Going up like a Ferris wheel and looking about.

Ferrous? You mean *iron* wheel? *I* am whirling!

We talk about Neruda's three-day visit to New York City and his huge success at a YMHA reading where he read "The United Fruit Co." and revealed his new poem "The Mermaid"—"Her eyes are the color of distant love." Carlos translated for a Chilean literary magazine my *Evergreen Review* article about this event. But now I wonder how many of my colorful literary feathers he caught—or perhaps just winged with his imperfect mastery of which and who. Carlos thinks Neruda's communism hampers his chances for the Nobel Prize. He laughs, But Neruda thinks he is Greatest Living Poet! When you write to him, he never answers what you write about but always something else and a little curious.

Why doesn't he answer you straight?

I can no tell. He ees very curious man.

He wants to be a myth?

Of course. But you think McManis is the Greatest Living Poet, no?

My Neruda article compares McManis—a friend with a small but heartfelt public at Penn State where he teaches—with Neruda for the garland of Greatest Living Poet. McManis is Lowell's age and I've typed up a swatch of his poems to give to Lowell for his files this evening. My ambition wavers however before the awful and majestic blister Lowell's tongue can raise should I be too forward. He once answered a *Village Voice* reviewer of one of his plays with a thwack that left the page tingling. His irony—never reckless—staves in a man's ribs.

McManis? Or Neruda? Or Lowell? The Greatest Living Poet, Carlos? Up at that height, who can say? So Lowell knows you are interviewing him? It's not just tea and matzoth?

Of course he does! I can hardly believe my ears, he sound so kind on the phone. I tell him I bring tape-recorder and interpreters. So you must write me up the notes on what he says tonight which I don't understand or miss on the tape-recorder. What is his wife like?

She publishes under her maiden name, Elizabeth Hardwick, and is much respected—a first-rate literary journalist and Advisory Editor of *The New York Review of Books*. I open her *A View of My Own* and show him her elegiac "America and Dylan Thomas" essay: "He was one of ours. In a way he came back here to die with a terrible and fabulous rightness . . . 'Severe alcoholic insult to the brain,' the doctors said . . . He could be allowed anything. They would give him more drinks when he was dying of drink . . ."

That is very good, no? Carlos asks.

Here's her picture.—It's a photo of a thoughtful, dark-haired woman of piercing inner beauty. A few years ago I envied Lowell for having so beautiful a wife whose writing ever moved me as deeply felt and kind and brilliant. I once got a hand-written reply from her while Lowell was away. She said she was answering his mail during his illness. Her hand is jittery or spidery in this letter and reading it my sympathies rise as I imagine Lowell in the wards he describes while Mrs. Lowell sits—well, I admire her!

We all walk out into the wind and part—later to meet on Lowell's doorstep before going inside. Ice cinders the wind and Matilde's leatherette bell-bottoms. Early Lowell weather blowing from Boston Common to Tompkins Square.

The wind fifes and long-gowned women run for the Lowell doorway as Jackie and I stand and hope that each arriving cab comes packed with Chileans. Cab after cab stops at this swank front. They're partying, we agree, we'll never get an interview! My wife wilts in the chill. My beard mats with snow like Zhivago's at his iced-over country home. After a half-hour the ice drives us in without Carlos and Matilde and we find we're at the wrong door: this elegance houses the Regency Whist Club! Carlos has given us an East Side address, not West Side.

We slog across Central Park amid wind blasts over raw ice and at last find the right buzzer and a door opens upon . . . a graying bespectacled skulking man. He sees only a hairy ambush in wire frames and its frozen mate.

I'm afraid Carlos misunderstood me. We didn't expect you for dinner and we really don't have enough to go around. We're just sitting down now. Perhaps you'd like to go away and come back, says Robert Lowell. A baleful and majestic glare. But penniless past coffee shops I cry *Forget us!* and launch my wilting wife forward into his Lowellian fright-face and she stands drinking down heat, poor thing. Must think of my wife first. As for food, we escapees from the Siberian plains will settle for crusts like creatures of the gulag.

We glide into a soaring living room roof-windowed over tall chairs and a royal couch boat meant for Alexandrian revels. We shuck our frozen clothes—oh, so eager for this sauna's swelter after our hour crunching over Central Park ice through hard winds rivering down from Harlem. Above us a balcony overhangs the Olympian library-living room and from the heavens of invention I hear student fiddlers and a girl pianist on the balcony spring into the last movement of the *Archduke Trio*. Live Beethoven! But what else did I expect? Lowell and I anchor two ends of the publishing arch in Manhattan—uptown and downtown—his purity of live pianist and fiddlers and my rasp of aged stereo disks. At once I hand Lowell a bottle of Chilean champagne. Delight writ large causes him to miss that the gift is from Carlos and Matilde who now wave to us from a candlelit table in the dining room. Other guests drink and study us. Jackie and I move to sit out dinner in the living room but

Mrs. Lowell—gowned and apologetic—floats toward us.

Look, they've brought Chilean champagne! Lowell says. I'll put it on to chill.

It doesn't need to chill, I say.

But he fades off and leaves the hard part to his wife.

Flowing with embarrassment, Mrs. Lowell waves a hospitable dish towel toward the dining room. Have you eaten? Oh, I don't believe you! A Southern accent.

But why don't you sit with us anyway? We've set chairs for you.

After introductions we sit amid candlelight and Con Ed. My wife perches beside Elizabeth Lowell at the table's far serving end. I'm in a noble bucket of sticks beside Robert Lowell at the head. Elizabeth Lowell swoops out of the kitchen, loaded with a casserole steaming with cabbage and knackwurst. It's odd, sitting without a plate, and I cozy Lowell's ash tray onto my bare polished corner. The candleglow guests talk and my wife and I say nothing for a while. I pat and dry my beard as a kind of guest simian. Beside me Lowell looms like Beethoven, a dusty bottle of Margaux uncorked by his wine glass. He leads the table talk or—like the piano in the *Archduke*—announces each theme. He wears a fuzzy old peach-brandy jacket—its fibers strain, rounded to his bulk—and a candy-striped shirt with pastel block-stripe tie—the candlelit lord from Boston's hardly passionate Marlborough Street. He smiles—no veil. I find myself surprised and seated beside Dr. Samuel Johnson, literary dictator of London. Ahh, so this is courtly life, so unlike Seventh Street and Avenue B.

What is whist? Jackie asks Elizabeth Lowell. We wound up at the Regency Whist Club looking for this address!

Cal, what is whist? Mrs. Lowell asks her husband. [His nickname "Cal" is short both for the Roman tyrant Caligula and for Shakespeare's dark monstrous mooncalf Caliban from *The Tempest*.]

What is whist? he asks the table. It's a kind of Tory bridge or something, isn't it? Are they still playing it? Whist, whist! The words we use! I've just discovered that the stories I've been telling for years are canards. I've been telling canards! Extravagancies! Absurdities! Falsehoods! But why are my stories ducks, Charles?

A dark-eyed man down the table only stares at Lowell and says nothing.

Have you any idea? Lowell asks again.

Charles moves his untouched cabbage and knackwurst about in silence.

He hasn't the foggiest idea, a man named Jack Thompson says, whom I take to be a British grenadier.

Oh, I'm sure he knows, Lowell says.

Charles pushes his cabbage away, grips his side and fights an attack of bile. He mutters, It's a fine feathered bird that quacks but can't sing.

But my lies sing! Lowell says. Don't they, Lizzie?

During this bit of lexicography I note that the party has been going on for a few hours. Laird Weary, a guest, cries out something about women and canards and Lowell replies, Man does, woman is, Graves says. Isn't that what you mean, Weary? And bullyragging Carlos he asks, Carlos, you can't learn anything at a writers' workshop can you?

What? Carlos says, aglow with despair. I don't quite understand your question, ha ha.

I mean, surely a poet has nothing to learn in a workshop? Lowell says.

Laird Weary says, Cal wonders why you waste your time at a carpenter's convention.

Carlos says, There are many things I feel important about it.

Lowell broods over workshops with the grim smile of a lifeguard at the Flood. He sees poets all over the beach? What do you do? he asks me in a quiet aside.

I write.

Oh? Poetry?

Then I shove it away out of sight.

Lowell slumps in thought into his cabbage.

Elizabeth Lowell delivers a fresh bottle of Margaux to her husband and a glass for me. You write? she asks, bottle at my glass.

None for me, thanks. I tell Matilde beside me, One drop and my head floats.

Why did you ask if he writes? Laird Weary asks—he's Lowell's age, around fifty-one, and went to Kenyon with Lowell.

You have to in the States! It's the first thing we ask, What do you do? That's really Puritan—we don't want anyone around who wastes time. In Europe you don't do this, don't ask me why. But I always ask that of Americans. You could be talking all afternoon to a bottle maker, Lowell says pouring a little more, and find later he's been translating Horace for thirty years. Lowell translates Horace—or rather imitates him and adds personal little touches to Horace's stampede at Phillipi and red roses to his myrtle garlands.

You do write *poetry*? Elizabeth Lowell asks me.

Oh, yes. But it takes six months after writing prose to get your head saturated again for poetry. And then you can't write prose because you're over-condensing all the lines, and they take forever.

You can't do them both together, Don! Lowell laughs, and Uncle Cal's hand falls upon my shoulder while he forks his cabbage. I see that while Lowell lives as a conservative aristocrat, his hair has a frayed Beethovenian back-mat.

Lowell and Laird Weary set about nettling reputations and Laird Weary's clowning brings out a trace of boorishness in Lowell. Lowell asks Carlos if he's met an older bull-tongued poet of the plains during his travels. He's a sort of scratchy poet, he says. Wouldn't you say he was *scratchy*?

No, I don't know, Carlos says. When I first meet him in Texas, he was very heavy drinking. So I cannot tell too much about him.

He writes better drunk, Lowell says.—But still scratchy.

After this amusement, Lowell measures American poets against their thin-talented British counterparts and avoids direct critique of living American poets. Speaking of unsung college poets, Lowell grimaces—much like a weight-lifter with sore gums but about to make a fifty-pound press with his jaw while battling a hernia.

Some mute inglorious birds! Laird Weary crows over his glass and swathes his big brass grenadier moustaches.

The trouble is they are not mute enough, Lowell says, they write endlessly!

I see armadas of midnight poems sailing to oblivion across the plains of the Republic. Poets without those magic germ cells spreading down into subconscious inks, as in Lowell's elegy on Roethke:

> helpless elemental creature.
> The black stump of your hand
> just touched the waters under the earth,
> and left them quickened with your name . . .

Is that black stump hallucinatory drunken grief—or Roethke's creative use of his manic depression? As Lowell comments on poets this evening, he measures by God-given standards of aristocratic germ cells: has he not transmagicked into cloud-borne English the metaplasm of Baudelaire, Montale, Pasternak, Rilke, and Horace? And even Aeschylus! Lowell's *Prometheus Bound* is set for production by the Yale School of Drama and carries something of an attack on Johnson's Vietnam policy.

Your Aeschylus is being put on—that must be satisfying.

And quite up to date—but without cigarette lighters. Prometheus is the prototype of today's rebels. In adapting Melville and Aeschylus, I'm given characters and plot—such wonderful crutches, you know, Don, like having meter to build with—and I don't have to go on and on about myself. But good translation from Greek to English is impossible and I didn't try and cut maybe thirty pages of the play and kept it in prose and let it rip right along. When I was reading with Parra down in Venezuela, I asked him what he thought was the difference between German and Anglo-Saxon, and he said, *Manure!*

What did Parra say? Carlos asks.

There's not really much difference between German and Anglo-Saxon, the stock words are from the same roots. Laird Weary mauls over this suggestion despite Lowell's status as a linguist. Parra said, "When I think of Anglo-Saxon, I feel my hands and my nose are full of soft, swarmy, smelly ordure! German is not rich quite this way." Lowell crumbles manure over his plate, then sinks grinning and hungry for praise into the small of his chair and says, Parra understands language as gesture! *I see the first Angle landing on Britain's shore and* clubbing *the first Celt he meets*—Lowell's fist rises over his plate—and when the Angle finally has the Celt down—split-skulled and bowels spilling—the Angle cries, Ha! You language, me gesture!

Laird Weary roars, awash in the blood of Celts. [He will die in 1975 of barbiturates and liquor.—DN]

Lowell glows into the turmoil of his cabbage. His mouth flies kind, gallant flags that droop bit by bit as the damned Sisyphean rock begins to roll back over him. He keeps a stammer under flattening pressure and—too self-respecting for a cliché—hulks and suffers over every verb, his voice heart-strong and a tense deep tenor. He strives, wherever he is, to be worthy of his work—of the exacting, crude, rugged virtue that brightens his New England crucifixion. In a note to his *Notebook 1967–68*, he says, "In truth,

I seem to have felt mostly the joys of living; in remembering, in recording, thanks to the gift of the Muse, it is the pain."

Borges is the finest Latin American poet, Laird Weary says.

Has he written poetry? Lowell asks Carlos. How surprising. Next I'll learn he translates Horace into excellent Spanish.

He is a very good poet! Everyone knows him for his stories, but I prefer him for his poetry.

Borges' late-blooming marriage comes up. Since Borges is a hermetic writer, I try to lead us into talk about writers' wives, with Nora Joyce and Georgie Yeats worn dry by their husbands' dips into dark secrets of the English tongue—hidden stuff made known only to those sucked into the cosmology of dream upon which rest the meanings of words used daily. Aside I tell Matilde, who is a writer's wife untroubled by dips into hidden secrets of the Spanish tongue, We talk as if we know what words mean—but the words we speak only glint with the meanings below common speech. She eyes me and nods but somehow I feel my remark strikes her as smelling of the lamp—too studied, cunning, and mercurial to mull over. Or perhaps she needs to read more Neruda and Borges!

What was that? Lowell asks.

Forget it. Maybe later—

What do you think of Ben Belitt? Carlos asks Lowell about a Neruda translator.

His ear is a ball of dough with old razor blades in it.

Do you like Ben Belitt? Elizabeth Lowell asks she delivers fresh wine to my corner—my glass stays upside down.

Well, I first read Neruda in his translations.

That would make a difference.

Well, maybe not. I've compared many translations of Neruda and for me he's untranslatable—nobody does it well—just as Hart Crane must be untranslatable. How can you translate "The imaged word it is that holds/Hushed willows anchored in its glow"?

In another tongue you can't even hint at that supermix of surreal linkages, much less suggest the subtext of the love affair the lines rest on.

Lowell burns with a smile to his wife. I said Ben Belitt has an ear like a ball of dough with old razor blades in it, darling.

I've never heard that before.

Helpless Carlos leans over the table and stares at me.

I point to Jackie, saying, She speaks Spanish.

But he misses everything. I must bring my dull novelist's eye to bear on the details of this festival of chat. But since note-taking marks me as an Untouchable, I shall trust to memory and to echoes ringing with brilliance. Ah yes, down the table I fix on Charles, who says less than nothing all evening. Checked-vest dandy, he has the same round head and deep-sunken eyes as Poe and I see him as Edgar Allan Baudelaire—yes, yes, that shared skull-shape and spitting eye. He eats nothing, never lifts his fork but to move the cabbage about his knackwurst, but ever wets his spiteful lower lip with wine, not drinking, only sucking up whatever fumes arise off his lip. When Lowell laughs, E.A.B. turns his bulbous forehead toward him, the better to vent his pity on Lowell's gaiety and pain. The greater Lowell's laugh the more his guest's eye burns.

The trio ends the Schubert piano trio in E flat major and Lowell calls, Again, again! This is my favorite piece of chamber music! You can't have enough Beethoven and Schubert to light up a winter night. Again the piano enters and the big-toned fiddle and juicy cello lay a larky sparkle on the diners.

These guests, this dinner, this music, Charles's eye says, this pitiable "faculty soirée," is not pleasurable, not patrician, and not even up to Paris standards. His small hands and tiny fingers—naked of all power for work and fit only to lift a pen—look not only boneless but limp and cast out as they lie before him, open and crablike. Lowell's fingers—roped over his fork or pinching his wine stem—look massive and swollen with heavy desk workouts tossing off hundreds of his new Lowellian-form unrhymed historical sonnets. And yet Charles, for all his seeming unlikeness, answers to Lowell's humors with a grim almost biological likeness of wavering temper. My likeness, my brother!

Lowell asks, Carlos, do you know Randall Jarrell?

Randall . . . Ja . . . *Jarrell!* Ah yes, I hear of him this afternoon.

He was our best critic and wrote our best war poetry.

He is dead, no?

I thought you might want him on your list.

My list, it is contemporary. I have on my list . . . Carlos runs through his list of nondescript verse jockeys. I writhe for Lowell but Lowell takes the list deadpan—he knows them all. What do you think of them? Carlos asks.

Lowell cuts out a maverick academy dream-singer from the list, speaks well of him and warns, But catch him when he's sober. Now Jarrell, he was so enthusiastic and a great quoter. You wanted to read whatever he was writing about. That's the mark of a great critic—enthusiasm . . .

Laird Weary's birdlike wife tells Jackie that she's writing a thesis in library science. I'm tracing the influence of William Morris—the Pre-Raphaelite poet and craftsman—on American bookmaking and cabinetry. His poetry isn't read today.

I can't think of a single poem by him, Jackie says.

But his chairs still hold up? E. A. Baudelaire asks. He goes unheard but by the sharpest of ears.

Mrs. Weary tells Jackie, It's our sixth wedding anniversary. We were married in front of that very fireplace in the living room.

You lucky woman! Jackie says. And did your husband have that moustache already?

Yes, but not as sweeping. And your husband?

The same. But less furry.

Ees your anniversary! Carlos cries across the table. He rises—the gallant international South American poet-cultural planner—and circles the table and kisses her raised cheek. But second thoughts butter his glasses.

That ees what we do in Chile on anniversary, he says in comic opera mock-epic and is cheered.

Interpret! Interpret! Laird Weary cries at Jackie. What the hell are you here for?

Carlos plans to run off with your wife, Jackie says.

And build cabinets with her? E. A. Baudelaire asks.

Mrs. Weary's mother, up visiting from Tennessee, takes a Tareyton from a silver cup. You're stopping! Laird Weary chucks at her. She says nothing and looks for a match. Lowell cries, Laird, your whole family must be stopping because all they do is grub cigarettes.

Matilde's hand falls on Laird Weary as she says in Spanish to Carlos, Laird reminds me of Octavio.

Interpreter! Laird crows at Jackie.

Matilde says, I say you remind me of our friend Octavio in Santiago who ees great lover.

Laird Weary kisses her hair, his hand on her leatherette thigh. She laughs.

Yes, that ees Octavio.

Watch out, Carlos, Lowell warns.

Laird Weary's hand drops from her thigh to the carpet and comes up with an eight-week pure brown Burmese. It's the cat! The cat! The cat is a leather freak!

The cat breaks loose and bolts into the living room.

Lowell facing the living room points, Look! My laurels are fading.

He nods toward a life-size white marble bust of a boy-man on the living room table—a wreath of russet laurel crowns the bust.

Those were green laurels when given to me on my fiftieth birthday. Now they've turned brown.

Ees that you? Matilde asks of the far bust.

No, that's Richard Wilbur.

Laird Weary roars, flagging down the wine.

Through the laughter Carlos says to me, Richard Wilbur!—You must tell me more about Richard Wilbur.

I join Mrs. Weary's mother in one of Lowell's table Tareytons as Edgar Allan Baudelaire's glance pricks me. My wife smiles from her bare polished corner two candle flames away. E.A.B.'s glance assures me that all is vanity and that of writing many magazine articles there is no end—and it is good to keep one's trumpet humbled.

Lowell looks at him. When did Shakespeare retire? At forty-six? I'm fifty-one...

How would you like to write *Hamlet* at thirty-six and *Lear* at forty-one? E. A. Baudelaire asks Lowell. And thirty-four other five-act verse plays in sixteen years? Which is impossible...

Of course Middleton's hand is obvious, Lowell says. But Shakespeare wrote the greater part of his work in a ten-year period. From about thirty-six to forty-five or so. He had run down by *The Tempest*. *The Tempest* is a disaster, don't you think? It only has about 200 good lines. Lowell digs up the good passages for E. A. Baudelaire. Peter Brook wanted me to tinker with it for a new production—Lowell holds the seashell necklace of the play up for us to look at—do away with that masque and the most boring parts. Nothing happens during the masque! It just shouldn't be there.

Oh but it should, E. A. Baudelaire says with a mild glance at the musicians above us. The whole play is one thought in the mind of Prospero—one drop of water like *A Midsummer Night's Dream*. All the colors and hues keep changing so that everyone sees everything differently, with a different tawniness or green or blue—and the masque is the great moment of clarified light before Prospero pulls the clouds back over it.

That's very interesting. I'd never thought of that.

The masque is the reason he wrote the play.

Well, I knew it was impossible. I couldn't rewrite *The Tempest*, heaven knows. My God, I haven't . . . His shudder disclaims such overreaching. We know how he wrote. I mean he must have written like lightning, the pages blotchy and black, then gone back and filled in. You have to wait for it to come and it's such a miracle when it does.

E. A. Baudelaire wags a finger. You forget that he wrote each play without acts or scene divisions. We credit him with the work of centuries of editors. He just jumped in at the beginning and wrote until his hinder parts grew smooth and all knots were tied and the dawn rose over his last speech. But what if your best friend and rival—with Marlowe dead or in hiding abroad—has steeped himself in philosophical magic and written a play called *The Alchemist*? Wouldn't some of your best friend's interests rub off on you when you start out to write about a philosopher on an island? And—

But Jonson's *Alchemist* is such a great bore, so over-written and dense. Of course he wrote the best poem we have about Shakespeare, but I think Shakespeare knew—while Jonson was merely pedantic.

Ah! But what if you also had a king whose edict can open or close the theaters and who literally believes in all the spirits, witches, fairies, magicians and fishman creatures you write about and who himself has published a book called *Daemonologie* in which he describes the little magic beasties on this island that he rules? And—

Did Shakespeare know James that well? I mean, behind the scenes—or did he know him just at court and from his books?

I believe they're mentioned being together twice. But what if—in excess to living and writing on an island with a king who writes about demons—you have this king who as well institutes the conception of the divine right of kings and thinks that he has been touched by God and that God talks through him—just as Moses—who stammered—spoke to his people through his brother Aaron—who spoke well. James must speak through someone, such as his Bible translators. Your James is so sublimely touched by divine rapture that he's lame and can't walk because he's with the Spirit. He has to be carried everywhere and the clothes practically have to be peeled off his body—I mean they are rank! Now you, William Shakespeare, have just written thirty-some plays about kings—and the qualities of aristocracy and nobility have consumed your life as a poet-dramatist. So, when you have a king who, in his mind, rules not by the consent of the people, but by divine purpose—with God at his ear and speaking through his tongue and his translators as surely as He spoke through Moses and Isaiah, and who in the vulgar view might be thought a reeling idiot but who in your view might be a great deal more, then you, as an old spineshaker, would be *inspired*. Then you might very well create a play about a magician ruling a small island—a play written for your James the First on his island and for no lesser mortal—and include a masque of fairies both for James's delectation—and for another purpose. Don't think Shakespeare was writing for the audience by then. And what seems crotchety to Peter Brook was not crotchety to Shakespeare at all. Look at it this way. The masque created by Prospero shows everyone in the play as an aspect of Shakespeare himself—much as the figures in the masque all spring from Prospero's aerial mind. Miranda is the innocence Prospero would like to recover but himself lost while delving into non-Christian magic in Milan—and perhaps lost as well to the wicked witch Sycorax on whom he may have fathered Caliban, a creature of insensate lust who tried to rape Miranda. Prospero sometimes tells another story about Caliban and Sycorax—but he also tells the audience at play's end about the beast, "This thing of darkness I/Acknowledge mine." It's no great stretch to see all the characters as Shakespeare—who creates the masque as a form of uprooting and dispersing courtly evil—the function of these wordless masques was always to let figures of courtly vice be defeated by figures of courtly virtue. Only through this ritual could Shakespeare exhaust his own guilt and at play's end ask James himself as the play's audience, "As you from crimes would pardon'd be/Let your indulgence set me free." An "indulgence" is a remission of sin from the Pope—a role James now plays in his empire. And let me remind you that James believed absolutely in detestable slaves of the Devil and witches like Sycorax and enchanters like Prospero. You might say that Shakespeare is playing to the gallery in *The Tempest* and especially in its masque.

What's all this chatter all about? asks Laird Weary as he turns from Matilde's leatherette glimmer.

Lowell says, Did Shakespeare write *The Tempest* for the audience or for James the First?

E. A. Baudelaire adds, With his head severed by genius and floating off of his body. And while taking advantage of vast audience interest in the latest island discoveries in the New World.

Oh that tripe! Laird Weary says. And what a place for Shakespeare to place the play—the Bermudas'll never sell.

I hear invisible Ariel say, Hey, old magickmon, whot you want next from your see-through houseboy and all his abilities?

Poof on the Bermudas! says Laird Weary.

Blissful Carlos and Matilde—wide-eyed with wonder—listen through candlelight.

Elizabeth Lowell serves coffee ("It's the maid's day off!")—and bourbon-flavored chocolates signal meal's end.

I think I'll take mother home now, Mrs. Weary says as the

party moves toward the living room. I have some blessed coffee and head at once toward the pot for a second cup.

Mrs. Weary's smile pours over Jackie. It was such a pleasure to have met you and I do hope we can see you again. Lowell leaves to escort the two women home. Laird Weary fills his glass. E. A. Baudelaire leafs with slow pace through a new illustrated edition of Lowell's *Imitations* on the coffee table. He skims Rilke and Lowell's stab at Charles Baudelaire. Lowell's novelty in *Imitations* stuns with its immense daring as he imitates rather than retongues famous works by great world poets in French and Italian and Russian and so on.

E. A. Baudelaire looks at me and says, Well, at least he doesn't touch up the "Grecian Urn" or "Ode to the West Wind."

He'd give them a little more grit and dynamite?

You know he would! Have you tried the bourbon cordials?

I am a bit hungry.

I prefer absinthe.

I face away from Jackie and pop a bourbon chocolate. A rainbow bursts against my palate. My God, it's needled with real bourbon! My chemistry prickles. First sauce in eighteen months and it's awful: chocolate bourbon. I sit, dizzy. The juice crawls through my cells in a red blaze. I reach for the coffee pot and it's empty.

A deep breath. I can hardly walk. I go out to join the others in the living room. Severed, my head floats above my body. My hips bump about. I suck on the past.

The student musicians switch to Beethoven's Piano Trio Number 5 and delight rouses me back to my second and last bourbon chocolate and now the Lowell apartment looks sort of immortal and dream-varnished. The ceiling rises to Wagnerian heights and tall buckets of spears bristle in each corner. Here sweeps an artist's studio such as no poet in America dwells in. The balcony overhangs the living room and far up the north wall a skylight rises embedded in Lowell's psyche. [Indeed, in nine years he will die in a taxi from the airport while returning from England to this very apartment and to his daughter Harriet and divorced wife Elizabeth.] The great skylight mounts very high up and spreads large as myth. Two walls tower with slabs of books, each fifteen shelves high and ten feet broad, and arched against each library wall Cyclopean traveling-ladders ascend attached to ceiling rods along which the angled ladders roll. Stripped of and untainted by bright dust jackets, the books shelve themselves in long banks and show battered dusty sets (*The Rise of the Dutch Republic* for one)—Lowellian books, old clopped covers, foundering books, halved and salvaged, hammered pages zigzagged and jagged, smashed, fattened, suffering, scuffed, razored, savage, dynamited, torn, lolling, spilled, cracked, numb, grizzled, sunken, pocked, huddled, burned out, groveling, dragged back, trembling, hopped up, suffocating and lunging—*books*—in hunt for a man to strike down and drown in. Oh, who could ever leave such a library? Look where the Wagnerian evening filters through graying puritan patches of spirits adrift in the air, and lights up Brady's framed large gray Civil War photos, and rouges one wall with a red-velvet Pre-Raphaelite painting of two nudes for a dash of purple decay and Swinburne. Here sits the white smooth marble bust of Adonis crowned with Lowell's russet laurels. A far wall rises blocked and covered like The Gotham Book Mart with small framed photographs of family and ashen literati. Another wall holds blowups of Lowell at his readings and a group of Pasternak rarities—photos of Boris at twenty, bony and sensual. Here hang high black-and-white line drawings by Sidney Nolan, many times larger than their first appearance in *The New York Review of Books*. Behind the couch a tall Christmas tree spires with handmade paper ornaments, while hung from the ceiling a knobbed brown wooden chandelier curls and rocks, an heirloom from the *Mayflower*, lost in the high air.

Laird Weary walks about with a wineglass, a captain in mufti who has wandered into a liquor ad. Elizabeth Lowell stands moaning over the record collection. We don't have the new Beatles album! It costs twelve dollars. Well, that's too much! But we have the last two Beatles records. However, she plays an organ-rock record and the Wagnerian twilight crashes with a *Götterdammerung* of Southern howling: The day destroys the night, Night divides the day. Tried to run, Tried to hide, Break on through to the other side.

Matilde rolls her blue beetle eyes at E. A. Baudelaire. Music is stronger than death, he tells her—but not this music.

In wineglass and gown, Elizabeth Lowell chases the kitten which has escaped from the kitchen and now snatches at Lowell's laurels. Her accent's galumphing Kentuckian and—a Tennessee Williams heroine—she cries over the music, That cat! Until a couple of hours ago I had control over that cat and I was faster than it. Now it's faster than me! It keeps getting out of the kitchen faster than I can close the door. I'm sorry, people. Oh, I give up. She and Matilde sit and talk about The Machine Show at The Museum of Modern Art.

I circle back though Lord Lowell's castle to refresh myself at his table. Somebody has eaten all the bourbon chocolates! Elizabeth Lowell groans by with the coffeepot into the kitchen and I follow. The yellow kitchen curves boomerang-shaped with clutter. At the stove our hostess overpours boiling water from a saucepan into a dripolator and misses.

This pot!

She descants on coffeepots, dripolators and filter tops. We weigh my filter drip grinder and coffee beans. With pot in hand she sweeps by into the living room. Here's more coffee, everybody! I plant myself first in line while she rushes off again to shoo the cat from swatting leaves off Lowell's bust of Adonis.

Lowell returns and sloughs his greatcoat. You know, Matilde says, I always think of you from your pictures as—

How? I look older than my pictures?

Much *colder* in them, she says.

As like engineer! Carlos says.

Oh, here are some better pictures, Lowell offers, to correct their poor impression. He shuffles through a stuffed closet for pictures and stretches over a chair for one off the wall. Framed, he with fingers raised as if conducting at a reading—his figure at a chiseled Etruscan slump at once upright and glorious—and in the other he's trim and Apollonian with golden haircut. Neither suggests that baleful and noble anger in many of his published photographs.

I hand him a two-record album—*Mozart's Complete Masonic Music*—as a gift. Mozart is my favorite! he says. And I've never heard this. Pleased, he holds it out to his wife. *The Marriage of Figaro* is the greatest music ever written, he says.

The door buzzes. Lowell opens it and his twelve-year-old daughter runs in and heads at once upstairs to bedrooms beyond the balcony.

Lowell calls up, Harriet, come back and met our friends from Chile. Well, she'll be down. She was with us during our trip down South.

Elizabeth Lowell tells Jackie, When Harriet hears you're from the Lower East Side, she'll flip to meet you . . . . I see Harriet's bedroom dreams of The Electric Circus, bushy-headed guitarists and folkies and motorcycles and pads for poets . . . but not dreams of our glacial igloo heated only by steam from our lungs.

By heavens, Lowell asks Carlos, have you read da Cunha?

With Carlos shy on da Cunha, Lowell and wife join in concert on *Rebellion in the Backlands* by Euclides da Cunha.

The Brazilian *Moby-Dick*—Elizabeth Lowell—in Portuguese. I've given away about a hundred copies! That dear old duck Samuel

Putnam translated it in the Forties.

It's very much like *Moby-Dick*, Lowell seconds—reading the air and funding a peace drive on the Forty-Second Street Library's front steps: The same Melvillean pace of description of the Brazilian heartland and epic brooding about the nature of man and a narrative about an insane rebellion like Ahab's quest.

I'd give you one but we've run out—she. It's a Lowellian duet.

Harriet comes down. Lowell crushes her in a turn. This is my daughter. Harriet, these are our friends from Chile.

Through the guitar drench, Elizabeth Lowell delivers a monologue about Harriet to Jackie. My wife seems to be losing weight this evening—no knackwurst, no chocolates. Now Lowell boards a library ladder and sits on the ceiling and winces at us as Elizabeth takes over and tells us, Harriet goes to Dalton, she's in sixth grade. Do you know what they're doing?—They're computerizing her. Before she even has lunch at one-fifteen she has Latin, Spanish, English, science and math—and after lunch, dance and study hall. Her favorite's Spanish because of our maid. But the appalling thing about today's private schools is that the children work so hard. Harriet's not the best and not the worst student at Dalton, but she's up each night till ten! And do you know—they know so little . . . And not just the children. I teach one of those creative writing courses at Barnard and they don't know any more than I know with the worst Southern public school education!

Now Lowell from his Promethean height beats off a vulture tearing at his liver. Or is he about to declaim Aeschylus?

Elizabeth Lowell goes on with Jackie. I'm not sure I believe in the importance of those early years. I think children can learn the difference between "I saw" and "I did see" when they're older. What slum children need most, for example, is tenderness, don't you think? And how can they get that when there are so many children in the family—no money, no husband? That's the danger of teaching slum children, one can get so *much* attached to them—they are charming . . .

I feel very tender and hope he won't jump.

Harriet stands gimlet-eyed beside me where I sit. My nose twitches—a free question! Say, what's the cat's name?—She can't believe the Hairy Ambush has spoken.—What?—What's the cat's name, *heh heh*?—Sumner.—I rack my brain for Civil War memorabilia. Oh, after Fort Sumner? I ask. She stares at me curiously and eyes my beard—am I Hairshert Hammersaxon? As she goes to bed it occurs to me that I'd meant Fort Sumter . . . I'm not getting through. My mind's not right.

Swim! Try the couch! I sink into the Alexandrian couch and list upward through looming guitars—Carlos, Lowell (down) and Laird Weary above me.

Carlos, hectic yellow, asks, What do you say now we have questions to you we have written? On the tape-recorder?

I writhe. It's futile.

Laird Weary takes his cue from Lowell while Lowell transmogrifies into a bust of Beethoven on a bad day but gumming a melody for Christ on the Mount of Olives. His pride rises—he's unable to decide as Laird Weary mirrors the crisis: We're myths above the petty data of tapes. It's too computerizing. Too wracking. And too low-caste for the informal cadences of a Sunday dinner and evening. Carlos burns, his face reddens. Light Mah Fahr gargles over a thrombosis of drums.

It's too much thumping and throbbing and Elizabeth Lowell and E. A. Baudelaire slip on a Mozart Masonic record . . . *Wolfgang, Ludwig and Johanne Pere awake to music in the air* . . . Carlos shaken and at a loss about his interview, so, to help, I ask Lowell about his early connection with the Fugitives—the circle of Southern Renaissance poet-critics at Vanderbilt and Kenyon. The circle met at times on Nashville Friday evenings at the home of recluse linguist Sidney Hirsch, whose work I've been studying.

When you were at Kenyon, did you ever meet Sidney Hirsch?

I saw him a few times. Did he ever do anything beside appear in that Vanderbilt University Press book, *Fugitives' Reunion*?

Oh no, he didn't write—he wouldn't. He's dead now.

He was a mystic, wasn't he? Did you work with him?

No. I know his brother quite well.

Well, what did he do?—Laird Weary.

I'm hard put. He didn't do anything. Real mystics don't do anything. Others speak for them—aside from Krishnamurti and Madame Blavatsky. He was a master of languages. He taught himself Greek and Latin and a lot else and could follow a word or a thought through several tongues at once.

Some Fugitives thought very, very highly of him, Lowell says. But Tate and Red Warren I think couldn't take him very seriously.

What do you think about him?—Laird Weary, grimacing, my double in a sleeper's mirror.

Well, he lived alone for about fifty years, and just studied and practiced some kind of ecstatic spiritual exercises like Kundalini Yoga. Several times a day . . . so that he was in a sort of ecstasy of languages most of his life.

Laird Weary mutters and turns away. He turns back. What are your interests in this?

I'm tongue-tied and sunken on the couch. Sidney Hirsch piques me keenly. But the more I learn, the less loosely I speak.

To wake up, I say.

He digs down for a word to sum up his feelings. And you plan to turn into gold out of dross metal?

Something like that. I smile.

Laird Weary catches a goldfish in his throat. His eyes pop. Shit! he says.

My heart falls away, sliced by a weaver.

You really believe this shit? he asks from a great height.

My severed head floats and veins flood with radiant cordial. Ahh, now I know who ate all the chocolates.

Well, I don't have to stand here and listen to your shit. He's so full of fucking horseshit that I'm going home.

I say nothing, too surprised at having wounded him. He turns, huffing, and strides to the coat pile. Mrs. Lowell follows into his mutter. What's wrong, Laird?

On the couch with me, Carlos and Matilde sit with stunned golden smiles. My wife stands before me, amazed and smiling. What did you say to him?

Nothing.

Did you bring up that topic?

No. Not really.

Her head twists sidewise as she reads my forebrain.

I don't have to listen to that sonofabitch, Laird says now to Lowell and his wife as they try to calm him. He's into his coat. Lowell mumbles something to him, then leaves to walk Laird home. No goodbyes. Mozart sings, *Brothers, surrender wholly to the bliss of your feelings!*

Well! Elizabeth Lowell says in a flutter. He drinks a lot. He's not like that. He didn't mean all that really. Did you say something to him?

No! The hand-folded bluebird of innocence.

She sits in her queen-backed chair. *What* could have got into him?

No answer. She keeps peeling and stripping an apology. At last, Don't mind Laird, he just had too much.

He's passionate.

What?

He's passionate.

She looks away for something else to think about. What's your book about?

It's called *The Body Artist*. It's about a world-famous surgeon who's won two Nobel Prizes and has never lost a patient. He's a very spiritual surgeon.

Lowell returns and grins in agony. Well, heh, heh—Laird drinks like a fish.

He takes me aside. We stand with faces pale in a patch of snow light under the glass skylight.

Are you interested in alchemy?

It's a language, I say. I'm trying to get through some of these huge tomes on alchemy by Jung. If a man of his caliber puts thirty years' study into defining a subject, it becomes a legitimate language. It's about converting your spirit.

Lowell nods and I see it's time for journalism to be invoked. Would you mind saying what you're working on?

Lowell rubs his hair flat—orchestrating an answer—and looks up from molten snow light blanketing his back. It's real suffering and I'm ready to quit on the spot—no spirit for journalism.

I'm working on a great long poem that follows the seasons of the year. It's more or less finished. I'm putting what last I can into the page proofs. I've published bits of it already.

Intense search underwrites the feeling in each word he speaks— it's clear that an interview is Lowell's Gethsemane. He looks jellied and tinned in the phantom snow light.

What do you think of Mailer's description of you in *The Armies of the Night*? It was very funny when he had you falling back on your head and there wasn't any headrest. Were you embarrassed by his gratuities?

No, in fact I was quite flattered! Norman really didn't have to say all that about me. Lowell smiles—eyes ringed with good humor.

Do you still think Jewishness is a major American theme?

I think we're over the crest. That generation has inherited the tremendous backlog of European culture to dump here in the States—and now they've had their vogue—like the Southern novelists had theirs.

Whatever became of your interest in opera? After your Ford Foundation grant...

Oh, I wrote plays instead. He eyes me askance.

I didn't accuse you of not writing operas, I say.

Besides, I stopped out to see Stravinsky and there was really no hope of doing anything together. It's not really possible to write anything that survives the music. The words are wasted.

Ah! Not if you write sacred music, E. A. Baudelaire says as he joins us. Something *a capella*, like Palestrina. The possibilities in oratorio are immense.

But Stravinsky and Benjamin Britten both write unaccompanied songs and the words are still lost.

But that's it, says E. A. Baudelaire. You have to write something very clear and stirring! He waves toward the stars which are not out. Like the Stabat Mater or those Masonic texts, O Sun, O Soul of the Universe—like that—sweeping, mystical... They'll remember you.

Lowell looks wine-weary and goes to sit on the couch with Carlos and Matilde. A male chorus sings Mozart into its brotherhood. Are the Masons still active? he asks.

Well, there are levels and levels, E. A. Baudelaire hints, and secret societies sparkle about him.

Of course, my father was a Mason.

Governor Rockefeller perhaps, E. A. Baudelaire lets fall. Roosevelt was—look at the pyramid on the back of the dollar bill, you couldn't ask for a bigger tip-off.

Lowell nods. Yes, I know. The pyramid with the floating eye. But there was a time when all our leaders were Masons: Adams, Jefferson, Franklin.

True! And there's still a Masonic level that the bourgeois Masons don't have the slightest idea about.

Don't you think Mozart just wrote Masonic music for ceremonies? He wasn't a high officer. Lowell cocks his ear. This is so beautiful! But *The Marriage of Figaro* is his greatest.

You have to think of the audience, says E. A. Baudelaire. This Masonic music isn't for sophisticates in the opera house. It's unornamented, de-Italianized, de-theatered, man-to-man—yet very elevated. All his life he was hungry for a brother-prince. He fell in with the Masons with their mysticism like an alky saved by A.A.

But, everything considered musically, *The Marriage of Figaro* is the greatest piece of music ever written. Lowell's interest turns. Carlos, don't you think Crane's *The Bridge* and Neruda's *Macchu Picchu* are similar in their density of effects? *The Bridge* is the only poem we have anywhere like *Macchu Picchu*. Of course we have *The Wasteland*, but that's not the same really. I mean these telescoped or shorthand double metaphors that overlap—*O Thou steel Cognizance whose leap commits/The agile precincts of the lark's return*—you don't find that in Eliot—and then Eliot could only do it once. You can only write one *Wasteland* and then you have to do something else entirely. You don't have the original impulse any more. But Neruda's surrealism in *Macchu Picchu* comes very close to matching Crane's denser logic of metaphor. And you can only write one *Bridge* and one *Macchu Picchu*. Has anything of Neruda's ever again matched *Macchu Picchu*?

Well, I think *Residencia en la Tierra* is better though I very much like *Macchu Picchu* in parts. And he write this very long *Canto General* which take him ten years. But *Residencia* is more deep from very down inside and have more visions.

But *Carlos*, then you'd agree!

Lowell lays into *Carlos*—flat and Yankee as his tooth sinks into Neruda's myth.

Don't you agree that he'd really done his best work by his late thirties? Lowell speaks of Elizabeth Bishop who knew Neruda in the Thirties and has made a like weighing. Carlos agrees with her. No, no, Matilde says, he still write very beautiful love poems. He is world's greatest love poet. I remind myself that Lowell has never honored Neruda with one of his imitations. I hear Neruda had a great response when he read at the YMHA, Lowell says.

Although, I say, one of his translators had a ball of dough filled with old razor blades in his ear.

I've heard that before, Elizabeth Lowell says, now listening.

E. A. Baudelaire's eye whips to flame. It was the greatest, longest standing ovation ever given to a poet on the North American continent! That's my modest assessment of the night. And it could actually have been grander than I suggest. Whitman, of course, in his later years, did very well at the Academy of Music with his personal memories of Lincoln—the whole house was sublimated. But it would be hard to put the two evenings on the balance scale. Neruda moved everyone! I was there and have also heard it on tape and, I must say, I am yet to come down from such heights. The applause—let me be clear—was like the end of the Ring Cycle at the Met. One sits in the twilight of the gods. People wept on both sides of me and reporters standing in the aisles dissolved. Meanwhile, Pablo stood there on the stage like a pink penguin in an Antarctic sunset—applauding back slowly at his audience.

I'm not sure there are Antarctic sunsets, Lowell says.

That may have been my tears.

Of course, Lowell says to Carlos, he's a Communist, isn't he?

Carlos agrees. I believe him very much when he says he is.

Lowell waits as oblivion in a wine-dark cloud of fatigue casts shadows over him but soon fades as the rainbow of his will launches him into memories of South America. He has great family feeling for South American politics. What I think is indispensable about any reasonable country, he says, is that you can vote your leader out of office. Carlos, I don't think much of Nixon but I do know we can get rid of him. In South America this isn't usually so. I was talking with a cabinet official in Buenos Aires one night and the next morning the whole government was gone and a new one in. I read about it at breakfast! It was a generals' revolution, no bloodshed . . . I like South America. It's so unspoiled in many ways.

But we are really out of it, Matilde says.

Out of it?

You know, nothing is there! No little civilization.

What's it like beyond Buenos Aires?

Nothing is there, Carlos says. Ees just pampas.

Kilometers and kilometers of grass, Matilde says.

Lowell's voice deepens. Well, I think 1968 will be remembered as a turbulent year of small disasters. Nothing turned out as I expected! I think in the long run it will be remembered as the year of Biafra.

Elizabeth Lowell says, We're trying to save up money for a trip to Spain. "Cal" has an offer for three months at The Hebrew University at Jerusalem. Then he can come and meet Harriet and me in Spain.

If the university isn't blown up beforehand, Lowell says with a nod at bad news from Israel.

The porcelain clock strikes eleven. We're ready to leave. But Lowell turns to Carlos and Matilde beside him on the couch and—deadpanning as the old virtuoso and national poet—without notice jumps into poetry and memories of poets. For the Latin visitors it is the full sonata—the improvisation that severs head from body. Lowell rubs his hairline back until his forehead bulks like Beethoven's, his hair matted and trailing. He weaves themes and fragments from everywhere on his keyboard into a ten-minute monologue. His voice just scrapes his cords and breaks out in a sulky whisper, all tones inner—he has closed the lid to muffle his pianissimo. Admiration creeps over me. Here is the germ stuff itself. Jackie's jaw drops and—lost—she shakes her head at me. Carlos melts, raked limp beneath Lowell's faint deep rasps and sonorities. Matilde sits straight up, eyes brimming and misted. Lowell—blue eyes lecturing as they swell his glasses—his kindly grim mouth compelling us to his mood—weaves on. A hand limps to draw the earth and cloudscapes before him but weak with sublimity falls to his lap. His head floats.

. . . And once you met the force in the green fuse that drove him, you were aware of active genius . . . Eager Carlos listens ablaze. . . . Of course these seeds on the sill after the burial are so great, you know it's genius . . . Carlos nods, sea-deep . . . he was so alive and fresh. I knew him. If you were in the same room with Dylan Thomas you gravitated toward him. I did. He was a great performer. *Actor*, really. If you heard him declaim a poem once, you knew you'd hear it four more times that night. He mostly read other poets aloud. At a reading only about one poem in nine was his—he was really modest about himself. He had about ten great poems—of course, he was a minor poet—he took one quality of Yeats's and blew it up and used it better than Yeats—he admired Yeats profoundly—but he became the narrower poet for it—really minor. His best poems were about five—you couldn't say just which five—with another five shifting and changing as his second best five. He's the only one who did anything with prose. Of course he couldn't hold an audience or penetrate it as completely as Frost or Eliot, and he really wasn't as good a poet as Auden or Pound

Matilde—a toothpaste ad—sits reacting with her teeth. She has never heard of Swinburne.

Lowell's memories curl off into heaven. E. A. Baudelaire's head tilts back in sleep, his sockets scraped with peace. Silence. Time to tiptoe out.

I launch McManis.

In this very long article on Neruda I published two years ago, my title calls him the GLP, the Greatest Living Poet—

Lowell smiles, grim.

—but in the text I explain that he is only the Greatest Living Poet after my friend Jack McManis of Penn State—

Alarm fills Lowell's glasses.

—who is the real Greatest Living Poet and—

Lowell glowers into the carpet, wishing I'd finish.

—throughout the article I keep alternating passages of my interview with Neruda with passages about McManis and quoting Jack's poems—

Oh, you really do think he's good?

I nod, happy. —And of course no one's ever heard of McManis!

Oh, of course not! Lowell chuckles, sighing.

Well, no comments necessary. I've brought a batch of his poems for your files and I hope you might look them over yourself sometime.

Well, I can't fail to do that! Lowell says and accepts my McManis gift.

Sad to say, I say, one of his greatest poems is lost. That is, I've lost my copy and it's not in my McManis files. Seems unlikely, huh, a great poem being lost? Something quite the equal of Villon? It's called "Elequy for Big Bill Tilden"—I asked Jack what an elequy is and he said a queer elegy.

I see, Tilden was gay, everybody knows that, Lowell says.

And he served time for trying to pick up a male prostitute minor on Sunset Boulevard. Jack himself was ranked seventh and eighth national tennis champion in the early forties. Well, Tilden was voted the greatest player of the first half century. But he had a harsh rival, René Lacoste, who was a mechanic, an unbeatable player, often a champion, and on the court he never smiled. For

Jack or Big Bill to find himself up against Lacoste was to be tested past your limits. When Big Bill died, Jack wrote a poem which begins

> The Vice Squad
> was helping God
> guard Hollywood

and the poem goes on to tell of Big Bill's arrest and jail time. And it ends with a couplet from heaven:

> Implacable as Lacoste, death made him fall
> who lent such measure to a tennis ball.

Lowell nods. Saying, It's like Ingmar Bergman! Death comes as a tennis mechanic rather than as a supernal chess master.

I knew you'd appreciate it.

I hope you find your lost poem. I look forward to reading these.

Our revels are now ended and we rise to leave. Sober and charming, Lowell fills with warmth—his handshake large and manly. I love those Mozart records! He tells me.

Watch out for the hidden symbols.

I was afraid of that, he says into the rug.

On the street Carlos releases his huge high. But you know that last ten minutes on the couch, I don't understand five words! Just the force through the green fuse. His talk was like James Joyce. It was difficult, no? he asks Matilde.

I only sit and smile, she says. But his voice—

Ahh! Carlos sighs, his black lamb headpiece afloat.—Ecstasy! Nothing do I understand what he say—but that voice is so moving I know he is very deep man and become convinced he is very great poet. Just by his voice! I never have experience like that. Such deep feeling, you hear it ring from his bones! Yet like the softest cello, like music, like Beethoven, no?

Afterword

I have tried not for word-by-word likeness in this retonguing of an evening with the Lowells, but rather tried to catch the echoes still banging about my brain. Tone is everything and a reporter can make any tone come through that he chooses. I have been reckless with dialogue. Strict dialogue reporters still exist, of course, apart in a world of pure objectivity, like sausage-makers and style-obsessed taxidermists with their owls and deer heads. I believe that poet-recording—call it re-agonizing—calls for much luck in catching the heart's heat and crackle. I take some strength from Lowell's own imitations and his comment about his adaptation of *Prometheus Bound*, ". . . half my lines are not in the original." My licenses have been many. I have stripped Mr. Lowell of half his speeches and expanded mine to twice their length. Much of what was obscured or muffled by his speaking into the rug and most of his oration on the couch I've left out. Laird Weary has given me special problems, and I have rashly tried to improve on the original by giving him a moustache. I hope I caught something worthy of his all-important tone. I have been almost as free as God himself in finding ways to make this evening unique and ring right for me. I end with a kiss to my wife's sharp ears.

—Edgar Allan Baudelaire

Epilogue
[from *Those Drinking Days: Myself and Other Writers*]

Whenever I heard about Lowell after this evening he was just going in or coming out of a hospital and couching more of his disasters into free rhythms. Returning from England to his ex-wife Elizabeth and daughter Harriet, he died in a taxi coming from Kennedy International into Manhattan, of congestive heart failure. His more public poems, such as the superb "Waking Early Sunday Morning," had rhyme and meter. He was a high-minded, private man, a Boston aristocrat who enjoyed the mortification of getting shitfaced and writing about it. He was puffed up with humiliation. Self-abasement was his meat and drink, and his last years were a banquet of it as his last books make plain, with poems quoting Elizabeth's agonized letters to him about his new marriage. His writing, of course, shows a dry hand. There is nothing slovenly about his verse. He could bring springlike freshness to suffering—shocking brightness to self-recognition—moral force to self-loathing. Of this kingly man we may say, he was every inch a drunk—a grim Marmeladov on his knees in the family doorway. A man with enormous power over language and early formal discipline, a gripping speaker who brought electric doom to his best and his worst lines, a charmer who could show you his forebears with loving vigor—his Navy father in the bathtub, his mother's body wrapped in tinfoil and being shipped home from Italy for burial—a man highborn, educated by the finest teachers, friend to distinguished philosophers and connoisseurs, intimate with the most celebrated writers, composers and poets of his time, himself magnificently well-read and distinguished in languages, a scholar-poet when he wished, who dared to imitate the gods of ancient and modern tongues and English them, whose own tongue could leave welts on his critics, rend them with slow carnage, stave their ribs in—you feared him—a loving father, the spellbinding teacher and lecturer, acclaimed playwright, a large-boned, robust, tall, commanding man, his every word authentic, rooted in the past, deep-spirited, a poet loved and honored, a Nobel Prize at his fingertips, to be all this and casually, knowingly, relentlessly, to step aside from himself, that man not the real man, only a supersensitive bubble of a man, the real man rising from wine, grand, his feelings slowly inflating, Caligula appearing, the tyrant of unhappiness, or satyr with a racing ego, brain humid, no longer hamstrung and straining, but smirking and baleful, bullyragging, brooding, grim, slumping, doleful, translating some patch of Horace or Catullus in the back of his mind while listening or talking, his big fatherly hand falling on your shoulder from the heavens of fame, grinning, joking, glowing through some veiled turmoil, a kind, gallant smile suddenly clamped, keeping a stammer under flattening pressure, hulking now, then tensely ardent, striving to be worthy of his work, burning, his eye spitting fire, something writhing within him, his ropelike fingers clenching, his face swelling, then deadpan, boorish, worn-looking, foundering, halved, salvaged by a deep breath, then hammered, jagged, smashed, fat, suffering, scuffy, razored, savage, dynamited, torn, lolling, spilled, cracked, numb, grizzled, sunken, ashen, huddled, burned out, groveling, dragged back, trembling, hopped up, suffocating, hunting, lunging, drowning. Where is our Pulitzer Apollo with the golden haircut, fire-breathing and twenty-seven, his gimlet eyes aerial, puckish, blinking?

Trusting in his recuperative powers like an elephant's. And then the power died. A man laid bare and every inch spread-eagled.

Who took the wristwatch from his wrist?

Trumpet
Evergreen Review, Vol. 13, No. 72, November 1969

LARGE ABILITY FOR LITTLE SUICIDES!
    The old American know-how that brought us The Depression!
    A handiness to survive among ashes!
    And like a fifty-gallon drum dropped from a wharf, you've got to bounce—whatever the labor!
    This suicide fable, my farewell attack on fame, begins as a documentary...

My cameraman Jaime Barrios edits. He's just so beautiful, dancing film back and forth through the moviscope, unreeling rhythms—a Balanchine, a Nureyev of spinning filmstrips. Joining rhythm to rhythm. We are cutting the motorcycle coda. What would otherwise be commonplace—a cycle crossing Brooklyn Bridge with a horn player perched backwards on the rear wheel—leaps into verse in Jaime's edit. We've shot this scene twice—once in black and white and once in color. He opens the film with the b&w cycle zooming toward the camera—he shot this hanging out of a cab window—and ends the film with a wine jump onto the horn player on the rear wheel in color! Thirty minutes of film pass between these shots. Between them come the marvels of *Trumpet*. Are they marvels? Perhaps not when we shot them. But as Jaime edits—a craftsman of cadences!—and zaps film back and forth through the pygmy screen of the moviscope, motorcycle and trumpet leap forward and splash the eye—it's clear he's a poet.

And wouldn't it be spring if art were all there was to moviemaking...

Invention is not enough. Nor the high spirits—the enZeusment!—of genius. Look at Welles, the most enZeused director on earth—but a prisoner of abilities that bind him just as the sea-serpents bind Laocoön and his sons in the famous sculpture. He is *too good*—the more he strives, the less happens. Where is his Don Quixote now seventeen years in production? Nowhere. Well, I speak here on a more modest scale, and ask: Where is Newlove's *Trumpet*? Beached...

This morning a rap on my door lifts me afoot from my floor mattress—and face my elderly Ukrainian landlady I must.

Hey, wot you going to do? You owe me two month rent going on three! I have expenses! De heat goes on and you don't pay me. Wot vill I do? I am old woman. I can't climb up to top floor looking for you week after week. I am old, old woman! You never think of that? Just slip by my door, don't say nothing?

Mrs. Maria Ouspenskaya [a disguised name], I've lived here six years—*six years!* Long before the hippie invasion and haven't I always paid you? Sometimes you've had to wait, yes. Yes, *I admit it!* But I've always come through—there I am, dancing in your apartment with two or three months rent from one of my magazine sales [fictive]. Or book contracts [fictive]. Or temp jobs. *Trust* me. Just trust me. I am known far and wide as an honest man—and now as a movie producer still more so. You've heard of movies, I'm—

You going *to move* in de middle of de night!

Remember the last time I paid, how happy we were, and how you smiled, how much better your back felt [her spine curves and grieves]—and there I stood, dropping dollars all over your kitchen table.

A death in my family, sad to say—but it led to an amusing if heartbroken day of deliverance. *Our* day of deliverance! And what can I say about your cherry vodka, Mrs. Ouspenskaya? Our joy at the kitchen table—

I am broke! She tightens her babushka and winter shawl for warmth. Dis is de expensive season!

It's only the first of November—still Indian summer.

She peers into my digs to check on my furniture.

Here, look at this picture, I say. This is Cynara Rosewine, the star of my new movie.

Dot girl is in your movie? I see her visiting you. She don't mind climbing five flights?

Some dish, eh?

Dot dish don't pay my hoil bill. You marry her maybe? She works steady?

Well, she is married. But from time to time she visits me—her old friend.

You too old for dot girl. And married?

Yes. We called off *our* engagement some years ago. But the rent is coming! Look, Mrs. Ouspenskaya, I hang like a sick dog at the mailbox every morning—but that bastard my publisher [fictive] is simply holding back on my royalties. I will go up today and speak with him quite roundly. I'm only waiting for my socks to dry.

Socks? Mrs. Ouspenskaya looks down at my bare feet in flip-flops. Her face drains as clouds darken over my rent payment. She turns in her slow gray shuffle and with a hand on the hallway rail growls, You need a second pair of socks, Meestair Nooluff.

I close the door but at once reopen it.

Would you carry this bag down for me? These melon rinds are really ripe. Thanks.

At nine A.M.—as your self-esteem flakes away on every side—sleep is the cheap narcotic. From my bedroom I watch a waterbug big as a beer can waddle down the kitchen, lift up the stove and crawl under. I recall my brushed short hair and eager youth and sharp blue suit and blushing pink tie when I first rented this top-floor walkup from Mrs. Ouspenskaya and explained how I am a novelist [unpublished] who needs the seclusion of a great height for my work—and the $28 monthly rent. But now my two mewling, hunger-ridden, pity-mongering cats beg for supper and breakfast. *Shut up! You'll eat when I eat.* They see me light a cigarette and know I'm cheating.

 I lie testing ropes too frayed for freedom from my shame as a budding but directionless movie director. My marvelmovie *Trumpet*—now filmed in its entirety!—lies undeveloped in my cameraman's apartment and needs

$$$ONE$$$
$$$HUNDRED$$$
$$$AND$$$
$$$SEVENTY$$$
$$$DOLLARS$$$

to develop—a fortune these days. I haven't seen $170 in one piece since I was discharged from the Air Force seventeen years ago. I am fagged flat for money and march on empty pockets. Meanwhile, the film—much of it exposed over two months ago—lies developing in its own chemicals. Once exposed, these chemicals go on working. After awhile they bleach and if you wait too long you have a fish-belly-pale print. At this very moment my triumphant *Trumpet* may be paling out of existence.

I've written a scenario for this, my first flick—and its subject is trumpets. No stars, just trumpets. Trumpets in playgrounds—trumpets in apartments found—no, *unlidded*—in odd crumpled corners of the city—hearty trumpets on roofs or far off in parks—easy-riding or demonized trumpets—children huffing trumpets at their first lessons—myself blowing a rented five-foot Aïda trumpet under the Washington Monument—a girl on a pocket cornet—a naked Negro glimpsed through a window and running scales—and then a historical sequence, about sixty cuts scattered throughout of trumpets from stained glass windows and old paintings and old engravings and the Met's antique horns collection—melancholy trumpets in pawn shop windows—men blowing horns in the St. Anthony's Day parade in Little Italy—lads blowing in practice rooms over the Academy of Music—that horde of beauties of all varieties in 48th Street store windows, the Selmers, Bachs, Conns—trumpets at the lips of masters in pavilions of the wealthy, from the balconies of Carnegie Hall and back wall of Lincoln Center and as the Valkyries ride over the horn section, banked players playing—a wooden mallet coming down on a bent trumpet bell in a repair shop as the bell gets banged dentless on a cloth-covered iron form—old green rotary-valve trumpets—Michelangelo's *Last Judgment* with Gabriel blowing souls into hell and horns in Velásquez and Egyptian horns and Roland at Roncesvalles and Frederick Remington and the U.S. Cavalry charging the Sioux—*and* an erotic sequence with horns while Cynara lies on a white couch in a white Harlow costume, her skin in clown white, with a white ostrich fan and six-foot white feather boa and . . . and . . . white rug! White cat! An ecstasy of white on white on white—and all shot at white heat! Let's use the adagio from Mahler's *Fifth* for the erotic sequence . . . although that's all strings without brass . . . and we can't afford the copyright . . . well, a toughie scene to score . . .

    We shot this scene. Costly! But without this movie, I might still be a wretched wine-drenched unpublished novelist—a fishpeddler of empty dreams and scratching about for the rent and boosting my bent soul with Piaf singing the French national anthem. Instead, I have made what financially stands on its own two feet as an underground film and the rent is minor news to my nerves. Oh, I may never climb up out of Welles's footprint, I grant you—even in the sublime inanity of the underground. And it's true I have yet to lift a finished work to the screen for my credentials. But all that glory waits just around the corner.

I dump the Mahler adagio and phone Louis Armstrong for the erotic sequence. My movie will be a shambles without a snatch of Satchmo somewhere. Get Joe Glazer, Louis' agent, on the phone. Sure you can have Louis, Joe says—one hundred thou... [In rough figures that's $100,000.] What's your budget? Joe asks.—Less, Joe, much less.—Look, Joe says, Louis hasn't made a picture for under a hundred thou in fifteen years.—This is art, Joe.—*Wha-a-at?*

So I go to the bank for $1,000 to film my idea. Meanwhile, I've fallen in with three Chilean paparazzi. I mention my project to Jaime Barrios, with whom I'd had dealings while interviewing Pablo Neruda two years ago. Jaime'd been filming Neruda's trip to Manhattan for a reading at the YMHA. Now he wants to see my scenario. Jaime is ring-leader of the camera-mad Chileans: skinny, narrow-faced, brown eyes burning, brown crow's wing over his forehead. I thought him twenty-eight. Later during *The Second Great Bank Loan* (which flopped) he turned out to be a twenty-year-old legal minor. What's your budget? he asks.

It may run up to a hundred thou. More likely, three hundred dollars.

With sound? he asks.

Well, it's about trumpets, Jaime.

Forget it!

He draws me my budget—I am treating him in Downey's, my first expense—and it seems I need at least $1,000 for filming, sound-studio rental, processing the optical track, editing, final dupe with special cutting effects, renting the moviscope, reels for the film itself, cab fares for equipment, floodlamps, building the white-on-white-on-white set, Harlow costume rental for Cynara, electric camera rentals—and on and on as he itemizes—and I won't bore you with all of it, although he keeps me electrified. Do you realize, he asks, how much those historical shots are going to cost? Michelangelo's Gabriel, you have to shoot the detail with a still camera and blow it up and film it with the movie camera. That's one single detail which takes maybe three seconds of finished film.

So, OK, I want all those wonderful trumpet details to flash by. Gotta have 'em.

What's this "Mass Mess in Central Park"?

That's the climax.

I thought the Erotic Sequence is.

Well, they both are. Have to see which comes out better.

Yes, yes, but what is this "Mass Mess"?

I really can't contain my delight about this, Jaime. We invite everyone with a trumpet in New York City to Central Park to blow. Ecstasy, man! And we'll film it. Thousands of captive trumpet players. Think of the sound track! And it costs nothing, just getting the word out.

Wow. That's very ambitious. It will take advertising. Now what is this "flutter technique" in the Erotic Sequence?

You remember *Last Year at Marienbad*—Renais's transition from a fancy saloon scene to Delphine Seyrig's bedroom where she's standing in black ostrich feathers? The transition is blinding—*blap!—blap!—blap!* From this dark saloon you are gradually led into—a few frames at a time—this gorgeous white bedroom. Dark, white, dark, white, dark, white frames, then white, dark, white, dark, white white white white. I'll do it in color and black and white. We snip snip snip the frames in a transition from a black and white Negro kid in Tompkins Square Park blowing a horn to this fantastic erotic white-on-white-on-white color scene with Cynara in a Harlow costume. You get the fluttering image of a kid in the park swapping snips from the Flaming Erotic Sequence until we're at last wholly into the White Room.

That could be very moving.

My heart warms to this Chilean. We flutter?

That, man, will be expensive.

We just *edit* it that way, Jaime.

Oh, no. When you come to have the final dupes made, the people uptown will have to stop all their equipment and *insert* these little pieces of color film. They develop film very fast, the film just runs through the developer, a half-hour film is done in less than ten minutes. *You* want special attention. You have to have every frame marked. It has to be done exactly. The man who is developing will have to stop the film maybe thirty times to insert the color flutters until the full transition is made to color film. That's money, that *costs*.

I guess it must.

No, man, I think it's a great idea. Let's do it.

Couldn't we get both color and black and white done separately, and do the editing ourselves?

Oh, we have to do that anyway. But then we have only one dupe. When we want to get a final neg the same problem arises all over. Don't worry about it!

You want to help?

Help? I want to shoot it. Do you have a cameraman?

I like to be Napoleonic about equipment. Hundreds of guys all over the Village are dying to use their gadgets in your service. Welles says, "There's always someone around for that." So you want to work on *Trumpet*?

Put your hand to it. A pact!

We swear brotherhood.

My God, Jaime! We're going to make a glorious movie!

That's what's important, Jaime says.

Sitting in the Chemical Church Bank of New York on Fourteenth Street and Seventh Avenue I say to Mr. Richard Nixon [a disguised name], Yes, I work for the city as a social worker and for the Virginia Kirkus Service as a book reviewer and for Trident Press as a manuscript reader and for Paramount Pictures as a reviewer of story materials. My income is $8,750 annually.

To explain the funny stuff behind this figure and the editing and splicing together of these jobs would be to harass the reader with a freewheeling income layout whose source wavers between Bleak House and New Grub Street. For show—with a fresh hairwash and fray trimmed from my shirt-collar and sleeve cuffs and shirtboard inserts covering the holes in my spit-shined shoes, I earn $8,750 a year—a phantasmal financial statement. But I am out to outrace the swift and make mincemeat of this rather waxen-looking loan manager.

Dick Nixon studies my beard. You want this money to make a movie?

Indeed I do. That's where the money is, I say scanning the bank and its giant safe door. In movies, Mr. Nixon! I have the scenario right here. I intend to sell the finished picture to educational TV—to an agent—and to a distributor with Canadian, South American, Asian, and African outlets. Do you watch PBS? You'll see it there, I'm sure. PBS appreciates the higher things—and, I might say, is thankful for that touch of genius that injects extra meaning where we least expect it. As with Orson Welles! Not that I pretend to genius, ha ha—only to that extra enthusiasm and burst of spirit that can be, well, as infectious as a horserace.

This sounds quite interesting. But why don't you go to a studio for backing?

Studios bar the distribution of non-union movies, Mr. Nixon. And quite often we underground—uh, *independent* filmmakers—are forced to pay off the unions for workers who never existed as we shot the film. We pay for ghost labor.

That doesn't sound very honest.

The unions are the biggest crooks in the world, sir. And their heavy-handed dishonesty is vexing to the $1,000 film producer—a burden almost meant to keep us from getting our money back.

But won't your actors be unionized?

Well, our leading actress is an amateur but extremely talented. Her name is Cynara Rosewine and I just happen to have her picture with me. Here she is. But don't let her demure appearance fool you. She has unrecognized talents. I might add, we plan to marry once the film is in release. Ah, the age difference? I've weighed and weighed it. But there's no fighting her, once her mind is set.

I see she'd be hard to fight off.

And so Mr. Nixon and I laugh and chew the fat as I forge an honest face and sink into Capitalism.

For front I've also brought with me a manuscript galley from Kirkus about *Twentieth Century Guns* and leave it out on Richard Nixon's desk. His waxen face more or less lights up and he slaps his desk.

Are you a gun enthusiast? he asks.

Actually, this is a galley. I get paid for re—

I was up in Canada just last week on vacation! Wonderful hunting, beautiful guns. You'd have loved it. I love expert craftsmanship, superior mechanism. Shot a few quails and pigeons. It's remarkable to find someone sitting at my desk who understands guns. What's your favorite?

Oh, I don't know that much about it.

I've got three antique guns as a basis for a collection. Hand guns. I'll bet you're just not saying what you know.

Why should I tell him that this is a prop I've filched from the Kirkus office? Instead I say, I like a rifle as tight as a pistol.

Ah! Oh, sign here.

I take his pen and, amid rising dawns, sign. Is there any question? I ask.

I don't think so. We'll let you know in a day or two.

Oh, very good. Happy hunting, Mr. Nixon. I stand, calm and composed, shake his hand, leave the bank in my blue suit and banded hair—and at once run to the corner booth and phone Jaime.

We got the Chemical Church's bread, babe!

Our first day's shooting opens with the buying of film, renting equipment, buying filters, tape for sound and other desiderata Jaime stamps Necessary. Jaime's crew of Chileans has worked with him on the Neruda film for release on South American TV. Luis Prieto returns for sound and Juan Ureta, camera. Jaime directs. I do too but Jaime has nothing else to do—as he'd planned—so he directs while I bloom in the Slot, which means I Produce, Hold the Purse, and Talk with Cops. What do you think about This, about That? Jaime asks. Glorious, I say, producing. Then he launches into Spanish, telling the crew what I/he wants. Man, are we going to make a movie! He says this in English.

Juan questions me in staccato Spanish about focus. Luis asks something forbidding about the sound. You're speaking in Spanish, I say to Luis.

Oh! Oh, forgive me. He bows. Do you want to record these horns? He sounds awful.

That's the fun of it, Luis.

Luis, I find, is eighteen, Juan, the camera signor, is twenty-two. I have entrusted myself to adolescents. In a language I can't speak.

As the day winds on I turn phosphorescent with loneliness. We—I—he make lovely shots as the day flicks on and off in a cloudy light. During the cloud-flicker I rush off to get a business permit from the city—billing us as Prometheus Productions—and a fresh gallon of cheap red—and then I get street shooting permits from the Department of Commerce and Industrial Development, City of New York. Armed with these and back with the crew, I am the target of every snotty cop in areas where we shoot. He's the man, Jaime says and points at me, go see him. I, David O. Selznick, indeed have the papers—the movie rolls as I refine the art of producing.

The cop studies my scenario and throws me a hard look.

We're just making a movie, officer.

What's this "Mass Mess"?

In Central Park? Oh, that's way way up in Central Park. We're having a few horn players for an afternoon concert in the park.

It says "Mass Mess—Mad Trumpet Rally without Parallel!"

Somebody's overstating the whole affair.

"Everyone in New York City with a Trumpet Invited."

It's really a chamber concert.

You are planning a *riot*.

Oh, heavens, no.

We shoot this knotty old man who walks up to us and says he learned to play in Florence, Italy. His lip slips and wind dims but he plays "The Carnival of Venice" with rococo verve. Best opening shot possible, not even planned! There he stands at St. Mark's and Second Avenue—adrift in hippies and blowing his heart out as we capture him. Ah, *Trumpet* is rolling.

Cut! I shout in English. The camera rolls on serenely.

How's that? asks Juan, camera.

Excellent. Now let's hit those pawn shops.

We move over to Third Avenue pawn shops and shoot sad windows of poor old dead horns hung behind window scum.

I don't quite understand what we're doing in this sequence, Jaime says.

It's a happy movie.

Yes, man, but all these pawn shops.

Shoot them all, the ones with horns.

But I need a kind of clue as to what we're doing.

Jaime, right now we're making a happy movie about trumpets. We gotta be fearless. Large-minded. And rhapsodic.

He looks at my rhapsodic pawn shop and shakes his head no.

Well, I say, part is *contrast*. We have to show horns in limbo as well as the happy side. I see these wretched windows as butcher shops hung with legs of meat.

Wow, man.

One window triggers my heart. Amid banked trumpets hangs a flugelhorn, a kind of trumpet with a hernia—all twisted up in its guts but calling my name. When the shop owner tells me it's only $49, I zap out my checkbook. I take Sheba my flugel delight and move on, blowing "On the Sunny Side of the Street." But it turns to suffering.

I'm not working, I tell Jaime. I'm not directing.

Sure you are, man, you're behind everything that's happening!

Don't feel it in my veins. Heavy sigh. Don't feel like I'm directing anything.

Oh, man, that all comes in the editing. This is just raw footage. This part here, this isn't directing.

You don't think so?

That's why I'm doing it. You shouldn't have to.

Who makes the shots really doesn't make any difference?

Do I tell Juan which lens to use? Sure, we talk it over. But that's his job. The real directing is with the moviscope. Cutting, man, that's the thrill.

I should just go on pursing and producing? I rub my flugelhorn's bell. I wish, I wish—

No, man, don't go rubbing that horn and wishing. Wishes have a bad way of coming true. You just go on doing what you do best.

I always wanted to be a movie director.

You *are* a movie director!

But I always thought I should be like Orson Welles and say what should be shot from what angle and who stands where and what's happening.

You're doing that. Aren't you saying what's happening?

I really am. Yes, I am.

So what are you worried about? When you get into the cutting room and start counting frames, you'll *know* you're a movie director.

That's where the real guts of it all is, right?

Of course! This out here is child's play.

Gosh. I always felt that *this* is where real movie directing is—the things you shoot.

This is it too! The whole movie is your *movie*.

I wrote it, yes—talk with the cops—do the battling, for God's sake—set up the next shot ahead of time. But I *feel* I'm not directing.

Don—he plants a hand on my shoulder,—you can only do so much.

By evening we've cabbed all over the Lower East Side and laugh with joy while worn flat. We retire to my pad and turn on with a variety of stimulants and depressants. As shooting goes forward, it works out that Prometheus Productions foots a heavy tab for imported Holland liquors and tobaccos, alkaloids, acids, and a resinous Turkish fuel for visions—and strains do show in the budget. Thinking about Mr. Richard Nixon at the bank, my stomach, thinking, trembles, hops—stifles my breath. Shadows race over Paradise. I find myself talking to Mr. Nixon and saying, We must invite executives from Paramount and Warner Brothers to the premiere. Perhaps you'd like to come? But don't bring a gun, ha ha ha—

I rock with worry. Jaime, baby, Jaime, next week, baby.

What, man?

The climax. We want to shoot it so we'll know where we're going. The Mass Mess in Central Park!

Do you think we can arrange it in a week?

Look, *el budgito* says we've got to.

OK, man, but when are we going to start developing film?

Not until we get the last shot in the can. The important thing is to get the film shot before we run out of cash. Worry about developing later.

That's dangerous, man. Be frank, how do you think the movie is going so far?

We're following the scenario but the movie isn't intimate.

He looks disappointed. What do you think's happening?

I thought we were going to make an intimate, wistful, melancholy, flamboyant movie with an historical spine that is also a happy picture that people'd like to see over and over for its uplift. All we're getting so far is a happy movie, sort of. We've set up almost every shot—but we haven't *crept* up on a single horn player, Jaime.

My Chilean brother looks injured. But that would take a year and hidden cameras and the money would never last that long.

That's the crux. We don't have the cash to shoot the full original conception.

Okay, so tell me in a few words what we're making.

A happy movie, I say—but am hollow.

It's decided? We make a happy picture?

Happy.

Launching into the Mass Mess, I lift my flugelhorn and tell the world about Prometheus Productions in an ad in *The Village Voice*. It's a loopy ad and sets the company back about $86. Its look on the movie page restores wine-shredded nerves.

COMING ++ COMING ++ COMING
Out of Palatial Railroad Cars in Transit
& Men of Rambling Gorgeous Intent
**PROMETHEUS
PRODUCTIONS ANNOUNCES**
Filming of the Eternal Classic Film
TRUMPET
by Newlove
Camera & Sound: Jaime Barrios & Luis
Prieto and Juan Ureta * A Film That Velazquez Might Have Liked * A Film Dotty and
Obsessed by Trumpets * Filmed with the
Whole Soul * Warm Hearts and Blue Horns
* Horns Antique, Beaten & Crushed *
Freshly Minted, Silvery & Lirruping with the
Greatest Mass Mess of Trumpeters in the
History of Music * A Thousand Horns
Aggregated Blowing Against Each Other *
The Trumpet Film the World Wants Finally
Filmed * Shiny, Blue & Clear-belling Trumpets.
FILM IN PROGRESS

Now that's telling the world! I tell Jaime modestly.

For good measure, I take out a separate ad about the Mass Mess:

SUNDAY SEPT. 11TH
11 A.M.—on the Mall in CENTRAL PARK
MAD TRUMPET RALLY

& MASS MESS OF HORNS
EVERYONE IN NEW YORK CITY with a TRUMPET INVITED

Greatest Gathering of Wandering Horn Players Ever En Masse *
$50 Grand Prize For Best Trumpeter Who Shows Up for Filming
of Climax of Newlove's Epic Film
"TRUMPET"
*Trumpet Battles on High Rocks!
*Cavalry Charges from Cleopatra's Needle!
*Mad Trumpet Morning without Parallel!
WBAI'S Larry Josephson ("Get that egomaniac off the air!")
Sole Judge of Trumpetry *
A Prometheus Production

When I hand in the ads, Howard Smith, a *Voice* columnist, stops me and crows his delight about my Mass Mess project and arranges for coverage. Next I dodge uptown for another shooting permit from the Department of Commerce and Industrial Development. Permit in hand I speed to a printer's and have worked up a rush order on a blazing red poster on gummed paper. The cost stuns: $35 for a $15 job. I dash home in Full Producer Mode and rent an electric typewriter for $18 a month plus $50 deposit. Time—which hath an art to make dust of all things—does not spare that $50 check now worthless as Methuselah's winding sheet, though there it lies in the store and here—with keys rapping as I type this very page you now read—sits the electric typewriter with a month's rent overdue, *Miserere! Miserere!* I've never with malice aforethought written a bad check for *Trumpet*—it's just that the checks decay, the checks decay and fall and after many a check dies the bank account. When Willoughby's wants a $400 deposit for an electric camera, it's best to rent the camera after banking hours Friday and get it back amid early birdsong Monday morning so that check remains unquestioned—and Prometheus Productions keeps in good odor at the store.

The immensity of our dream infects all of us. I set to at snapping out original letters to disk jockeys and news desks. My spent legs rise to a punishing day of notices hand-delivered to editors while at corner phone booths I hang on the line with my newly-rented answering service. Now pale I plunge into talks with national news desks. *The New York Times* interviews me for over an hour. They promise to bring their own kids and horns. The dream sweeps me up. I leap out of bed at three A.M. to write the Ford Foundation for a grant. I call Chemical Church and the account is rocky. Well, mashed. I don't have a penny to flip or whistle with. Do you know what it's like—bills piling—and not a penny for front? Feel a bit flat. My jaw grits all night as blind Samson agonizes and groans at the millwheel. O broke, broke, broke amid the blaze of stars.

Why do I make this movie? Because it is a poem that I hear and see.

Midnight blooms again and armed with a made up poster-plastering kit I paper every stop on the Lexington Avenue line—from Bowling Green to 125th Street—ride empty trains, sip brandy, and plaster MASS MESS all the stops one side uptown, all the other side downtown—and near dawn rise as a fagged Orpheus from the underworld of Astor Place and head home. But I still have posters. So, hollow-eyed, I go to Times Square and plaster the long white tunnel tying East and West Side trains, then slog and plaster from Sheridan Square to the East Village—and again home. And still have posters left. Wash, check the answering service, phone an accomplice to act as cop lookout—cops weary me with advice to move on. My partner in crime, Chris Johnson, twelve, shows up and out we set to paper the East Side. Then cometh the thunderblow.

Oh, harrying, harrying, harrying! *HARRYING!*

The answering service—or rather the Coordinator, Permit Division, Department of Commerce and Industrial Development—catches me during muscatel sunlight over Houston Street. I am to call her. Oh, thank God I've got hold of you at last! I was going out of my mind, she says. The sun sputters around my outdoor phone booth. I swallow—my stomach goes hollow. What about? I ask—a whisper, a hop frog croak.

Mr. Newlove, I have exceeded my authority in granting you permission to use the park on Sunday. The Borough Director of Parks has disapproved your request.

The bright sun goes blood-red over Houston Street.

Disapproved? How can you disapprove an event before it happens? I've got a *permit. SIGNED!*

I'm telling you, I exceeded my authority with your trumpet rally movie. You simply can't hold it, and especially not this Sunday.

Madame, I have to hold it this Sunday. *I couldn't stop it if I tried!*

Why not?

That rally is just going to take place, heaven and hell couldn't stop it. Gears are in motion—posters are up all over Manhattan—announcements are in newspapers—on radio and television—people are coming and *Life* magazine!

Can't you take the posters down?

I couldn't even find them again! They're gummed onto stanchions and lamp posts and subway walls from Harlem to South Ferry and Bronx to Staten Island.

Oh, lord!

Even if I personally don't go within three miles of the park with my crew on Sunday, these trumpet players are going to show up—*and play!*

Mr. Newlove, this may cost me my job.

That's possible but I button up.

You *can't* revoke my permit. I've spent a lot of money [I mean spirit] on this. It's the climax of my movie.

The point is, she says, I didn't know at the time I granted your permit that the Parks Department had already granted the Jehovah's Witnesses a Sunday permit to hold a mass memorial service on the Mall at the very hour of your trumpet rally . . .

Horns wail wall to wall on the green pastures.

. . . *OHH, GAWD!*

Two Mass Messes at once!

But—I can't stop it, I whimper.

You've got to!

You don't understand. Things are just . . . all out . . . of my control.

Mr. Newlove, I wasn't even supposed to let anyone anybody use the park on Sunday. There is no commercial activity allowed in the park on Saturday or Sunday. You told me there would be only two handheld cameras and a sound man and that the picture is only a tiny home movie and *not* even commercial.

I doubt that anybody in the movie business would think of this as commercial.

But were you honest with me?

Madame, movie producers rely on honesty.

I'm sorry I ever got into this. I'll never put my foot into a mess like this again. Do you understand?

Yes. I hang up in a stupor.

I am caught up in a spun-cotton absurdity—something sticky and stretchy in the sunlight binds me. Samson fuzzes over at his mud-bound millwheel. Chris and I drag toward Sheridan Square. And then rebellion buzzes and drums along my nerves. *By God!* I slap up a red poster on the red side of a wetly painted fire-alarm box. Prometheus Productions will be in Central Park on Sunday morning if we have to use hidden cameras. Viva! Viva! Blow, *Gabriel, blow!*

Howard Smith shouts, No! It's unbelievable! He howls in joy and beats his desk at the *Voice*. This isn't a movie, it's a legend! As he twists in place in his dim quarters and stares out at Sheridan Square in noon light, he masks his eyes as if before a firing squad. His head shudders, malarial, as his desk chair weaves. I thought your Mass Mess a *great* publicity idea. But this—who could even *plan* this? The Jehovahs Witnesses!

Howard, this is a movie-poem, not a stunt. I even talked with the Commissioner's top assistant. He says no. I tell him I can't stop it. He growls, Young man, we have a very efficient police force!

Oh, you know these middlemen in the pecking order. Let me call him. Howard phones the Commissioner's assistant and screams, You can't do this! Howard leans into him, his mouth a devil's. Both elbows push. We can't stop this! Howard hectors the CA for over half an hour. The CA backs off. We can shoot *down the park* on Sheep Meadow—not at the Mall. My heart lifts from mud and pops free into pure sunlight.

The Voice guards my ass as I pick up my plastering kit. All of New York's lamp posts stand outside, places to stick fast my red posters. With Goliath stoned, young Chris and I go forth into burning daylight.

Urgency inspires and drenches us. Lamp after lamp gets slapped. A bloody cough splatters the city with red *Trumpet* posters. SLAP! SLAP! SLAP! The Word goes up. On Saturday night we rage with love for our event as the whole crew blows horns and marches with great red and yellow two-man signs through the Village: MASS MESS IN SHEEP MEADOW!

Doubt troubles me in bed with my gallon. What if no Mass Mess takes place? That disaster would be my fault. Wine nerves ache in my elbows. I watch a waterbug waddle across my grave, lift up the stone and crawl under.

Ill met by sunlight, we survive our Village march and gather into a knot of raccoon-eyed moviemakers on The Sunday Morning of the Incarnation of the Mass Mess. We breakfast at a quiet matchbox restaurant—our forks naked artifacts—horns ring in our wired nerves. We swim in equipment—banks of wonderful electric junk jumble down the aisle—all of it underwritten by the fantasizing weekend checkbook of Prometheus Productions.

Wow, Jaime, all this junk—and yet the movie—it's so intangible.

Man, Jaime says, you're making a classic.

Well, call it a verse from the heart.

Great, man! Call it anything you want.

Luis asks Juan, What is "intangible"?

A powerful production, Juan says.

Ah, big budget! Luis says.

Jaime on the company tab eats like a Greek bent toward Thermopylae. He studies me with great seriousness. Do you have any of the, uh, stuff with you?

I slip him a packet of amphetamine.

This is going to make the day, he says.

We each get in gear for the day and zap up to the lower rung of Fool's Paradise. Jaime's genius shines. He says, I could fight King Kong. Luis and Juan have jesters' smiles—their eyes bounce and heads dance. I am Atlas bearing the Mass Mess on my shoulders. In dreams begin responsibilities, Jaime says—his last gasp before the coming storm, and we leave. We split cabs and Welles up to Central Park. Jaime, I ask, is this a raft of feathers or the world's first balsa-wood taxi?

Don't come down, he says. Stay with it.

Right. Down there is for mice, not moviemakers.

We reach Sheep Meadow and debark. Huge haunches of equipment hang from our shoulders. We strike out for the Big Rocks in the Meadow.

Where is Sheep Meadow? Jaime asks.

I don't know.

We are looking for some sheep? Luis asks.

We come up to a cop on a looming beast. He looks down at us. What are you doing?

As producer I say, We're having a rally.

Do you have a permit?

I show him the scenario and permits. Stunned, he reads the whole scenario on the horse. He reads the permits with pointed eyes. Studies the Chileans' shepherd-like haircuts. He sees through thickened air that he can't throw us out. Not until we screw up. What's the name of this picture? He asks.

Arthur, Jaime says—referring to John Lennon's Arthurian haircut.

The horse prangs up its head and swizzes its mind our way. We can see that it's bred to herd hippies smelling of pot—not Chileans on pink pills. The horse dances back—its eye-globes print us on its pea-brain. It will remember us should our joys beat down Sunday prayer.

Jaime digs at his crotch for crawly earthworms. Which way to Sheeps Meadow, man?

The cop points heroically over his horse's head. That way.

Thanks, Jaime says. If you like Beethoven, stop over.

Our Lewis and Clark team heads toward Sheep Meadow. At last we find one magnificent area we call *our* Sheep Meadow—a flat place fitted out with a mammoth rock or the molten end of a tractor trailer done in stone—a Tyrannosaurus rock. Here the Mass Mess plants its flag.

Man, let's turn on, Jaime says.

Aren't we?

I mean before the people get here.

We tamp down a bowl of Promethean Gold. I light it and swallow and whisper, *Try. This.*

He swallows a cloud and nods. This is *good* stuff.

The Promethean Meadow fades underfoot.

Jaime, I would climb that rock but if I fell off—as I might at this moment—I'd get hospitalized and you'd have to do the producing. Do you think the world is ready for *Trumpet*?

He whispers, Mister Dylan, I don't think it's ready for *Mouthorgan*.

Thought maybe some trumpeters would be here ahead of time. Blow for awhile. Maybe you'll attract them.

I put my horn together and blow the racetrack Call To Colors.

Man, don't let the horses hear that! Jaime warns.

Luis and Juan carry our big red and yellow signs to the Mall to redirect the millions to Sheep Meadow. It is ten-thirty A.M. Away down the Meadow two soccer teams kick a ball—figures on the plains of Marathon. A young Negro lad—maybe twelve years old—shows up with his mother and his horn. The lad warms up on Gershwin's "Summertime." The kid has tone.

Why don't we film the trumpet duel? Jaime asks. You know, as if you and the kid are meeting with pistols or swords. We could filter-in a six A.M. dueling hour.

I don't think he and I are quite up to that. That little duel takes really sharp players, Jaime, and I think he would outplay me.

I can't work up any feeling on my flugelhorn and switch to trumpet. My screechy Maynard Ferguson 13C cup pierces the soccer game an acre away. A player arrives with his Selmer glowing and whales into some gorgeous scales but saves his good stuff for when it counts. Two mounted cops—who look bound in stiff leather—sidle up and study every letter and dot on our permits.

The horses loom and sniff the Promethean air.

Jesus Christ, one cop says to the other, read this permit. He looks down at me. You don't like mounted policemen?

Why not?

"We really don't need any police," he reads, "and we especially don't need any mounted police, i.e., horses." You don't like horses either?

I am pale and stammer through fear, W-We thought the horns might frighten them.

Well, I'm afraid we might even madden them when the full power of the Mass Mess turns on. One horse's eyes question me. He does not like my aroma. Has the NYPD horse patrol sniffed us out?

These horses don't frighten, the cop says and turns his mount and the two cops amble off above rolling haunches.

The young lad playing "Summertime" shines but looks shy. Compelling excellence comes more from tone than from agility, Satchmo says, and my heart cracks at this lad's molded shimmer over mellow depths. *Roll, Trumpet!* This kid is why I'm making this amber movie. A man arrives with a professional soft leather bag I'd die for and takes out a Bach shiny as silver herring netted from the North Sea. He drips and larrups through fantastic scales I'd also die for and begins playing Handel's "A Trumpet Shall Sound" from *The Messiah*. The glorious smashing climax of our *Trumpet* epic will happen, dammit!

Where is this Larry Josephson cat? Jaime asks. I look about for our contest judge. Do you know what he looks like?

The Meadow fills with bewildered but bemused enthusiasts of the grass who wilt into picnic position—yogis approaching satori.

No, I hear he looks like a bald bear.

We watch the morning spring up and away on the haunches of Prometheus.

Jaime says, We got to get this show on the road pretty soon, man. Before the Jehovah's Witnesses ask us to shut up.

I'm nervous, having little organized activity in mind—but also a familiar powdery effervescence fills my arms. People from every part of my life—current and past friends who don't even know each other and whom I haven't particularly invited—show up in their Sunday spirits and with their families stretch out on the grass as their children hop about, all eyes aglow and amused. Ah, wine, puff, gulp. I am all waves and slip back into a sunny day from childhood. Old times spin up in a flushed card deck of faces.

My senses stir and life gathers in smoke-hewn serenity at the calm rise and fall of horns warming up on sunlit tunes and scales. Slow but building, *Trumpet* broaches the limits of deep disharmony—a Hiroshima of wayward horns looking for or awaiting their heavenly WBAI bandmaster's descent from the great blue bending above. Kids trade my two horns and wail from their own corner of the storm as they plumb their first music lesson and their lobster eyes pop. By Jehovah, they are players too! The day explodes as the sun shakes out all the chords from *The Scythian Suite* and scatters rosy silver iridescence about Sheep Meadow and all crash and dance en masse. Men shine on brass and women sit happy in their bones. We the mad makers of this morning-blast bear up under our joy. Yes, someday the breath will fail but now the eyes mist over as day spills delight and the crew shoots fragments of heaven fallen about us—for the Mass Mess is in flower.

Good God, says young Chris Johnson's mother Becky, this is what people *should* do! Chris, my fellow poster plasterer this week, blows my flugelhorn. This is so lovely, Becky says as her other kids blow among men who rip and lust to bang the sun. The world cries, Yes! Yes! Yes!

Perhaps three hundred people sit on the grass about our towering Rock. We have about forty trumpeters with horns but many other players as well who borrow instruments back and forth. Forty is far from the five hundred we'd hoped for. But recall how Hampton's or Basie's bands lift off the roof with just four trumpets powered by a drummer. Then bring to mind forty horns wailing "Ciribiribin" and "The Carnival of Venice" and "I Can't Get Started" and "And the Angels Sing" or just pumping their hearts out on Yiddish klezmer music in major and minor keys or climbing scales in a Parnassian goat dance and some of the messy but weird disorder and originality of the morning will blow through your senses. Ah, Milton, thou shouldst be with us at this hour! Manhattan hath need of thee, pure as the naked heavens, majestic, free.

Noon blooms with a gay flood of happy Botticelli faces banked and tumbled about at the wedding of the wine satyr with the angel of fame. Cynara Rosewine blows my Civil War bugle. I launch an assault on the Rock.

Up we go, every player as we hand up horns and haul each other summitward. At last we stand clustered on the Tyrannosaurus and now the Mass Mess bunches with power. The Rock roars. Din splatters the sunlight. Each player finds his private ecstasy as the Mass Mess exults and sweeps up listeners in a devil's orchestra mangling the sunlight. My foot beats with a life of its own. I play but barely, my lip by now a swollen primrose. We lift a punch-drunk Pamplona and run with the bulls. The Rock turns altar and anvil as Dionysus's liver gets cut out and lies bleeding by brightness of noon. From the Watchtower of our Rock we spy afar the Jehovah's Witnesses over their Bibles and at prayer that bloodless surgery be begat upon us.

A bald bear in a bulging yellow sweatshirt and rumpled pants heaves to below the Rock and shakes his head in a stupor. I grip his hand. He circles us, digging at his grand muff of a beard, and weighs the work before him. He comes up below me and cups his hands:

I'M NOT SURE I CAN REALLY JUDGE THIS CONTEST!
Do your best!

At nine o'clock A.M. Mrs Maria Ouspenskaya knocks and begs and chews me out as my stomach trembles and drums and, in a sneak attack at nine P.M., Richard Nixon strikes at my weakest point with a telegram: "URGENT YOU REMIT $96.35 TODAY ON YOUR ACCOUNT TO FORESTALL FURTHER ACTION OTHERWISE YOU WILL INCUR ADDITIONAL CHARGES IN ACCORDANCE WITH THE TERMS OF YOUR NOTE." I drop this atop alike piles of death notices. One informs me that Chemical Church regards the Prometheus Productions account as defunct and in deep arrears. This night—every night—I stir in a restless grave. I see in my battle against oblivion the certified letter from Willoughby's: "We tried to reach you by telephone several times but have not heard from you . . ." The letter from Eaves Costume Company speaks in a less harsh tone but advises me that I have just battered my financial reputation with a rubber club. Bond Clothes debits me at $31.50. Actorfone, my answering service, says I m $9.20 from perfection as a client. But not only these firms chase me: my Polish grocer wants $50, my vintner has turned off the spigot at $70— and me his best customer!—My camera crew hectors me daily for $170 to save our exposed film. Household Finance and Seaboard Trust have both turned me down on a $500 consolidation loan. My grass contact harps at my door fruitlessly to make a sale he needs to keep up his reputation with his dealer—and now I check my mailbox only at midnight—Raskolnikov on Stairwell Despair. I am so involved with the movie that my Kirkus book-reviewing income piddles into pennies. Every cent I scratch gets spent just on liverwurst and cheap white bread and the sobbing of my wine cells.

As Prometheus Productions swells with reel after undeveloped reel—our horn-filled soundtrack is now longer than *Götterdam-*

merung—I suck in a deep breath and sell blood at the blood bank and hock my two horns and plunge into the Erotic Color Sequence which spins me into a Chinese torture chamber of debt. Creditors' shops checker my neighborhood: I shun daylight and keep an eye sharp for dark mystic cracks in the sidewalk. In conference with Jaime, we throw out the historical sequence altogether. Goodbye, Met collection of antiques. He asks, How are you going to finance the color sequence, man? I tell him, Trident Press owes me $140 for reviewing manuscripts—they've simply got to come through.

Then go up and see them.

They'll think I'm a fishpeddler.

You've got to do it, man. We've got to finish this film!

We've shot twenty-seven reels, over ninety minutes: a raid on the Statue of Liberty—dancing trumpets in the Sunday silence of Wall Street and in the fountain at Lincoln Center—a dazzling and magical sequence as the lights boil in Times Square during the theater hour. Still waiting for the big Trident check, I spiral $200 deeper into credit disaster and produce the Cynara Rosewine sequence on three reels of color in a rented studio with rented camera and rented costume and fund production values on a Promethean scale that down at our level nonetheless rival those of the Lana Turner epic *The Bad and the Beautiful*—and we've got the shots to prove it. Friday night we build the white set, stream upon stream of white satin at five bucks a yard and dizzy ourselves with lights for our folly. Costume tryout at Cynara's on Friday night leaves me spinning with excitement—she's such a sex-goddess she defies words. I am about to out-Stroheim von Stroheim and set fire to her beauty in a blaze of ostrich feathers, flashing fantasy, mirrors, color, trumpets—and Cynara over Cynara over Cynara in an impasto celebration and passion of triple exposures.

Hellish nerves grab us as we shoot. The night wears on. At last we break through Cynara's shyness and wring image after flaming image out of her as a combined Queen of the Night, erotic enchantress, a dream figure glimmering out of Baudelaire, sensuous white witch, Strauss's Elektra and Salomé—all in a burst and swirl of color and white laugh upon laugh upon laugh—doubled in a mirror!

Next week we shoot a trumpet and motorcycle coda in color on Brooklyn Bridge and *Trumpet* wraps.

No relief takes for ahead. Mrs. Ouspenskaya still waits on the stairwell. Richard Nixon knows my address. No creditor's been paid. Now in the middle of the film—with Chemical Church snapping at me—Prometheus Productions needs as much for final dupes as is already spent in the making. The picture sits in its glory—as with Goya's once-hidden *The Nude Maja*—and lusts to be bared. All that editing faces us and then—Jaime assures me—I will truly become a movie director. We need more sound track recording to match the track to the picture. And there'll be esthetic spats as *Trumpet*'s thirst for money, money, money goes on. Honestly, it is painful and nerve-wracking to produce a happy picture.

Epilogue 2014

Jaime went quite far in editing *Trumpet* but the end money never came and a finished negative was never assembled nor was sound added—or I don't think it was. All of our film and sound clips went into his files. I was given a dupe of the Cynara sequence which is in my desk drawer as I write forty years later. My dupe is watchable but less pure than the negative it comes from—and is all I have left from my wonderful adventure. The dupe has no sound. Or trumpets.

Jaime married Cynthia Brown and had a daughter, Emilia Barrios-Brown, who still lived in Manhattan at my last knowledge of them. In 1989 he died at home of a heart attack at 43 years old, having had success as an experimental film maker. He invited me to see his *El Blocke*, an impressive and poetic documentary about a Spanish community in East lower Manhattan. In black and white, his film starts at dawn on the deserted cobbled street of a block and flows through the block's changing light and life through daylight into the evening. After President Salvador Allende's overthrow in Chile, Jaime turned to documentaries about human rights and Latin American politics and culture, many of which—*Missing Persons, Operation Bootstrap* and *Onward, Christian Soldiers*—were shown on public broadcasting.

Perhaps fifteen years after our work on *Trumpet* I met him with Cynthia and Emilia passing my front door in the Village and was invited to visit his studio. There he showed me sequences from our movie and gave me my dupe of Cynara. After his funeral I lost contact with Cynthia, nor could I later find her address. Today I'd very much like to recover the lost negative and see what might be done with it, if anything. He had a fat library of finished work filed in his studio and *Trumpet* was only a folly from his charmed youth. The Mass Mess still exists—somewhere.

I miss him and am sorry I did not get together more often with my lively, gentle friend.

Cynara, too, is dead. She was fourteen-year-old schoolgirl Leana Kantor when I met her and later, Laura Hurvich, after her second marriage. At 26 years old—in deep depression six months after giving birth to her daughter Elizabeth—she took her life in woods near Mill Valley, California, using a .38-caliber police pistol. This was her third attempt at suicide. That pistol report has echoed throughout my life—and needless to say throughout the lives of many others.

The Black Eye
Evergreen Review, Vol. 14, No, 77, April 1970

In memory of Marvel Marie Carris Newlove Berger Chambers Allan, from the great grape orchards of Lake Erie, who in her ninetieth year lay down in the Florida sunlight under orchard-coverings of long cloud.

For six ginswept months I've been living with my mother in a toy, flamingo-colored house near the gorgeous trash heap of Daytona Beach and by now my animal spirits are blue as a Bowery wino's in midwinter.

The hero lover?—flat out of women! My mother's built this rosy-white matchbox—with sliding glass doors that open onto a pink-pebbled patio—and surrounded it with orange trees and a thousand-dollar lawn that wads like currency under my toes. The Nile-green living room has a TV and Jackie Gleason highlights my week. This Saturday evening I'm stone sober with the blue devils—paralyzed by our meteoric bottle problem—while she starts in at four-thirty on a ninety-proof juice. Dejected, I lie cramped in her floral American Beauty love seat and wait for Gleason and for some word to seduce spirit out of my dead womanless legs into my heart and head. My body can live without women but my spirit can't. Not that I hate my body—it's just that this *valse triste* of revelation turns on my animal spirits.

We've incorporated ourselves with my married sister in the antiques business. We own our own shop but have lost money footstool over highboy. Mama's depressed. It gives me pleasure to learn a trade at last, at thirty-four. Burning off a finish satisfies like bringing out the grain of a paragraph. My sister decorates each piece with antique red lacquer or Chinese black and always with "stressed gold" and Oriental vignettes she invents. She passes right into these gardens and hillsides when she paints them—illusions have eaten her brain since childhood. They run in the family. I think it's glandular.

Just as the rippling metropolitan trumpets rise and smear Gleason's theme, my mother—who's drunk four husbands into the grave—also rises and floats about me with great butterfly wings of blame and finds all three of her husbands' faults enclosed in me. I said I think it's glandular. If she were mad, I might put up with this. But she's just drunk and ranting over the abuses she's endured from her battery of husbands to keep my sister and me in the style we've known growing up. In one breath, she's chaste as the trademark for Columbia Pictures—and then a ruined woman rising pure again from the ashes of brute after raging brute. *And away-y-y we go* Jackie cries, doing his walkaway behind her, and I ask Mama to stand aside.

But she kneels beside me and harangues and wraps me in chicken wire. I love Gleason. Now he's outdoing himself to make up for the poor critical reception of his opening show. There stands Art Carney in a Prussian spike-top helmet, stunned by a Gleason insult. What—what did he say? She harangues.

After thirty-four years, my mother's harangue hits me at last. *Will you get away from the fucking TV so I can watch!*

Donald, you don't know how I love you.

Will you get off my fucking back and let me watch this goddamn fucking TV program?

I love you so much.

Suddenly her face loses all human illusion. I see two million years of growth shimmering on the gene pool and staring at me. It's like when the lights go up after the movies and you wake up and the theater's bare but for you and your bagged bottle—or maybe it's like your first sight of a woman's nakedness in a late afternoon hotel room: the veil is lifted. I see her sticklike bones and cranial bowl with its cauliflower as a kind of love-filled puppet, her face a knot of sensory organs declaring love for me. I, Cro-Magnon, my brainy sober glare says—you, witless Neanderthal.

But her palm splays over me like Columbia's torch—she hovers on her knees and when I can't move her aside from Jackie Gleason, my blue devils drive me berserk and I backhand her cheek. She falls aside but at once rises back onto the love seat, exhorting, Don't you understand how I love you?—Good God, I can't care less, I don't give a shit!—Don't be like that, Donald, not you.—Oh, please. Shut up and let me watch.—I love you more than your sister, I always have.—Will you get out of my line of sight?—You're my favorite.—I want to watch Jackie Gleason!

She slaps me and turns off the TV. Gleason's binocular rage fades.

You can't do this, I say.—I am your mother, young man.—Turn that set on.—You can watch it tomorrow. Go to bed.—It's seven-thirty, Mama, I'm not going to bed, and I am going to watch the TV.—A gladiator, she stands before me, legs spread and set. You are not.—Oh, yes I am.—Around my dead body.

I rip out of the love seat, rap her shoulder and turn on the set. I sit with my face right in it. Frank Fontaine sings—his mouth a dolphin grimace—while Jackie the bartender as straight man, his hair in Gay Nineties curls and eyelids at sentimental half-mast, wipes the bar. Frank sings *I love you as I never loved before-r-e since first I saw you on the village green*—as the small sea-mammal comedians swim in the tube. My mother, who's not fallen—she's goaded each husband into beating the Book out of her—stands at the telephone and dials my sister. But she hangs up rather than complete the call. Now she stands over me—superior and silent—her fearless queenship a bleak threat from on high. Her hand reaches down to flick off the set and I grab it and pick her up and throw her majesty onto the love seat. She lies stunned and her face swells. I watch Gleason arf-arfing—a false-mustached animal imitating an animal—talk about gene pools. My heart empties. I go into the kitchen, lift the high-proof juice and let cool spring-water bite and gush onto my parched soul. Even Jackie's blown his illusion. I feel frenzy and swallow and moan. When I return, she lies watching me.

Oh, Lord! What ironies she must feel! Her suckling baby, her schoolboy, her brilliant son the class vice president, her military school cadet, her Marine, her college student, her married son, her airman, her son the father, and then her divorced son, her unpublished son, her drinking son the reporter, her whoring son back from Europe, her fat bearded son in Manhattan, and now her mother-beating son—heavy legs in Bermudas, puffy eyes without pity.

Now who's stripped of illusions?

She says something incensing, and I don't really hear it but next I'm slapping her face right, left, right, goaded by her into a fit—not of madness—of loving salvation. This pain is an electroshock series to save her. Again she incenses me but I cannot beat her anymore and so smash the table lamp down onto her spindly powderblue writing desk. She's unmoved. I pick up her cream and gold floor lamp and swing it straight down onto her slippery concrete floor on which I'm forever twisting an ankle. She starts bawling. I eye the sliding glass patio doors but instead rip out the desk telephone and smash that onto her tessellated pink-and-blue concrete living room floor. In many ways, I'm lovesick.

Then I leave for a bike ride.

The roadhouse I bike to in the moonless night lies two houseless and empty blocks from my mother's house. We live on the outskirts of a hamlet and in Florida no houseless outskirt has light. The flat countryside is black. My nephew's bike has no lamp. I know where I pedal by the feel of asphalt under my tires. Some nightwalkers carry flashlights but the possibility hangs that I might bust into some lightless idiot—like myself—and as I guide my tire away from the asphalt's edge, ideas creep up my ginswept back of a black man jumping out and killing and robbing me, in that order. I grit my teeth and pump on blind into a night crushed of starlight. In that blackness I ride a membrane of darkness of soul—utter night within—and beside—and ahead of me. Darkness pools the very intersection where the signless snug roadhouse spreads Pabst Blue Ribbon neon from a single small window. I pedal up and park, thankful in the red and blue beer-glow.

As I go in—the bar sells only beer—I carry with me William Manchester's *Portrait of a President* which features a cover photo of JFK. A man beside me at the bar snorts at the book at my elbow. He rises up straight, a thirty-year-old Korean veteran with no love for JFK.—Whutchu readin' that fer?—I like the man!—Yew like JFK?—He's our President and he's interesting.

This cracker has a whip body and cheekbones of rock and smoky gray-blue eyes shot through with Confederacy. I see pure, bone animal and an overbearing hawknose.—Yew know, he says, running back his blond hair, JFK is for the niggers and I was in Korea and I never saw a single nigger there.—Maybe you didn't. But I'm sure they were there since fewer Negroes go to college and more get drafted.—Ahh, yew know about the niggers in Korea, he tells me politely.—No, what about them?—They was all kept back so us white folk could do the fightin', yes sir. We couldn't have them in there fuhkin' everythin' up!—I saw photographs of them on the front line.—Who's been feeding yew all this bullshiyut. *Life* magazine?—The Army has no segregation, there had to be Negroes on the front line. But he sniffs, shaking his head at my sad innocence. By God, you are a queer one, boy, how come you don't wear blackspecs an' dress like a' aighead insteada runnin' around in these bitty shorts? Huh? Course yew do have some chin whiskers—thayut goat-tee like a Mayunhattan aighead.

Enjoying this banter I buy us beer—icy and headachey. Very straightfaced, he pulls my leg around the crackerbarrel. But as I stare into his face I hear William Manchester describe him: ". . . born into an illusion which works hand in glove with his instincts to keep him bound to both without hope of insight." Despite my humor, I admire that part of him which feeds on illusion and instinct and hates with the power of fury. And as he just breathes, I sense this bone-breaking force. He'd whip into half the bar if he'd a mind to.—Buddy, you sure are all fucked up, I never heard the like—'cause I never saw one nigger on Pork Chop Hill.—You were there?

He draws his shirt down a shoulder and shows me a red puncture scar. Ya-is, he says.—Well, I believe you, but you must have seen a few Negroes.—Why, *hail*, you must mean those messenger boys! (I laugh.) Why, hail, yes, I saw some niggers—quite a few. He drinks a gulp. They weren't none of them totin' a rifle, of course, he says very politely. I am just as polite and ask, Why do you insist on this when the Army's table-of-organization doesn't separate Negro riflemen from white?—I know you aren't doubting my word.—Of course I'm not! I drink. But why say you didn't see them? Okay, I'll shut up.

I shut up but William Manchester goes rigid and right on speaking and the vet hears him in my eyes. Bill, I say, shut up, you can't convince him.

We wind up playing eight ball while I buy him beer by losing matches on purpose. And by this time I no longer care about niggers in Korea. I am seducing him into letting me out of the bar alive—but fear has collected into shiny dimes in my eyes and I know it. He now has three or four crackers backing up his every straight-faced smear—calm people as insane as himself, forked, warped animals—his troops of genetic trash—and I can't make a gesture that doesn't glitter with fright. I am losing more illusions than I care to lose.

A cracker studying my book says, Naw, Kennedy ain't goin' to buy the next election. He ain't even goin' ta get nominated.—Why not, I ask and by accident—damn!—sink a ball.—Boy, he's a nigger lover, that's why. Look what he's doing for that Meredith nigger.—Well, I'm not a nigger lover, but if a man pays his taxes he deserves to be educated. Isn't that just and reasonable?—Ha! All them fancy words just to talk about a plain animal, it don't make sense ... I want to shut up but they wait.—Even an animal, if he pays his money, he deserves to get what he bought. Isn't that true?—Donald, you are talking through your asshole. Another cracker says, I think you really are a nigger lover, fat boy.—Me! A nigger lover? Never. Seriously, I don't have a single nigger friend.

But the asshole and fat boy insults telegraph black-bordered news to me. I walk up to the bartender-owner of the roadhouse and say, I just want to buy a six-pack and g-get on my bike and go h-home in one piece. So will you help me?

The fat little redroundfaced foul-souled bartender-owner smirks. His pig eyes snicker like a merry lil shaver's and smile up. He says, They ain't nothing going to happen to you in here.

G-give me the six-pack.

I pay and head to the door. Then every light goes out—even the neon beer sign. I'm so surprised I think it might be closing time. I go to the screen door and, as I open it and step out, I see many men and a woman press toward me in the moonless dark—ghosts in white tee shirts. They won't let me step down and the inner door closes tight and locks behind me. The woman and her short husband by her—who grips my nephew's bike—harangue me as a nigger lover and with muck and filth work over my ignorance. I make a roguish dismissal of my faults but her soul shrieks in the dark, You ain't gonna git outta here without a fight, you stupid *buhg!*

Great! I'll fight him, I say and nod at her short husband.

She sneers, He's too small to fight!

He can whip a nigger lover, I say with serene certainty.

I'll fight, I'll fight, her faint-hearted husband says.

A figure comes around the now lightless roadhouse and moves toward me. It's my Korean veteran and stripped to the waist.— Bring him around the building, he says, and the band herds me around side of the roadhouse where the lawn lies bordered by a hedge. My fright tempers itself with fatalism. They're too eager and many hands jump me at once and pound glancing blows. I don't hit back. I don't want to anger anyone. I think they'll let me go once they finish. I don't mind pain much and stunning pain short circuits the nervous system. After a suitable half-minute, I take a dive to my hands and knees. They kick me but I've covered my vitals. Somebody knocks me on my side and I look up and see a patch of stars—inhuman blue stars above our animal planet—and I go back into my crouch. The hedges! I kick off my Japanese flip-flops and dive into the hedge, scrape through and find myself in a driveway. I hit the drive and gazelle up the midnight highway and run past all the people on the lawn. Oh, God, I cry, breaking down, Gun it, Donald! Bare feet don't mind the pebbles. Leaving beer, book and bike, I am Pheidippides hotfooting from Marathon to Athens. Fat boy runs.

The highway looms in lampless and lightless black space and I run but not toward my mother's damned house. I half sob and run by intuition into darkness from pole to pole.

Then as I run I'm lighted up. I look back and see cars, many cars. Chasing me. Whoo, my heart drops. They are really going to do it, I wail within. They want a fat northerner to stomp and dip their sprits in.

I run harder and come to a curved driveway to a horseshoe of houses. About twelve houses half-circle this development, all alike. I run to the first house, which lies dark, and beat the door and ring the bell. No answer. I run to the next house and beat and ring. No answer to all my noise. At last I run the whole horseshoe and no one will open his door although—or because—I'm shouting, They're trying to kill me! You've got to help me!

Now the whole development lights up. Every picture-window blazes. The cars turn into the drive. I stand disappointed in humanity. Then I run into the center of the horseshoe and hold my fists between my knees and sob and cry, Oh you motherfuckers, oh you bastards! Won't one of you help me and call the cops—you bastards, you cowardly bastards—these sons of bitches are going to kill me and you won't let me in or help me call the cops! Feet splayed and hands locked between my knees, I vomit my brain out.

Men walk toward me from a crowd of cars banked with their headlights on me. My eye catches a screen door lighted from within. I swallow my heart and run toward that house. Somebody shouts behind me and I find myself whimpering that they might catch me before I reach the house.

I hit the front steps and then the screen door and hurl myself straight through the screen and carry most of it with me right into the house and yet don't lose my balance. I'm in this living room where a man stands and I stand scraped raw from his torn screen.

You've got to help me! These men are trying to kill me!

His eyes—pale buttons on a plant.

Just let me use your phone to call the police, that's all.

You'll have to git out of here.

I see car headlights moving to the front of the house. My God,

I cry, they're out to murder me!

He's unmoved.

Oh God! I study him and see thick mulatto lips and brown eyes. You're one of us, you're a Negro, help me!

His wife stands in the bedroom doorway and goes rigid in her nightgown. When I say this she shrieks. Her shriek rises. I am a nigger rapist who has trapped her in the bathtub? Horror draws her face into a white mouse point.

Did you call me a nigger? the man asks.

No! No! I cry. I didn't mean that. You're not a Negro. I made a mistake.

But with that red flash I turn and run from his living room and hit the front doorway and porch where the cars huddle and leap the side rail and run around the corner of the house and out back and into a swamp. Again I'm sobbing and still barefoot, and as I wade through the swamp I think of snakes and cry to myself, I don't care about snakes! I don't care! Which way in this swamp lies my mother's house? The swamp sinks deep and dense. A root catches my foot and I go under, then rise and fight to a far side and find myself in a trench against the highway. The trench stinks waist-deep with water and muck. Nobody's on the highway. Sucking in breath I run across the highway to the far side and throw myself flat into another trench of muck. It's a swamp draining trench and slick with oily creosote to kill insect eggs. I lie there and gag on the creosote. Down the road the whole horseshoe burns against the sky much like New Year's in my beloved but far distant Times Square. I know that nothing good will come to me staying where I gag, and so I dig in a deep oily breath, jump to the highway and begin running straight toward where I'd come from—the lighted houses.

I've seen a county patrol car pull into the horseshoe. As I run, the roadway pebbles chew my feet and my eyes swim. I pass rebels swaggering under their flat-topped garbage brains. How they've relished beating and kicking me. I get very close to the patrol car before anyone sees me—hell-bent with knees high—running toward them and I slam myself fish-flat onto the hood with a loud thunk and scramble up the patrol car windshield and slap my arms against the roof and clutch the red light whirling on top. The Dixie cops turn and look at me. They amble up in Stetsons—all law, all smiles.

Barefoot, I bleed head to toe—hair spiked with swamp crud, legs slick with creosote—and shirt and bitty shorts shredded by hedge and swamp and wire screen.

You the boy? A trooper asks under his stiff brim.

I need help, I gag, saved. These people want to kill me. They been chasing me with cars and nobody would help me.—We'll help you. Let go of that light, you're filthying up our patrol car. Now turn around and put your hands behind you.—I don't have any weapons, officer. Handcuffs snap closed behind me on my slick wrists.—Officer, it's not me, I say. It's them.

The cop opens the rear door of his car and bending my head down shoves me onto the floor.—Boy, *do not* sit on that seat.

He slides up front to drive. I lie bent and vexed with my wrists cuffed over my ass. A second cop gets in beside me but keeps his distance and the car pulls out of the horseshoe. As we glide down the road the backseat cop gives up and pulls me onto the seat's edge, saying, Stay forward. I sit bent forward. The over-tight cuffs burn. The cop cleans his hands on a rag.

What's wrong, sonny? he asks.—These people were trying to kill me. Back in the roadhouse. I really didn't do anything.—You must have done something or they wouldn't have been upset with you.—They weren't upset, they were out to kill!—You musta done something, the cop says. I sit hunched and silent in my cuffs.—What did you say? I begin crying—All I said was that a guy who pays all his state taxes deserves to attend the state university! The cop drags in a huge breath.—Well! he says, don't you know better than to say a thing like that down here?—I DIDN'T KNOW BEFORE BUT I KNOW IT NOW!—It seems to me you were asking for whatever happened you.—Look, I'm a citizen, I sob.—Oh, I appreciate that.—A goddamned citizen and I can have my ideas!

The incredible handcuffs may yet cause suicidal rage. We pull up to the county jail and the cops arm-cuff and waddle me in. I see stiff-brimmed animal robots. I'm convinced I know their real intent. My best hope: hide my identity.

They give my soggy wallet to the desk sergeant.—Name? he asks and gives his jaw a sound scratch.—I'm not talking to any of you bastards.—Come on, boy, what's your name?—I know all about you sonsofbitches, don't think I don't.—We're going to book you anyway, so you may as well tell us who you are. Your name is right in your wallet here.—That's it then and I'm not telling you another fucking thing. *Why do you have ME in here anyway!*—Keep your head, sonny.—Keep my head! I nearly lost it tonight in this motherfucking county of yours! *Oh I know all about you kill-happy goons,* you're all members of the White Citizens Council and so's your D.A. and so're all your judges who are going to run me up forever for doing nothing. I won't get out of here for six months and I know it!

I now keep mum but they are kind to me, even gentle and fatherly. Very kind. A hatted animal walks me off into a dark passageway. That hat frightens and makes me timid.

We come to an elevator and he pushes a button and we wait.—Yais, he says, I been North. We ain't all so unalike as you might think. But—blinking—his heavy-lidded sheepish eyes turn sober as William Manchester's and look forward and I stiffen with the clear knowledge that he sees me bound by birth and illusion into a Northern stereotype without hope of insight. My spirit teeters. The elevator opens in absolute electrical silence. The doors just split open before us without a sound of bearings, and this sleepy-lidded lamb and I step inside. On foam or cobweb, we go up three floors without a single sensation. The doors again open—upon blackness absolute.

Come in, he says. He walks me into the black. I now glimpse heavy, heavy bars beside me—bars thick as peaches. We come to some place in the darkness which the cop sees though I am blind. A key rattles as he opens a cell door. At last my cuffs come off. A hand comes into my back and pushes me lurching barefoot into a cage. My head thuds somewhere into heavy bars and I fall onto concrete and pain leaps from stubbed toes. I lie there. I don't know it but this is the open cell for twenty separate cells. All the cells are unlocked and anyone who wishes can walk around in the large open cell. Down the darkness I see three cigarette butts glowing. I just lie where I am and get my breath and suck some pity for myself from swollen lips. My heart pounds under my breastbone.

The three cigarette butts get up from cots and glide toward me down the general cell. It is black. Three embers hang over me. My fame goes before me. I'd thought that perhaps I could hold my own in this cell. I've been in cells. But one ember at last lowers and crouches by me and I smell a plume of smoke over my face and a tenory soft voice asks, *Are you the nigger lover?*

I give up my life.

I will not leave this cell alive. Thanks to my very own and kindly personal troopers. I choke. For one minute, when hanging onto the whirling red light, I'd thought I was safe tonight. But not until now has the full cup of peril gone down my throat. My great fear is of bashing my skullcap and brains against those terrific bars in a scuffle or melee in the black. No weapon is needed, just these bars. The safety of my poor cantaloupe hinges on not fighting in here. But just as piercing as the possible mode is the certainty that my shade may well shut in here and I better face up to it—though no thought of prayer crosses my mind.

I'm no nigger lover. Why'd you say that?

A drag on a cigarette by my face lights me up. You sure look like a nigger lover. And you sure *sound* like a nigger lover, Donald.

My name! I lose the power of speech.

Speak up.

You c-can't even see me really. If you could you'd know.

Ah, we know you're a nigger lover. Pretty name like yours—Donald Newlove!—you'd have to be. What say you get up and come over here where we can get a good look at a genu-ine pussy-eating New York nigger lover.

In the great cell's center sits a picnic table and one prisoner lights a white stub of candle on the table. I sit alone on one side and face three prisoners in the still small candle flame. This is kangaroo court.

They inquire why I am a nigger lover and I smile and give a soft laugh and deny it and laugh again and smile through creosote in the comforting darkness. Of the three the Grand Inquisitor is the oldest, about twenty-three—lean, blond, brainless—and he unfolds the leaves of my each answer for its truth or fancy. Wind tosses about his dull wits and makes his each question hard to parry. All three are bruised and nicked and need taping up but my inquisitor, the leader, looks so slack-jaw and hang-face battered that he has nothing to lose *whatever* happens to me. The second prisoner is a baby-faced blue-eyed blond shark whose perfect teeth bulge with pearl. Shadows twist his broken nose as he smiles and his curiosity glows at me through a big bruised eye and one glass eye absent of curiosity that rolls about at free will. The bruised eye puffs out swollen almost shut but in candle flame both eyes hang enrapt by seeing in captivity a pure specimen of double-talking Yankee nigger lover. I'm just too rare for his child's spirit to grasp as he smiles shark-like with his rows of pearl. The third lad—the tallest and meanest—has a Mohawk clump of frizzed hair or wide loaf of pumpernickel on his skull and lacks any joy of life. For in his palm lies a knotted sock full of metal cot springs and soon he gets up and stands hard behind me and slow-raps the sock into his palm six inches from my ear but so I won't get too upset varies the ear he socks nearest oh so slow. I don't dare stir during the first five minutes of this sock-beat and try to mask my flinching but my heart races as its dial turns up and the two crackers' beautiful mugs in the candle flame deepen with cosmic wonder. These three know I am already so slicked over, scraped and beat that a few blows from the sock won't be noticed among my cuts and scratches and spiked hair. Palsy panics and unnerves me. My slightest word slip may sink me.

M-m-y f-feelings about niggers are that they are t-t-terribly untrustworthy people—or animals—I would trust a dog first. And—and they're always trying to g-get you to like them. But we know whom—uh, who—the jails are filled with. These snaky-minded, two-faced niggers. There is no doubt in my mind that niggers n-n-not only lack honesty but c-c-courage. Did you know there wasn't one nigger on Pork Chop Hill in Korea? I mean aside from the messenger boys who weren't allowed to carry rifles or ammo. They were all shipped back to the rear lines so we white folks could w-win the war. Lotta people don't know that. It's g-good to have a r-r-rational chat with smart folks like you.

Were you there, Donald? asks the long-faced battered Grand Inquisitor, whose spiritual parts are at low ebb in this universe. His head's swollen half crushes his face to one side and the squinting side—bashed by shadows—is brutish.

No, but it was spread all over *Life* magazine. And I have a close friend who was wounded there who was telling me about it just tonight. I tell you, until I heard the true f-facts from my friend—and all of it confirmed by *Life* magazine—I even liked a nigger now and then. Not that I ever had any good buddies, no, no! But that, by God, is all over with, I swear it is. It is over! The veil is lifted from my eyes. I am undeceived.

After I recant my nigger-loving past with a fury of table slaps, they switch to their main goal and peaceful purpose: extortion.—Well, the cops have all my money downstairs, I say.—How much you got? You tell the truth because we know already because a friend of ours counted it, Donald.—About three-seventy.—Three dollars and seventy cents?—Uh, no, hundreds. I thought you knew.—Don't tell me what I know and what I don't know.—Of course not! And I have about two thousand in the Orange and Lemon Growers Trust.

How the gods laughed at that.

The kangaroo court goes on for an hour during which I lie and re-lie and cover my tracks and make new tracks and at last leave them all dizzy with promises of personal cartons of tailor-made cigarettes. They know I can't get money up to them but that I just might return and leave them the cigarettes since they have my phony address and can come and beat the nigger-loving shit out of me if I don't pay their kangaroo court fine of cigarettes. Court adjourns. They pinch out their precious candle and go back to their cells in the blackness. Baby-shark lies smoking far into the night. I don't move—unable to—and turn to dust. Then, in the middle of the night, the whole world dead—a fresh cigarette gets up and walks into the general cell and comes toward me and stands behind me. The sock strikes a palm. No talk is needed. I abandon any idea of resistance, not wanting to be the object of a manhunt in a cage. I sit palms flat on the table and seesaw between despair and grief. At last he leaves and I wait in the dark, not quite sure where he's gone. There is no sound. This is worse than the sock. I sit in the black and wait. And wait.

One window . . . just past the picnic table. I stare at the window while it goes through the degrees of night and at last deepens to blue-green. Beyond the bars now rise palms and my heart goes out to one heavenly yellow star like a bulb on a tall gas-station sign pole. Toward five—as the cell lightens—I see before me a ragged red book, the only one on the table. As a dodge, should I be watched, I draw it to me and attempt the first page. It is *The Moon and Sixpence*—a romance about trading social illusions for pagan illusions—but as I read I feel caught up in lunar drift. The opening sentence is piled rocks. The whole first page flows with fog over rocks. In three hours, grind as I do, I cannot lift the earth-crust of the first page. Its weight buckles my brain.

As I look up with neurons frazzled raw I find that I have faked myself again—for that wondrous yellow star is a light-bulb on a Mobilgas pole with flying red horse. A white-haired man gets up and washes his face in his cell sink, combs his hair and steps out into the general cell. He is an old retainer out of Chekhov, his hair parted to a perfect edge not unlike Jackie Gleason's curls as bartender. He goes to the far reaches of the cell, finds a push broom and begins to sweep. One of my three inquisitors gets up—forked in tight denim. The old man sweeps on and on. This, I think, is worth the whole disaster. To watch this gray-haired old Florida retiree push his broom down the cell. The cracker comes up behind me and begins slapping the sock into his palm. My back prickles but I watch the washed out old Wall Streeter. He is quite thorough as cell patsy for cleanup and clearly likes to start each day with a clean cellblock for visiting bishops. I sit out Sock-man's interest by focusing on the old man, his face calcified into a faithful dog mask.

About eight-thirty, a man walks by the cell—like a U.S. cattle inspector—and many prisoners get up and plead with him as an old acquaintance. The bail bondsman. Even I, when the way is clear, plead—though head to bare feet, in shirt ripped and shorts stinking of creosote, I am a column of crap. But speaking in an unconvincing *sotto voce* so that my inquisitors will not hear I have no money downstairs, I plead with him to go see my mother and get my bail. He studies me over like a pawnbroker—shakes his head with disgust—and leaves. So I begin considering fresh lies for my cellmates.

About nine o'clock a cop comes down the cellblock and calls my name three times.—That's me!—You haven't had your phone call yet, he says and bites his lip. Do you want to make a call?—Hell, yes, I do.

He unlocks the main cell and lets me out. He is a barrel of beef, his face a slab of red steak with two brown eyes squinting in the meat. I barefoot after him down a passageway and we come to a wall phone.—All my change is downstairs in my wallet which you took from me when you booked me. Can you lend me a *dime*?— The State does not lend prisoners money. There's the phone, he says ending it. I stare at the phone for which have no dime.—You won't lend me a dime?—No. I stare at the phone still. Then I remember that even if I did have a dime . . . *I had torn out my mother's phone* . . . I nearly weep as vacant days in the Florida penal system rise before this famous nigger lover's eyes. Take me back, I say. I follow his strapping uniformed haunches back up the hall.

I pick out an empty cell for myself—with empties on each side—and weigh how my injuries might multiply or not multiply if I can keep this door closed. I'll have to lie to those animals after me and work up a sugartit for their imaginations to suck on. William Manchester—now interviewing me for the postage-stamp drama I've become—tells me as a brother: "Each of us has a tiny gland which emits insulin of illusion to keep us from seeing nakedly." But I'd always known that. I am about to wash when the cop returns and calls my name. Yes, I say.—Come with me, Mr. Newlove. I walk down a corridor with him, knowing I am about to be mugged and fingerprinted for a long stay. The doors of the electric elevator split open on silent foam. We go in. It goes down in blood-ringing silence.

What's happening? I ask my stiff-brimmed robot.

Your bail's been paid, sonny.

I look up to see if he's pulling my leg.

The doors part like cobweb. That marvel of a bailer stands before me, not a foot away.

She has a black eye.

Princes of the Switchblade: Trembling on the Street

The Village Voice, January 7, 1971

Midnight on Tompkins Square Park. I pass from Avenues A to B on shadowy 7th Street. Two dark figures leap the steel park fence ahead of me. One moves into the street to hold off my turning back and—drawn knives silvery in the dark—both shadows close in. My blood fails to pound but my nerves go weary. The two blades waving at my heart glimmer with Avenue A's far-off streetlight. Soon, to my relief, I am being robbed—not mugged, or murdered wantonly in some ritual blooding. Hungry hands dig into my every pocket and rifle my person for anything hidden. They take everything—bills, ID, lighter, small change. My cigarette package holds my stash of a lone joint. All their success will be capped with a mind-lifting smoke.

Danger, yes, and I agree to and answer everything they ask of me. I don't miss the $14 with which I've set out to score a bag. My calmness surprises me after my huge and spurting but guarded madness—whetted by grass—which ever goes with me on any dark city street. I've been robbed and attacked so many times in dream that the real thing comes with much less furor. I have no thought of fighting back. Or calling out—to whom? I wish no harm to my victimizers—since they are the victims.

Two blacks in their mid-teens do the job on me. All their boyish swagger and faith spring from the bravura of a blade. At their age they've found the one money-making job that works. Two black teens from uptown who subway down for a midnight cruise of this white and Latino Park. I have sense enough not to walk into bushy park spaces scrubbed of footsteps and echoes in these late hours. Lamps glitter along empty walks but these paths are the left side of darkness. Keep to the street, Don! I walk down the middle of the paving when the shadows leap the fence. As they clean me out I see in these lads restless and rolling white-eyed fear of standing out and being stopped and caught down here that stills all my impulses. Intense and innocent, they whisper in the dark and with the shoulders of dirty angels demand my silence. Cloaked by night, they are princes of the switchblade.

Their innocence strikes me deepest—a discovery which makes this robbery more valuable than not being robbed. The smudged innocence of their boy-faces robs me blind. My own sins rise up before me, spindly and black. I've lost my innocence. I am a girl undressed in the dark by strange hands.

How full the irony. A year ago I move from my apartment at 7th and B where I've lived for almost ten years. During my last two years of tenancy my apartment has been robbed four times by young Latinos new to our all-Polish-Ukrainian neighborhood. We have few blacks. My wife Jackie has been attacked at knifepoint by Latinos and robbed by knife blade at our downstairs mailbox—molested—and raped under our lowest staircase. We've been victimized seven times in two years, each time by teenage Puerto Ricans or blacks. Once I came upon three young Latinos who'd split my door down the middle with a crowbar, knocked the floor bar aside, and gone in. Another time I surprise two Latinos in my top-floor apartment. As I unlock my three locks, I hear them move about. As the door opens they scramble out the kitchen window they'd opened from outside and monkey up the rain pipe over my gaping airshaft and scamper away over the roofs—with my cornet! I vow I'll never return to this hideous neighborhood. Madness drowns my once quiet street. You have to call daylight molestation, rape, repeated robberies and fear of walking your block at night or entering your own hallway—and putting up with it—some kind of madness.

So we move to the Bronx. Though we now live by airy Joyce Kilmer Park with its trees and robins, the vandals here turn out to be even younger. A publisher reads my first fifty pages and I'm given a contract to write a novel about the Lower East Side. One Saturday morning, as I sit and type in my back room in the Bronx, rocks burst through my study windows. This happens on three different mornings—once almost blinding me. I hear voices and through the window I see a rock coming right at me and the five-year-old black who threw it with the whites of his eyes boiling. I shake. We get rocks in the study and rocks in the bedroom and beer cans against the living room windows. I spend my first six months in the Bronx trembling on the street—trembling at my building's lobby doors being set far back from the street—trembling in the lobby as I wait for the elevator—trembling at the basement Laundromat—and trembling by every window in my apartment. It's a low tremble—a sort of palsy.

Gunshot fantasies crack—triggered by each shadow—as my imagination arms itself. I thirst for a knife or gun. A razor blade lodged in my shoe tip. Knives up my sleeves, a small pistol in my armpit. A throwing knife slung to the back of my neck. Where on my body can I carry a weapon that will not be seen—something to wound attackers with as they flee? How arm myself, weapon unseen? Repeated robberies in both boroughs, rape of your wife that builds her fears even deeper than yours, and with your home a target range for rocks—all that can get to you.

How arm myself indeed? Only within. But my loose trigger holds off nothing. I am all fantasy. No faith in non-violence can withstand the murderous chemistry of a shadow. One free shadow—one dark alley—and my brain spurts. Fires. Cuts.

But how can *my* Tolstoyan non-violence save my wife? She, demoralized utterly by just fears. No argument that she give over to a safety within means anything to her. She dare not return from anywhere by subway in the evening and must be escorted everywhere she goes after the first shadow falls on Joyce Kilmer's trees. She fears the Laundromat. She fears the elevator.

These Bronx kids don't like my beard? The trumpet practice in my study? I go for a lesson and tell my teacher I can't blow the simplest scale. I've lost all my breath, all spirit. My wife has died, I tell him, but still walks about and sleeps in our apartment.

I vow I'll never return to 7th and B and yet I do. To give an advance copy of my novel to one of the characters in it—and perhaps at the same time to score from him. I am led back both by swinishness and generosity—a hard team to beat.

I pass the building owned by my old Ukrainian landlady, Mrs. Maria Ouspenskaya, who beat my door for the rent for ten years. In this very doorway my wife thrice met her fate and in this hallway the girlfriend of my Chilean director Jaime Barrios got raped and was hospitalized while a block away we shot our movie *Trumpet*. Meeting my switchblade princes this night completes my irony— for the novel I have with me holds my own warnings and many of the incidents I've spoken of and is in part a record of my struggle against hatred of the bold creatures who see fit to harm and rob us—and dismember or just bruise our spirits with rocks. Impersonal as these crimes may be, I take them personally—despite my twenty years as a Tolstoyan—and seated I find my fists balled and unnerved. My novel spills with disgust and hatred for these "dynamited banana brains, genetic defectives—all their sperm is cut with Rheingold!" And so on, for which it's panned in *Kirkus Reviews* by an uptown 23-year-old Columbia girl grad. How legitimate is this hatred awakened within me? I expect to be taken to task for it.

What am I to do? Pour cream and honey over knife blades and rocks and crowbars and monkeys stealing my trumpets?—I've had three stolen. Still another time my door gets split right off its hinges—a time when my wife might by chance meet the thieves at their business and be—what?—beaten aside? Murdered? Or just raped again? Ever hear your wife wail her story just after a wild kid at the mailbox has been at her throat with a knife and you sit powerless listening? I just tell you here what happened and how it felt and how madness and hatred awake and how I still fight these daily. Should I soften these scenes? In fact, I do. But the bile flows. What's to overcome if my enemy isn't awake within me and my hatred of its scales and colors doesn't show? Must my spirit bottle itself and withhold perils it thinks should be seen and felt by all? I can't do other than I do. Need I say who my worst enemy is and with what cunning he undermines and divides me?

But I lay the racial theme out cold and offer no defense for myself. There can be no defense just as there can be no lasting coming together with my "enemy" unless I give over my wife to her own tactics for living among "the barbarians." She must not lean on me. The only defense is defenselessness. But this is much too metaphysical for my Jewish wife from Queens. I think of her as my soul's guide and my spirit made visible. She is very weak.

Getting Unpickled
WIN Magazine, Vol. 7, No. 12, August 1971

I

I fall onto the subway rails at 96th and Broadway. Lying there Saturday two A.M.; a train roaring toward me. I'm paralyzed. A man leaps down from the platform and lifts me out. Next morning, thighbone cracked against the skin, leg purple from knee to hip, I can't remember the man who saved me.

A summer night. Zooming down Lake Erie's superhighway; my three-year-old asleep beside me. Sixty miles to home. Suddenly I'm awake and bouncing uncontrollably. I've driven into oncoming traffic, crossed off the highway, and sailing through a tomato patch at 70 m.p.h. Extracted at dawn by tractor at the cost of my watch and manhood. The farmer stares at my son on the front seat.

An education reporter, I drive through a metal lamp post in front of my home town high school. A howling night in the cooler and lost license.

One sunny morning I wake up and cough blood for a week.

Only then, I stop drinking. At 38.

And I'm yet to come to my senses! Though 43 this week.

I begin writing at nine, drinking at thirteen. My stepfather, a restaurateur and high-pocket lush. Our wine cellar cools the finest liquors, wines and liqueurs, a strawberry field of flavors. Wine doesn't interest me. Later I sell blood for it in gallons.

A barfly in ninth grade, at 17 a Marine with beer at $2.40 a case in the slopchutes. Afterward, finishing high school, joining the morning beerklatsch with hardtalking GI schoolfriends. Folding in college during first semester. Trying twice again, forever the brilliant sophomore.

Come Korea, back with the eagle and drinking daily. My marriage fails, a blessing. My wife Scandinavian gloom and my spirit black as Beckett with Truman and Eisenhower on each shoulder. Everyone too stupid on a horse of money to see how black life is.

A boiling lad, sending my first book off and being rejected. Twelve years and I finish another. A wino masterplaster, still on my shelf.

Turning thirty and, my God, still in the same Lower East Side pad, now pushing forty! Shelf crammed with unpublished work. Drunk tanks and mishmash agony of wine crutches. Tears in the movies. Battering my typewriter with marshmallow boxing gloves. Love-starved hog!

Oh, that miserable drug. Not moderate, I'm its victim for life. During great happiness, I unfailingly boost my joy to delirium with a bottle. For me, alcohol is not an intellectual problem. It is a disease and seduces my spirit, not my reason. I don't drink to think, I drink to float.

But juice depresses, no matter the gaiety of the first jolt. Memory fuzzes over. By evening's end I bark for sex, heartstrings whining. Morning, I rise like Frankenstein from his sulphur pit, cells burned waterless, skull cracked, spirit iced. Abstain all day and go to bed dry: the juice show comes. My apartment fills with dead men in the night. I lie awake trembling. They sit in the livingroom, at my kitchen table, and sometimes stand over me beseechingly. What do they want from me? Drinking, I rarely stop short of unconsciousness—then can't handle my nightmares when I dry out trying to stop! And that's when my egghead pride and powerful conviction about Dionysian uplift become absurd. I cross over in the real world and join A.A., after the example of a great friend.

Getting unpickled, my chronic insomnia vanishes. A midnight pint of ice cream is vastly fatiguing and a tremendous sedative. Rest, self-care, vitamins and meetings, plenty of Whitman, avoidance of bars, new visions, typewriter blooming with candlepower, first sales, marriage. And after a few months, I kick ice cream.

Facing me as I write this are seven unpublished books. Seven drunken books I spent 20 years writing. It's been a saucy youth, nearly all sauce. And one day I'm 38 and belting blood into the sink. More red telegrams follow.

II

An alcoholic is a drinker who admits that his life is unmanageable. Before that recognition, he is a "heavy drinker" with a deep belief in his saintliness and five powerful reasons to drink: despair, self-pity, anesthesia, emotional starvation, and for business purposes. My business is with my spirit, so what better reason to drink? Artistic dedication, for God's sake. I have to be rough on a bastard like me. I'm supersonically alert for any sanction that will let me keep my bottle—even writing this article deserves its reward. Gray Friday outdoors. This despite seven volumes of sentimental cant and baroque gurglings. I still think each book can be the one which rescues me from wine and puts me on a whiskey basis, so that I can take better care of myself while drinking at a higher proof. How lucky I am to fail!

Norman Mailer, trying to rewrite *The Deer Park* on lush and drugs, finds pills, pot and the bottle the worst enemies of his talent:

> ... But the punishment was commencing for me ... the attrition of the drugs and the possibility of failure began to depress me, and Benzedrine entered the balance, and I was on the way to

wearing badly ... I did not know that I was no longer as large to others as I had been. I was always overmatching myself ... With each week of work, bombed and sapped and charged and stoned with lush, with pot, with benny, saggy, Miltown, coffee, and two packs a day. I was working live, and overalert, and tiring into what felt like death, afraid all the way because I had achieved the worst tired, I was more tired than I had ever been in combat, and so as the weeks went on ... there was only a worn-out part of me to keep protesting into the pillows of one drug and the pinch of the other that I ought to have the guts to stop the machine ... But I had passed the point where I could stop. My anxiety had become too great. I did not know anything anymore, I did not have that clear sense of the way things work which is what you need for the natural proportions of a long novel ... Knowing however, what I had failed to do, shame added momentum to the punishment of the drugs. By the last week or two, I had worn down so badly that ... I was reduced to working hardly more than an hour a day ... Then my mind would wear out, and new work was done for the day. I would sit around, watch more television and try to rest my dulled mind, but by evening a riot of bad nerves was on me again ...

—Advertisements for Myself

I listen to a woman whose son dies while she's recovering from alcoholism. She's wept, but kept off the sauce, and takes death with some vigor. "Those are salt tears, not alcoholic squeezings. I was glad—that I could weep over his death with some dignity and awareness of grief. I paid him the tribute of experiencing his loss. Now he's dead and, thank God, not mummified in a bottle." What artist would not be the better artist for experiencing his losses instead of dehydrating them for his inner knickknack shelf?

My spirit needs no obsession with the bottle to give it insight into hell. Everyday, hell is under the breastbone. See that drunk typing in my pad?—his hysteria isn't joy, it's agony. What's it all about! he shouts at his machine. Hilarious exhaustion surging on juice.

Hell, crazy people shouldn't drink. Not even with his willpower. That man has so much willpower while drinking that the 81st Airborne Division could be against his taking a drink—but that arm would get up. Listen to him laugh and cry at that machine. He cries aloud, I don't need another drink, I need a dam! That man is a damned saint to resist the effects that clear-headedly. It's his laughing that exhausts him.

He's laughing about his zombie jobs? Or impossible sex life? Or wine trots? Or empty house loud with music? Now he's hysterical again. He really gushed a beauty that time. Whoo! he cries, oh God! Ripping the page out and rising to read it aloud, prancing a circle, clearing his pipes with brackish gulp of burgundy, beaming thankfully to heaven, he floats on genius and vanity like a stereo needle, declaims to the empty pad, then toasts his triumphant nuance. One more facet to his perfection! He sucks his teeth to ventilate the arsenical wine flavor. His tongue is purple and losing buds. Goes to kitchen and sucks Tabasco bottle, sighs vigorously, returns to work.

This Napoleon erases typos meticulously as they happen. You know this rigid perfectionist?—whose juicing is above criticism, in no need of modification, his self-esteem as metaphysical as a world conqueror's? Any hint that he's a lush makes him incredulous, agitated, hostile. But our Bowery is full of perfectionists, as is all Manhattan, and his Waterloo of stuttering typos is suffering he must bear. And year after year he bears it, erasing, erasing.

III

All those bar mirrors to recover from—not to mention the works I've ruined. Vacant days in Stanley's, waiting for my ship to plow

through the window. Or Mercury to come with my silver message.
Not willpower, only be willing.
I strive to give this message away to find out what it is.

Be not forgetful of prayer. Every time you pray, if your prayer is sincere, there will be new feeling and new meaning in it, which will give you fresh courage, and you will understand that prayer is an education.
—Dostoievsky

Suffering is the sole origin of consciousness.
—Dostoievsky

I began to see that I had no right to rely on my individual reasoning and neglect those answers given by faith, for they are the only answers to the question.
—Tolstoy

Truly transforming spiritual experiences are nearly always founded on calamity and collapse.
—William James

What is lost in time is gained in power.
—Thoreau

Always losing money. My pocket picked frequently, rolled in the park, my pants slit with a razor while I sleep on a four a.m. subway to exotic places. I know my destiny's to die of drink, but I can't afford the research.
—Anonymous

I can't slip again. Next time it's padded walls and police guards 24-gray-hours-a-day, every day, forever. I can't afford that, not for a drunk.
—Anonymous

The thought that judges works its way self-tormentingly upwards through the pain, heightening the torment and helping not at all. As if the fundamental architectural problem were raised for the first time in the house that is burning down to the ground.
—Kafka

Even Gallo's seems like vintage wine today. Sneaky Pete's at my side, waiting for action, but he has to wait until the Ole Ballantine, his ale roan, cools off from his run home from the grocery store. Ah, glasses of cold muscatel and ale at hand!
—Bob Grapevine

Case Study, Male, 50 years old: Dependent, self-pitying, unable to come to grips with his problems, extraordinary immaturity. Everything he says in general category of rationalization. Three months in A.A., quit drinking whiskey. After these three months, began taking codeine terpin hydrate, seconal. Brought into hospital via stretcher. Sense of impending disaster. Paranoid delusions, which he recognizes as false but can't stop having. Diagnosis: Alcoholic. Suspected brain damage. Prognosis: This patient will probably need to be hospitalized for the rest of his life.
—Case Study

Afterward, the harsh hell lights at the Port Authority bus terminal . . . bathroom tile ashine.
—Anonymous

Alcoholism is daily suicide. I'm not afraid of dying, but not every day.
—Anonymous

Sobriety has given me Today. When I was drinking I never had Today. It was always ten years ago, or next month, or some other time—never today. When I'd start seeing people I hadn't seen for

ten, fifteen, twenty years—then I was on the edge of the deetees.
—Anonymous

The AMA rates Giant Staggerjuice as our third greatest health problem, led only by heart disease and mental illness. It knocks cancer into fourth place. When a middle-class alky dies, his death certificate is often falsified (with such euphemisms as hepatitis, gastric bleeding, pneumonia, tuberculosis, diabetes, over-enlarged heart, heart disease, mental disease—28 percent of all male mental patients are alcoholics—or auto fatality). Drunkard though he was, no family wants it in writing. So drink may well be our most serious illness.

An alcoholic is a permanent victim of a progressive disease, one that bears as little relation to willpower as does malaria. Neither guilt nor willpower nor insight can help him. Only fellow drunks who are recovering—and I think you know where to find them.

We need an alcohol corps to handle our over six million alkies in this country. A.A is too small for the job. There are five million smiling, fogbound drunks A.A. will never reach. Amazingly, the Department of Health, Education and Welfare is preparing a national attack on the disease (see *Alcohol Problems* by T. F. Plaut, $1.50, Oxford paperbacks, for an excellent report on this commission). It is working in cooperation with the Department of Defense, for the armed services are plagued with heavy drinkers—as is the U.S. Senate. One-third of all arrests in this country are for public drunkenness. However, untold hundreds of thousands of arrests are listed on police blotters as disorderly conduct, disturbing the peace, vagrancy and such euphemisms, while the number of alkies who never come under scrutiny but drink at home is staggering. Problem drinking must be dealt with drunk by drunk: these are victims for whom one drink is too many and a thousand deaths not enough.

Therapeutic pessimism reigns among doctors. Treatment services are disarrayed beyond definition. Courts pursue inhuman policies, dooming alkies to revolving door drunk tanks or "flight decks" at city hospitals. Lifeless, talkless drinkers of the lower classes are beneath clinical interest: among doctors, martini drinkers are more equal than stewbums. A true program must include the cast-off with the alienated Harvard grad. As in the army, everyone is the same age in alcoholism, for the disease is baffling, cunning and insidious to each according to his resistance. This disease is *progressive*: if you stop for five years and start again, you age those five years as if you'd never stopped, because you have five years less youth to resist with. Is it better to let these forlorn spirits drift unmanageably toward death, or to help steer them back to life?

My experience is that it takes one man to save another. I'm afraid these notes fail to show how deeply I was helped by others—by many, many others, fellow victims who recognize that they have a guilt-free disease. Their inspiration—and my wife—provides everything. If you think you may be a drunk, try this test: Don't drink for 90 days. You may find yourself rising from deep darkness into morning, or perhaps discover how far you've sunk.

Few people experience life with the daily alertness and vibrance of a recovering alky who has managed to unmangle his sensibilities. Far from smiling gamely through crippled eyes (a notion I once had), this man's control of his work and sureness of gesture greatly cheer him and are considerable rewards for rethinking his life. I'm not just paying lip service. I no longer need distort every activity to my drinking advantage, nor spend immense wastes of time justifying my boorish, suicidal behavior. All that once over is a relief beyond words—and another life.

Two Lines a Day
The Village Voice, September 30, 1973

I first met Gil Orlovitz about two years ago in a roomful of hardcore recovering drunks. A giant in a hanging but respectable dark suit and tie, who listened hard but always spoke from his private wrinkle in the world, he was distinguished, dark, stooped, and sallow with a high leaden beard he shaved nearly to his dark eyes.

We traded publishing backgrounds on our novels. Then, chewing a cigarette between his teeth and inhaling until his eyes disappeared, Gil told me about his black decades of paralyzing anxiety from which he was still not free, the nameless, soul-sick alcoholic fears which had at last crippled him mentally, physically, and spiritually, and left him with an unmanageable and unemployable life, a spine-deep, daily uselessness that has now laid him in a pauper's grave in Hart Island city cemetery.

During these last two years he had choices to make about sobering up, and the choices he made were almost uniformly self-destructive. There were vague gestures toward attending many more meetings; he hit a drying-out farm and was dried out for a few months; he went on welfare. But he was on a daily maintenance of "five martinis" (read that as five six-ounce waterglasses of gin—drunks "controlling" their drinking don't make those prissy little bar-type doubles). Month after month, with his large hands hanging with coffee and cigarette, his forehead heavily wrinkled with fog, he told me in utter seriousness about his cutting down. I'd suggest to him that recovery means Don't Drink and Go to Meetings.

He preferred the lone wolf role of the writer whose individuality was threatened rather than liberated by fellowship in sobriety.

Earlier this year I went up to visit him in Roosevelt Hospital. He'd just been dried out for a week in the Roosevelt alky ward. He was having surgery and the doctors hadn't wanted a 54-year-old man in alcoholic convulsions on the operating table—so they'd dried him out first. It was a dismal room but Gil seemed comfortable, even smiling, and he was genuinely gratified by a gift of my new novel. Boy, he was a tall sonofagun even in paper slippers, lank dark hair and intense brown eyes, always smiling with self-absorbed humor, self-concern, fear, self-hatred, paralyzing anger with himself (which he hid beneath his constant, defensive soft laugh), the smile of a tall, strong intellectual wiped out to his backbone by remorse and guilt.

Last week Gil's obituary appeared in the *Times*. He'd collapsed on West 108th Street with a 108-degree temperature, never regained consciousness, and died the next day at Knickerbocker Hospital. It'd happened two months ago. But no one claimed his body and he was buried by the city. Knickerbocker says he died of bronchial pneumonia, but the *Times* says the city medical examiner's office has "rejected" the hospital's findings and is awaiting completion of lab tests. I won't speculate on these tests, but I know that a guy doesn't get out of bed with bronchial pneumonia, an extremely sapping, bone-aching sickness, unless something stronger than his sickness drives him out of bed, especially in the "terminal stages."

Gil's reasons for drinking were the usual cop-out alibis: "chronic insomnia," anxiety, separation from family, writer's block, loneliness, even cigarettes (five packs a day)—all fakes, all part of a raft of self-deceptions that allowed him to float day after day on his maintenance "five" martinis. I talked with him many hours about his alibis. And no matter how strongly they got punctured, the fog and the quicksand rolled right back in. He could not give up the main alibi, for which the others were window-dressing: that being a largely unrecognized writer in his own country justified his self-destruction.

One night last summer I drove him home from an extraordinarily powerful meeting of our fellowship of recovering lushes. Gil was elated. He'd just returned from six weeks at a fairly rigid drying-out farm and was now eight weeks dry. It'd happened at last—his black cloud of anxiety had lifted! For the first time since adolescence. His relief was terrific, a new breath filled him. And filled me—here was hope at last. Even *he* connected the lifting of his eternal anxiety with the taking away of alcohol and the inspiration of fellowship. As he hunched in my Bug, a wonderful light was filling those great black shining eyes, the first hint that an indescribable confidence was being born by being honest with himself. Not the confidence of my prose will last forever, but the confidence of action, a fearless and searching look at his alibis.

It was a great drive through Central Park and so I was doubly flattened a few weeks later when, haggard and smiling defensively, he extolled to me his new five-martini method for holding back his disease and "functioning." He said his anxiety had returned full force but that he was writing two lines of poetry daily. I suggested that he was writing two lines a day despite his drinking, not because of it. He thought that if he quit smoking first, then he could quit drinking. If his anxiety would only lift again . . . But he *was* getting his two lines a day done, thank God.

So he valued his life at two lines a day and carried a mountain of towering darkness. Wherever he went he was gloom-fighting (and losing), nervous, protective of his habit, hostile to any fresh air upon his self-absorption. I can handle it, he told me, his three-day beard spiky.

Still, I was hopeful. I'd said the same thing myself. My oldest friend in sobriety told me I was the most hopeless drunk he'd ever seen in a lifetime of seeing drunks. If Gil wanted to hole up with his pen in his mouth and without our fellowship, we'd wait him out until he hit bottom and was teachable. It's the hardest job in the world, letting a friend drink himself to his bottom before he asks for help.

But the bottom fell through.

I've Got a Right to Fish the Blues
New York Magazine, Vol. 6, No. 40, October 1, 1973

After Jackie, my second wife, left last month in heavy rain and my new housemate Bonnie and I put in for food stamps, I hocked my trombone for two fares on a Bronx River "head boat" and set out on a meat trip in the heavy rain. "Meat trip" means fishing not for sport but for meat to freeze in the fridge and help spell out the food-stamp tins of fatty beef and flavorless five-pound blocks of American cheese. Heavy rain means another wife wants out. We'll always be friends.

Big-fish head boats, or party boats, leave every morning at seven from Westchester Avenue and right now the summer-fattened fall blues are running. The crazed pure energy of a monster bluefish pulling you over the rail is matched only by its bone splintering viciousness bleeding out on deck as clicking teeth look for a hand or ankle and you try for a grip on the acrobatic bastard's gills or to jam a foot onto a slimed belly while the blue leaps knee-high head over tail looking for water—well, this is a sure way to beat the meat-price glooms and poor-me blues.

You might wonder why—with a new housemate who plays the violin while I run scales on the trumpet—I should have the glooms and the blues. Although we live in a nice apartment building in the Bronx we often find vandals attacking our windows with rocks and beer cans. My wife Jackie and I left the Lower East Side for the Bronx after rape and robbers drove us out.

Even so we find the Bronx hardly much better and so my wife

pulls out and says she has to find herself somewhere away from me and also find a place to help her stop shaking. (She winds up teaching in Arizona.) I now work the slush pile of unsolicited manuscripts at Saturday Review Press, the house which has contracted for and will bring out my third novel, and has in the meantime offered me this slush post for cigarette change. Daily I scan opening pages and send back unsolicited novel and nonfiction manuscripts by the dozen. But one novel catches my eye—a strange tale set in prehistory and called *Builder of Bridges* by a twenty-year-old named Bonnie Brunish. It's her third novel! I send her an upbeat letter and as my wife leaves Bonnie moves in with her fiddle, duds, and portable typewriter. She doesn't work and the cigarette change from shoveling out my publisher's slush pile does not lift us out of food-stamp worthiness. So I got a right to fish the blues.

Bonnie and I are on the *Claire I*. The *Claire II* and other head boats at the docks will set out for porgies and blackfish today. We've done that but we've never caught a blue on our own though we've been trying for a month. The *Claire I* captained by Ed Berlin—a curly blond with the tragic rings under his eyes of a seaman who mastered some hard waters on land the night before—has sonar and without fail goes right to the big schools. But we don't need sound waves to know where the blues are. Just look for gulls circling and gulls madly hopping through wheeling bunkers being slaughtered by blues. Look for gulls walking on a broth of fins and blood.

The river wavers frog-green and rubbery in light rain. We'd gone out on the *Claire I* a month ago with a full boat of Puerto Rican and black party folk. Bonnie and I were the only WASPs aboard. We're not anglers—as I say, we need meat fish to eat—but it's an obsessive sport. We brought back porgies—so sweet to the pan!—two sea robins (winged uglies whose tails are chickenmeat)—and a giant blackfish and had great suppers for weeks. Today the icebox—

and cupboard—is stripped. This bluefish trip means survival until monthly food stamps arrive. And so now we are outward bound.

Raindrops cymbal the gliding green as we stand at the rail. Below a rainbow oil slick a school of brown bunkers passes, driven upstream by fear of marauder blues. Mud-eating bunkers—a scavenger too coarse and bony to eat—have tobacco-stained flesh you cut up for bait. How amazing that the blues get so heavy and healthy on such vile, tainted flesh.

Relaxing rain. We sit around with the half-load of fishermen and await the captain's horn that we have hit the fishing grounds. As before, we're the only WASPs except for a father who's brought his son on their first fishing trip together and to enjoy a reunion of some kind. The dad looks overeager to please his fifteen-year-old with a great day yanking in monsters. No whiskey bottles on board today, unlike the last trip—blues fishermen clearly are more serious folk than the porgy and blackfish anglers and our pleasure lies in the heavy strike on the line, not on strong drink in the veins. Still, these aren't called party boats for nothing. After the blues move away, sometime in October, the *Claire*s will go out for codfish—until ice socks the boats in. We look forward to happy days after cod.

Snag, a gap-toothed black, says, Two years ago I hauled up ten blues! I ain't haulin' no mo' than eight today—and then I'm cuttin' their heads off.

Howie, another black, says, Oh thass work too, 'cause they out to take off your hand while you cut they heads off. Of course, I guess you can always get the hand back once you gets the head off.

Bonnie—a creature of high fantasy—gapes in disbelief.

The soda pop and hamburgers steward Tommy, a tall blond about seventeen, holds up a white-scarred finger. A blue did this to me, he says, out at Montauk. At first I thought I'd snagged the ocean bottom that sucker's pull was so great. Took me twenty minutes just to reel him to the surface. I couldn't believe my eyes when he jumped and shook, he was so tall outta the water. He got me on the deck and the blood flowed like water—my blood.

Suddenly the engines rev, and *Claire I* moves on in a cloud of blue oil smoke. Get your money out, fellas, Jeff the first mate calls. A spunky, soft-spoken youth and somewhat embarrassed by Bonnie's bright good will toward him, he tells us, $15 a head today, fellas.

Hey, I thought it was ten! I say.

That's for porgies and blacks, Jeff says. Blues are $15.

I pay $20 and write a check for $10. Since I have only $8 in the bank, I'll have to hock my trumpet tomorrow—and do. Well, it's Bonnie's birthday celebration—the big two oh—and the icebox is bleak. (The reader may rightly ask, Don, why don't you get a better job?—I DO work! Five hours before we got on board, I wrote THE END to a 680-page longhand first draft of my new novel which I now need four months to type, revise and retype. Talk about work!) Jeff goes around collecting $2 more for the pool—biggest blue wins all. We pass it up. Since her bearded and aging escort doesn't cough up for her, I think Jeff would love to give Bonnie a free ride on the blues pool. Or maybe bait her hooks for her? Why that should be I don't know—she didn't bring her fiddle for our entertainment.

Rainyday fishing's the greatest. Last month, having a dull boatless day on the Hudson—with nothing biting from the rocky stretches of Riverdale Park—we watched a big black cloud sweep over and hit us with the area's heaviest cloudburst in 100 years. The water churned white with hard drizzle and the perch went mad for our oldest, most dried up sandworms. We couldn't leave! Bonnie had a raincoat—I stuffed my clothes into a plastic trash bag and hauled in beauties in my stark bare skin. The bait hardly hit the froth before our flyrods bent with hard tug-tug-tugs. We're rain freaks now. Fish just hop and sing in the air pressure change of a big blue thunderhead—and so do I! You forget all about rape, burglary and car theft normal to city life.

Down into the galley sizzle for coffee where Kitty—the busy-bee cook with hourglass waist—fries bacon and egg sandwiches in tiny pans on propane burners. At noon she'll turn out burgers, and peanut butter with jelly. We've brought our own sandwiches—Deaf Smith unhydrogenated sunshine-dried peanut butter with sweet Vidalia onions on toasted A&P half-price discount-cart English muffins at twelve for 32¢—real savings! And English muffins age nicely. They can turn green but our dozen doesn't last that long. Anyway, scrape off the mold on the oldest crumpets and toast 'em—no harm done.

A cheer goes up and everyone crowds the rail to watch three inshore schools of bunker whirl and circle like Conestoga wagons holding off the Indians—as fat blues hit the air with bloody scavengers flipping in their teeth. The flat bunkers grow from a foot to sixteen inches and their backfins click on the water as the fish race in circles. Many bunkers play dead and swim on their sides, white bellies up. Brown under water, they look brassy-green above—and about as abominable as bluebottle flies when lifted out. Their rusty meat may turn my stomach but it's a banquet for blues.

Jeff the mate stands near and tells Bonnie, Sometimes I feel sorry for those bunkers. Bonnie nods, but I for one don't identify with those hard-luck muck-eaters.

Maybe he thinks I'm her dad and will invite him below for a fish sandwich with her.

Look, fellas, Ed Berlin cries from his high cabin, there are three schools of blues in there but we can't go in—it's too shallow. I'll get as close as I can and we'll drift by 'em.

We watch hungermad gulls hover in place as their magnetic claws sink deep into the bloody clicking fin froth.

Now look, Bonnie, Jeff says, forget everything we taught ya

about fishing for porgies last time out. Let your jig hit bottom, then give your reel ten hard turns—and I mean hard—then let it sink to the bottom. Most of the blues are on the bottom, not up here eating bunkers. Keep your jig in motion—let me show ya. He jigs her pole for her and calls out, Keep those jigs in motion, fellas! He tells her, Blues are fighters and you'll need all your weight, little lady, even on a baby blue. And these won't be babies—they're fat with summer weight. You need any help, just call.

Oh, I'm pretty strong, Bonnie assures him. I play the violin for hours.

I'm sure that helps, I tell him.

And it's my twentieth birthday.

Jeff smiles at her and stares at me.

Gosh. Happy birthday, little lady.

The *Claire* rents big-fish poles ($1.50) and sells heavy four-inch silver lures with big hooks ($1.25). No live bait on the hook, the fast-moving lure mimics a small fish and the faster you wind your reel the more the silver flash excites the blues. Vicious givers of instant death, the blues strike absolutely without forethought or toying around and slam teeth shut on the lures—the dangling hook seldom gets swallowed, it bites into their soft lips or just over the jaw. This isn't like smaller fish that will down the juicy bug of a hook. Some think that it's easier to get a hook down a blue than out again—I don't agree. You'll see why.

We're a mile above the Whitestone Bridge, only a half-hour from our dock, and stand with our thumbs on our reels, ready to drop lures. Wait for the horn, fellas! Jeff calls to the men in the pool. Suddenly the boat horn hoots. Cries and cheers go up and Howie shouts, Ah got one! Ah got a *biggie!* And as my line hits bottom, I reel up furiously. *Harder, fellas!* Jeff cries. *Let's wind those reels!*

Coming through! Howie shouts and his rod rises over our

heads as the blue takes him around the bow and we duck under Howie's arms. *Comin' through!*

Keep on reeling, Howie, Jeff calls. Don't give that sucker any slack.

I got 'im! *WHOOIE!*

A vast fish flashes below us and sweeps by on its side about five feet underwater—a pole-bending beast of Cadillac power. Howie bends over the rail—lifts his pole a few feet—lowers it quick and reels hard on the slack. At last the blue breaks the surface—a washing-machine maddened and gone berserk. Don't let his head outta the water! Jeff cries and gaffs the monster's side. Now Howie's blue flops all over us as Snag slings another blue flipping high over the rail and just misses Bonnie's ear as the blue bashes against the cabin. The two greenblue whoppers boil over the deck with great underslung jaws agape and ravenous. Howie and Snag chase them about and try to pin 'em underfoot against anything handy. Another biter lands among us and snaps as we wind our reels HARD. At last Howie works his hook free and Snag rips his loose and they grab their blues by the tail and heave them head down into deep plastic buckets. High tails still whip and the batted buckets bang about the deck. Strangely enough, the blues fight so hard on deck that they spend everything and die fast in the buckets. But you don't reach in to comfort them.

Winding with fury, I watch a jumbojet lift into haze over Kennedy with big blue A.A. letters on the fuselage and hear a stewardess call into the business class, *"Eight A.M.! Martini time!"* From where I stand, I don't envy those business folk. I get my lift naturally today. An actuarial table I've read rates deep-sea fishermen as having the longest lives insurable. Boy, that appeals to me!

I got one! I got one! Bonnie cries.

The blue whips her bent over the rail as Jeff rushes up with the gaff.

I'm with ya, little lady!

It won't come up! she cries and reels in as line goes out again.

Just keep reeling it in, Jeff says. You'll make it, honey.

At last a massive gold eye breaks water—takes one look at her—and dives hard. I guess she looks big to a blue. Line spurts in a burning buzz. I'm amazed she can hang on. Again turn by slow turn on the reel knob she reels the blue up. Whammo, a bluegreen body smashes flat onto the water and Jeff gaffs its tail. Bonnie's blue—long dreamed of in the waters of the night—goes head over tail up the deck. She jumps onto it fast and fearless as a fiddler on sixty-fourth notes with both hands digs into the gills. Helpful Jeff shows her how to pull the hook out hard from the soft blood-spurting lip rather than work it slow with that mouth ready to swallow her girlish fingers. I watch her lug the hopping monster up the deck. Well, that's my gal—and it's a 20th birthday she'll remember.

We're out here in the flow and too eager! These days many nighttime hours pass as perch and porgies wriggle in our fingers—hours arisen in dream as hooked fish fight or glide in schools of sleep and we foresee fat blues in our bucket and many tiring but happy hours spent scaling and dressing our catch into fillets. All this as—helpless—I watch slippery bodies below me veer and flash far from my line.

This week I read *Esquire* founder Arnold Gingrich's blue-skies *The Well-Tempered Angler* for the second time, although his is just fidgety dry-fly trout fishing in country streams—not struggle on big rivers ocean bound in heavy rain—and yet my mania builds even for the sport fishing of Arnold's fussy streamlet anglers and artistes.

I hook a heavyweight, my first strike. Unbelievable power drags me right over the rail—this is no scrawny trout, Arnold! Here I go with the fish of my dreams and that blue is DRUNK down there! I'm a winner at last—and then *ZAM*—a yank like an anvil falling—

and the line goes slack. My silver lure comes up bare.

Bonnie's glance telling what a big sweet birthday this is would encourage a guy going over Niagara to wave her goodbye. She knows my hunger. I smile hard and am happy still to have the lure though heart-heavy. Now the kid with his dad gets a strike. The kid can't even crank the reel, his line's so taut. His dad cries, You've got one! Reel him in, reel him in! As the blue breaks water the kid doesn't wait for the gaff but tries to sling him aboard over the rail with too much line out—the blue falls free, plunges straight out of sight. The kid stares at a huge redpink accordion gill on his hook, which dad takes off in wonder.

You had 'im by the gill, dad says. Dad's brown eyes—so eager for the kid to know, or think, he's really had a giant on the line. We'll take it home to show 'em! he says and implores his kid to see this big pink gill as a wonder from the deep. The kid says nothing and does not grasp the surge his dad hopes to infect him with. I sense they don't live together. All dad wants is for his kid to be happy on their outing—but the kid had lost his fish. Or do I mean faith?

The horn hoots. We head for distant gulls. A stray bunker leaps up and disappears in utter terror—every fiber strains to outrun a blue. The bunker zips off with eye bulging and hides so fast I'm shocked. We near a circle of fins that draws chatter and screams from gulls. A heavy blue head rages into a bunker and shakes it high, blood flying. The circling fins whip blood to foam as two, three blues mash through. Wheeling bunkers leave behind ripped bunkers and those bitten in half, heads afloat. Gulls screech on the cauldron.

The horn hoots. Our lines fly into the bunker wheel, sink bottomward. My finger blisters with hard reeling. Bonnie hangs over the rail and reels with jaw clenched and rippling. Her face lights—her rod bends—she fights the reel. Soon her blue breaks high—she lifts her pole, the blue dances—shakes the hook with a tinkle.

You let its head get outta the water, Jeff warns. Keep it flat.

We reel hard, fruitlessly, for hours. But blues fly over the rail by the bow and buckets overflow. I try to dope Howie's method. The luckiest of us is a black-haired Puerto Rican in black rubber pants who looks like Spencer Tracy in dark curls playing Manuel the Portuguese fisherman of Kipling's *Captains Courageous*. I feel like Santiago who has gone eighty-four days without taking a fish in *The Old Man and the Sea*. I know that some days spent fishing are so heart-swelling you want to—well, this is not one of them. Can't figure it out. All these guys do is reel hard and pull the blues out. Bonnie—still aglow with her birthday adventure, which has cost me my big bright $400 trombone for a few weeks [actually, I never get it back]—pats my shoulder and with eager brightness dismisses the fall-off in our catch. I, Ulysses, scan the open sea as anxiety and fears lift and noon light blossoms through the rain upon our grand signors of the great waters in their search for food. My heart warms for them and I am tempted to read to Bonnie from my small pocket book of T. S. Eliot's *Notes Towards the Definition of Culture* when Snag whoops and slings one in high that smacks Howie on the cheekbone and leaves a big red patch raked by fish scales. Howie cries out dazed but gap-tooth Snag calls only, *I'm sawry!*

I pocket the Eliot lesson as Jeff warns Bonnie about Snag, That is not a good way to fish.

And reel hard with Birthday Girl. My God, we're serious. O wonder, a strike—but it breaks my line: $1.25 for a new lure from Jeff. Again I get a strike, the most massive pull of my day—but it's the propellers. Another $1.25 jig.

Hour upon happy mad hour passes as we plow horses pull hard and till the deep. We are Bellevue material—our brains swollen into our wrists. Meat trips, Arnold, aren't for flyrods.

When at last—as evening falls—we pull into the dock, Bonnie

and I have four blues—well over forty pounds of fish to freeze. Bonnie caught three, one of which Jeff gave her to land from his line as he stood quite close and helpful and said, I'm tired, honey, you take this one. He'd landed over twenty. So had Tommy the soda pop steward, and Wayne the second mate, and Captain Berlin too. Everyone, just about, sank under more bluefish than he could lift. I'd caught one.

Howie's happy, despite a big new black eye and his cheek's Band-Aid. Snag's passed out in the cabin from an ale too frequent, having first announced, Ah catched enough! Spencer Tracy in black rubber pants counts a fabulous haul that fills two huge buckets. As I stagger off the boat with our meager catch I ask Spence how the hell he does so well.

Oh, I come out twice a week. It's all in getting the feel of it, he says and then grips my shoulder. His good cheer spills warm and solid, full of the sun and night stars—courageous as Tracy. And, he says, I have a reel that winds on a ratio of four turns to a twist. Your reel only winds two-to-one. Not fast enough. It don't fool the fish, dad.

On the dock Jeff lowers his head and grins at Bonnie. Come back, little lady!

Bonnie's tennis shoes squish, grimed with scales and blood. I sway up the plank walk to our car as the world floods in again with its reams of pages for a sea of typing—hocked trombone and tomorrow hocked trumpet—divorce, food stamps, unpaid bills, rent.

It's a glorious day! And after dinner Bonnie will scrape her fiddle for me.

Epilogue in Lemon Butter

I scale and dress all four blues at once, fillet one, freeze the others—two hours work and cleanup for this amateur—and I dream about it later. The fillets I salt down overnight in table salt, keep 'em unfrozen on a lower icebox shelf. Next evening I rinse the salt off one fillet, swab both sides with a mix of safflower oil and lemon juice, sprinkle on freshly ground pepper. The fillet's too large—huge!—for the preheated broiler but I squeeze it in on aluminum paper. I give the skin side five minutes highest heat possible about five inches from the flame, and when the skin browns and bubbles, turn the fillet over for ten more minutes—don't let it get too dry! Before serving I swab it with lots of lemon butter.

After the first bite, we sit frozen as heavenly flavors soak our mouths. It's hard to smile through such piercing satisfaction or even look at each other. But after a while we look over the Xanadu of fillet covering our platter and really set to putting away the blues.

Those Havana-Chinatown Blues
WIN Magazine, Vol. 10, No. 26, July 18, 1974

You will never smoke a Royal Crown Flat. I bought the last five boxes on earth. They are now gone forever. The first Flat I smoked—a wavy piss-colored ribbon of tobacco—was worm-holed and hard to draw smoke through, and yet smoke arrived so mild that it ran over my tongue almost barren of taste or flavor. So mild that I thought my Flat the cigar God smoked. Too pure! Too . . . heavenly.

You have never seen a flat cigar and yet I once had four hundred of them. Each short Flat lay about four inches long and had two ribbon-like dips baked into its faded yellow wavy length. Yes, I repeat myself. That happens in heaven. You see, some time ago, booze and grass once gripped me with their sunny, smoky delights and—in my rotted fifth-floor walkup—had me goofing on the hifi into the purple dawn. But about two years ago I put both drugs behind me, hung my soaked youth up to dry and—at thirty-six—fled toward a superhuman rebirth. Call it my personal workshop to find mental balance. Even so, my hungry cells still fill with chemical ghosts and prickles flash through my nerves and sting me. My new superhuman manhood must endure a dry tongue and ghosts of the old dances and riffs that once bounced the big bands through my roof.

So in need of relief I hop down to Charlie Greene's Cigar Shop in Chatham Square, Chinatown. Greene's sells secondhand schlock cigars—mostly pulped floor-sweepings bound with low-grade leaf. Charlie Greene makes out by rounding up seconds from fallen drug and cigar stores. This is not a store Winston Churchill would seek out but it gives Charlie Greene a corner on legal though heavily aged Havanas. My Royal Crown Flats are pure Havana leaf boxed in 1942—still sealed—and ripened for thirty-plus years in some store basement. Unlike wine, cigars do not age well. Did I not say mine had worm holes?

Chinatown Charlie's dim store and raunchy windows sport crumbled and sun-burnt cigars aged and yellowed in cellophane and street-dust. There's no need to replace them with fresh stock every few years—these are seconds, just like the winos lying about out front with rotted linoleum for skin. Royal Crown Flats died as a brand decades ago, long before our embargo against Cuban cigars. So I buy a box of fifty—Greene's cheapest selection—for three bucks. For these cigars that's still expensive.

You stock up! Charlie Green tells me. This is great cigar. World's best, I no kid swell young man like you. Charlie Greene got only four boxes left. This is tiptop Cuban leaf, very pure. You float after you smoke this. See?—box sealed in 1942. Top year for Cuban leaf.

I think, uh, I think one box's enough. Look at these! They're *flat*, Charlie.

Ohh ho ho. They not flat.

Well, look at this. It's flat as an anchovy, And bent into waves.

You no want? I keep! Charlie Greene have special customers who smoke these only on holidays. Space them out. Velly special.

Charlie, I'm happy with one box.

You short on cash?

Always.

Charlie Greene trust you.

Charlie, please! I'm only smoking these for my health. They're just a crutch! I plan to quit all my bad habits, not stock up on—*on cigars!*

You got no idea what you miss. I hold them aside for you. When you float, you call me.

Home, I study my boxful of short, flat cigars with their weird—well, vulgar—anchovy-like double wave. The tax seal is perforated 1942. The cellophane wrappers have turned amber and split with age. Boy, these may really burn my throat out. I live alone just now but hope for a sports model replacement for my last wife, who was herself a sports model if measured against my years. I unlid a can of chili and chop a fat Spanish onion to bulk it up and let the pan warm while I break out my trumpet and set "Limehouse Blues" on my music stand. I run a few scales, though I don't believe in scales for a warm up. My lip feels pretty good. I spy the Flats on the table and unseal the box. Light up. Damn worm holes make it hard to drag in some smoke. At last—some mild smoke comes through. I set the cigar aside.

"Limehouse Blues" is not a difficult piece. Nor is it a blues. Its lyrics set the piece in London's Limehouse Chinese district. I have no grasp of chord progression and just sail ahead on the melody. But of a sudden I seem to have grasped the deep thrum of these mock Chinese chords for I'm delving into poor broken blossoms of progression and bring forth haunting melodic phrases with rings on their fingers, and tears for their crown, that is the story of old Chinatown. I'm really, really floating.

It's like my lungs have filled twice over and my lip become superhuman. What feeling—what lingering notes—what joyous insight unfolds into the real China blues buried in this ting-tong pentatonic scale. I am visibly moved by myself. I wish my wives could hear me now. They'd come running back, I know—somebody stole my—

I drag on my sun-yellow tape of Havana from the seeds and showers of thirty years past. These worm holes mean nothing. I've struck gold.

I stare down at my horn in one hand and my Havana in the other. Donald, get on thy horse. I rush to the phone and tell Charlie

Greene to save me the last four boxes, I'll be down pronto.

I go off to the blood bank to pick up some dollars and that evening sit home alone and womanless but wrapped in the amber self-satisfaction of having cornered the entire world supply of Royal Crown Flats. There are no more anywhere, Charlie assures me and shrugs.

Days of pure sunshine and obsession pass. These Flats only taste better the further down I smoke them. Not like round cigars, these give off flat rich blue-white tapes of fume. They fade into fume—a soft upward curl of tasty smoke—and disappear into a sun-colored cloud—matchless in aroma and lightness on the tongue, a richness of riffs and dances—*of whirl*. A Flat dies beautifully. Its flat white ash draws down to the tiniest roach of remaining Havana. No bitter tars ever collect. The butt itself, if there is any, stays sweet—earth-perfumed—still exciting. No hurry to crush or bury this butt—not even the last hot ember.

A Flat smoked on the street gives the day supersaturated intensity. Showers of pleasure arise in the rustle of leaves—with heart-billows of high cloud in Constable skies. Its smoke has a mouthwatering savor, a smack as heady as honeysuckle. And yet it is only smoke, purified leaf-smoke.

In the morning my Flat brings a mercurial mood of rising hope—fulfillment out of the airy blue—possible paperback or book club contracts. After lunch a Flat lends slow dignity to my work, a sense of firm insight, fitness of phrase—a high-intensity color and light to the page—even the hint of a self-admiring turn of voice or mood. By twilight I find myself quoting through an ultraviolet window open to backyard eucalyptus branches:

> *Full fathom five thy father lies;*
> *Of his bones are coral made;*
> *Those are pearls that were his eyes;*

> *Nothing of him that does fade,*
> *But doth suffer a sea-change*
> *Into something rich and strange.*
> *Sea-nymphs hourly ring his knell:*
> *Ding-dong,*
> *Hark! Now I hear them—Ding-dong bell.*

Did I write that? My God, it's been years since I wrote that well. But there is no question of chain-smoking—no hardship in waiting fifteen minutes for another Flat.

But to be honest . . . Flats soften my writing. The song of Havana forever sifts into the most exacting work—makes exquisite what otherwise should be sharp, hard-edged—even a fury of fact. I try to ignore the pleasure's afternoon dwindle, be patient for the unleashed sweet wash of five p.m.,—that unflagging evening savagery when I allow passionate release of my devils—the restraints are off! Forget the rent! Resolutions! Deadlines! Spend, spend! Face my cares squarely tomorrow. I'm resurrected afresh in the aroma rising and spreading to each room—just from the leafy sunlight on my tongue, the sweet light slip or even ragged rush down the natural gates and alleys of my soul. I live!—and my arm goes like a carpenter's elbow as I gulp Flat after Flat.

Now I swill two pots of espresso daily and to prolong my evening pleasure plunge into a horrific run on caramel custard ice cream. Goof on the hifi. Get fat, logy, shaky—my jaw grinds and grits without stop. Halfway through the fourth box, I get honest with myself. Quit smoking—quit eating—quit espresso. I give my remaining Flats to a fellow recovering drinker—an ironworker who chews Copenhagen on the high steel and smokes bent Italian stogies—and spits a lot. Four or five hundred yards straight down.

Three months pass without tobacco. My friend Sidney the translator returns from South America with a bundle of Canary

Island double coronas for me that has spicy Cuban leaf in the blend. He loves my golden tongue at the meetings and I haven't the moral force to refuse these hand-rolled premium glories with their gorgeously caressing draw—powerful from the first puff. In my three months of clean living I've broken the inhalation habit. No, I need not *inhale* these double coronas. I can smoke these cigars without inhaling and with a clear conscience—almost.

My real drug, though, is Flats—and their ghost returns. "Limehouse Blues" has lost its lift on my trumpet. In sudden helplessness, I'm into stores all over Manhattan and the Bronx, Mornings I sneak out of the house [sneak?—*yes*, a girl fiddler/tyro sci-fi writer has moved in!] "to go to the branch library" and find myself spending hours all over the financial district seeking Havana seconds [I live twenty-five miles uptown by Yankee Stadium]. Search out small Cuban cigar makers on upper Broadway—and down in Abingdon Square—rifle all the big tobacconists. I find bland, passable utility cigars. But these are not soul smokes.

Some fancy shops still have 1960 stock, pure Havana they say. I find 'em bitter, too prickly—I suspect a Sumatran wrapper. I try Brazilian for a week—they don't draw right, have little lift—no *whirl* at all. Some Nicaraguan cigars may help pass the time until a détente with Cuba frees us. The great cigar names are here—but their American versions are laughable beside the European. They are not Flats. They have no worm holes. Their cellophane has a clear strong shine and their fresh brown wrappers lack the sere and yellow piss-color of a Flat.

The fool is condemned to repeat his obsessions. I'm reasonably content today. I hope to quit. I've taken up fishing and about thirty miles offshore now seek to pit myself against the ferocity of a bluefish—not the sea-change of a Flat. It's wondrous, your line in the quicksilver as the sun lifts through blue-sludge clouds and the sudden boil of real life strikes on your line. You don't feel like smoking at all. No number you can do on your body can deepen the pleasure—not Flats, not grass, not whiskey. One day at a time, I think I'm winning.

Review of *Dog Soldiers*
The Village Voice, November 7, 1974

[Bonnie put up with me for two years and then went to Hawaii—a nice change from the Bronx. I stayed sober, cut off a pony tail down to my ass, shaved my beard, took off fifty pounds and despite this grievous loss of character met and married my third wife, Nancy, an Armenian and magazine fiction editor. This romance I retell in my novel *Eternal Life*, where she is Irene Hesperides. Some years earlier, when his first novel *A Hall of Mirrors* was published in 1966, I interviewed Robert Stone for *The Village Voice*. Seven years later, when his second novel *Dog Soldiers* and my third novel *The Drunks* came out nearly the same week, Stone and his wife Janice visited Nancy and me in our Village apartment and then he and I toured the Village book stores and signed our bright new books. He at first did not want to sign his, since these were my local book stores—but he gave in. Shortly before the Stones' visit, my review of *Dog Soldiers* came out in *The Village Voice*. I might add that Stone is one of the few novelists I've ever met—despite a half-century of book reviewing. I did join the Pen Club for a few years but to watch famous authors step out of their book jackets at Pen is not having a friend you visit or chat or dine with weekly. I've never had the close friendship with a working novelist Melville had with Hawthorne, which now that I think of it was rather lop-sided. Should I say Hemingway had with Fitzgerald? Well, that went sour—and in the pages of *Esquire*. Fitzgerald with Thomas Wolfe? They argued. Fitzgerald with Ring Lardner? Mm, bonded in booze. Perhaps lasting ties between novelists is a poor dog to chase. I did, by the way, go on to review three more Stone novels for *Kirkus Reviews*. My favorite is his short, neat *Bay of Souls*.]

In this novel's wondrous opening scene, John Converse, a feverish, malarial, fear-ridden writer who has failed to find "his book" in Vietnam, sits on a Saigon bench while on his way to score for three kilos of uncut heroin and finds an angel beside him. Robert Stone just says she's an elderly missionary but I know she's an angel when I listen to Stone's reverence in describing her and by Converse's eager desire to please her by his every word and gesture. He even thinks of offering her a joint or some gin. As they talk they agree that time's short and God should soon be arriving in His whirlwind. "It's now or never," she tells him. Converse is carried away with adoration for her. "Deliverance from evil would be nice," he says.

Dog Soldiers then plunges into its hero's journey into the whirlwind. Hell sweeps down on schedule, which is about as much plot as I can decently reveal. You deserve every ounce of surprise that Stone prepares for you in this bravura spiritual melodrama.

That old lady is the last person the reader meets who isn't hyped on some kind of dope spirituality. The novel is—among other strivings—one long parade of virtuoso weirdos, each with his post here in the heart of darkness. Not here in Vietnam—I mean in the heart veiled from God. Most of the story happens in Frisco, L.A. and in a Zen Disneyland monastery on a Mexican mountaintop. But what prodigies those weirdos are, each with his human or egoistic justification for evil—each alive and breathing rationalizations like purest air. Each evil to his backbone. Each forgiven by Stone.

Somehow, God loves His incredible psychopaths and Frankensteins—but allows each the choice of darkness.

He also allows them to live as his "dog soldiers" (dumb faith in life) who face daily the utter horror of personal and mass evil. One of the more likable characters says there is no evil—but I trust that old lady, who believes in Satan ("It's always surprised me," she said softly, "things being what they are and all, that people find it so difficult to believe in Satan." "I suppose," Converse said, "that people would rather not. I mean it's so awful. It's too spooky for people." "People are in for an unpleasant surprise." And Stone tells she said it "without spite as though she were really sorry.")

At one point Converse is stripped of his every last illusion. As a half-assed journalist he covers a patrol action with some Cambodians when by mistake they get strafed by their own pilots.

Converse lay clinging to earth and life, his mouth full of sweet grass. Around him the screams, the bombs, the whistling splinters swelled their sickening volume until they blotted out sanity and light. It was then that he cried, although he had not realized it at the time.

In the course of being fragmentation-bombed by the South Vietnamese Air Force, Converse experienced several insights; he did not welcome them although they came as no surprise.

One insight was that the ordinary physical world through which one shuffled heedless and half-assed toward nonentity was capable of composing itself, at any time and without notice, into a massive instrument of agonizing death. Existence was a trap; the testy patience of things as they are might be exhausted at any moment.

Another was that in the single moment when the breathing world had hurled itself screeching and murderous at his throat, he had recognized the absolute correctness of its move. In those seconds, it seemed absurd that he had ever been allowed to go his foolish way, pursuing notions and small joys. He was ashamed of the casual arrogance with which he had presumed to scurry about creation. From the bottom of his heart, he concurred in the moral necessity of his annihilation.

. . . His desire to live was unendurable. It was impossible, not to be borne.

He was the celebrated living dog, preferred over dead lions.

I avoid the evil of riding into a purple sunset about this novel. I admire the sheer hell out of its sensibility, art, insight, humor, plot, characterizations, and the weight of infinite horror it bears with such success, aside from its being a most reliably built picture of the dope generation. Its modest language lays bare the nerve-matter within each sentence. There's just one scene toward the end I might quibble about, a crucial scene—but they're all crucial in this wonder-bearing invention. (*Stop that sunset!*) Great novels absorbed into Dog Soldiers rise to mind page by page. It's been seven years since Stone's praised first novel *A Hall of Mirrors*, and more praise may deter his third novel another seven years, so let's shut down the band. *Dog Soldiers* has a rare certainty of purpose and absolute fix on its every character and line of dialogue. As Converse—laughing unsteadily, hiding out from the feds—tells his father-in-law, "I been waiting my whole life to fuck up like this." "Well," Elmer said, "you made the big time. Congratulations." "It's all true," Converse said. "Character is fate."

My only dopes are tobacco and espresso, so it's a measure of this novel's spooky grip that at one point I had to get out of my chair and in broad daylight inspect my rooms for their funny creakings. Closets, too.

A Fantastic Journey
Into the Psychic Frontier
Viva, Vol. 3, No, 3, December 1975

Ragged afternoon clouds glower on dark Massachusetts woods as our tires rattle a short board bridge over a stony stream. Light flickers and dims for we drive into spirit space.

My God, I've been here before! cries my third wife, whose name for this piece is Irene Hesperides since as a senior editor she got me assigned this article for *Viva*—the sexually liberated woman's magazine. *It's another life,* she says. *Talk about* déjà vu!

I swear I've seen every tree on this road before—though I've never been here. These shadows swim with the past. I glance at her dark eyes and sense some far pre-existence between us. Our very bones—now risen from some earlier day—and awake with flesh.

The deeper we enter the sun-and-gold gloom, the more the light films our skin with time lost in lands past. Our hands clasp.

Irene Hesperides and I head for the Elwood Babbitt farm atop Mount Opie near Wendell Depot, the Babbitt mail drop. Babbitt is a trance medium, born 1922, whose biography *Voices of Spirit* (1975) by Charles Hapgood has gripped us. Babbitt in trance lets the famous dead—Christ, Edgar Cayce, Churchill, Mark Twain, Einstein, Freud, Gandhi, John F. Kennedy, Lincoln, epic filmmaker C. B. DeMille, Bishop Pike, Socrates, Adlai Stevenson, Wordsworth and even the Archangel Michael and a much greater flock of the unknown—speak through his voice box. The spirit of Dr.

Frederick Fisher, a mid-nineteenth-century British doctor, acts as his "control" or helper. The control protects Babbitt from "blowing out his fuses"—dying—when the tremendous energies of the Christ force, the Archangel Michael, Vishnu, and like spirits from a high God-force burn through him. C. B. DeMille or Sir Francis Bacon he can handle straight—but the Angel Gabriel needs many screens or much dimming—or Babbitt could blow into the next world—which, he says, throbs very close by. You can reach out and touch it.

No *déjà vu*, please! I beg Irene. We haven't space in this article for *déjà vu*.

I sigh and ask myself how cram into our Babbitt visit all the scientific work on mediums—itself a book—that might give this piece some standing and authority? Those lab reports on out-of-body experiences? Or Ian Stevenson's dry and compelling *Twenty Cases Suggestive of Reincarnation*—wherein biology meet re-birth? Where will I have room for telepathy experiments? For moving objects by thought-force? Which, yes, sounds idiotic. How will I pack in the great modern mediums like Arthur Ford and Eileen Garrett or Anne Gehman or Doc Anderson? What about the thirty years of afterlife communications from Frederick Myers, the first president of the American Society for Psychical Research? Kirlian photography? Hard-edged Russian lab work? Telepathic emotions from plants? Jung's reincarnation experiences? Plus a brief history of mediums and spiritualism? *Tell me?* How will I then digest my four interviews with Babbitt, one with his wife Emily, a night with Elwood's biographer Charles Hapgood—and meanwhile give a full sketch of the afterlife as I've pieced it together from a dozen mediums I've met—all of it in twenty pages typed up for *Viva*— and fit in our *déjà vu* as well? She can't be serious about *déjà vu*.

Irene reaches over and with tenderness pats my leg. You'll do it. I look into the dark eyes of my Armenian third wife where time flows out of Eden into the valley of the Tigris-Euphrates.

It'll have to be a love story, I say.

Elwood welcomes us into his farmhouse. It spills with children and young commune folk, three big dogs—one a lumbering St. Bernard—many cats, a parakeet—and a spider monkey! Sheep and goats call from pens nearby and I spot five or six riding horses in a corral. I note there's no door on the bathroom, only a tacked up sheet. A young girl in the kitchen makes supper for Babbitt's army. His wife Emily, also psychic—as is everyone alive—is in Manhattan this evening. We sit in a mandala of moving flesh and fur and feathers. A very big collie sits up and begins—there's no other word for it—*talking* with us as he gives begging looks at sensitive Irene and psychic Elwood and new friend Don and sniffs at heaven and pats the rug and wiggles and tells us, I feel so alive and blissful! He rolls about the carpet in proof and whimpers in the pressure of joy.

Is he always like this? Irene asks.

Always. Elwood laughs at the dog. Oh, shut up.

Elwood and I have a bit of no-shit fellowship between us—we were both in the Marine Corps during World War II. He was, in fact, at Pearl Harbor and at five-thirty in the morning of December 7, 1941 he warned his base commander—to no avail—that he'd just had a vision of the Japanese about to attack them. He had many psychic experiences during the war, and none deeper than when—after a 500-pound bomb went down the smokestack of the *Arizona*—he witnessed the souls of several hundred men "going up in a huge white cloud . . . a very brilliant light that enveloped them."

He's had visions since early childhood—I was an abnormal child, he says—and his control, Dr. Fisher, has been with him since age five. His father had psychic experiences and was a convinced spiritualist; his aunt was a high Rosicrucian and clairvoyant; his mother "felt presences" but tried to steer him away from the "spirit people" who filled his daily world. His friendliness strikes everyone and he's apt to address a coffee-shop waitress with, "Hello, God!" And he means it.

For us he phones Charles Hapgood, his biographer—who lives in active retirement in nearby Keene—and tells him to come over. *They want me to pose for the centerfold, Charlie!*

At sixteen, Elwood had a driving accident that left him deaf, blind and speechless for a month—and also may have killed him. *I went into spirit and could have been declared dead.* He had a vivid out-of-body experience in the hospital, saw his dead grandmother in "full materialization" and could sense her spiritual force. *I heard the grandest music I ever heard. Then I got the beautiful perfume, and a huge golden ball that went from my head down through my body.* As the ball glowed and faded a very resonant and deep voice came, he says, and seemingly all-powerful it said, "Peace." *I went to sleep . . . Death is only a transition. It's like leaving this room and going into another room where things are brighter and more detailed. You look back and see yourself lying on the bed. You see the physical body. And connected to it is a silver cord which is spirit and has not been fully severed. And I could see a lot of different colors . . . and smell the fragrance of flowers.* Then he went into the temple of the Masters. Later, his grandmother told him he was not going to die. *I gave a deep sigh,* he says, *and was back in the body.* And he has never been sick since. *Except for* the first time he drew down the Vishnu-force, whose power left him shaken to the depths for two weeks.

Shaken? *I thought he was going to die,* Charles Hapgood later tells us. *I saw I had really overdone things, asking for Vishnu while Elwood was in dead trance. The sweat was incredible. All his veins and arteries were over-expanded by the pressure of Vishnu. At last Elwood's control stopped everything and Elwood collapsed.*

Later work with controls has produced a second Babbitt-Hapgood manuscript, *The Testament of Vishnu*, which holds thirty-seven talks with Vishnu, the Hindu All-in-all. Irene Hesperides and I have heard a Vishnu tape—quite powerful and amazing. Hapgood is now typing up a third volume—trance talks with Christ.

Babbitt is quick to admit his lack of education, a lack which makes the sheer range of his voices striking indeed. These are voices of people or authors whom he has never met or read about—nor has he any books in his house. Hapgood says that if Elwood reads two books a year it's a big year. He hated school, disliked English and history, and did not get a diploma until after the war. He does subscribe to *Psychic* magazine and says he has had a lifelong radiant cloud in his vision which makes it hard for him to fix on books, the rent, or workaday worries—or even people. What's more, he has total recall of former incarnations, and even of his last birth.

I can remember the moment of my conception, sperm meeting egg, then as fetus and later sliding down the birth canal. But the important thing is not to concentrate on your individual lifetimes but to see the whole picture of yourself as energy, as Spirit, and to see how these various lifetimes show where you're headed.

With Charles Hapgood joining us we eat supper, and then retire to Elwood's locked study for a taping (four and a half hours—about one hundred typed pages). Charles is seventy-one, a bit nervous and word-choosy, but enjoys himself despite some heart trouble ten months ago. He has been taping Elwood's trance voices for eight years and—since Elwood neither knows nor cares what he has said in trance and doesn't listen to the tapes—is often quick to correct Elwood or split a hair.

DON: You talk about seeing stones like diamonds and hearing the celestial music of the trees—even the song that each tree makes. I feel something like that in the middle of a wheat field—the lifeforce that rises from waving wheat. You take this in through your ear?

ELWOOD: Visionary too. I always wear etheric glasses. To look at anything. I see a white sheen of colors all of the time. I have to look *through*, and concentrate hard to see your face. Or it'll all flash out in color. The cosmic cameras turn on and I begin to sense clues to former lifetimes, hear talk someone's had with people of the past, and pretty soon I find myself—if I let myself go—seeing you as an atom with every picture that identifies you from your every source in this ocean of vitality we talk about. [*Atom means a being in the greater Monad or primal aspect of God. Voices of Spirit has a glossary of such terms.*]

DON: Way I see it, man is in the image of God because he thinks. He thinks and breathes. Thought and breath are the image of God.

CHARLES: God is no more. *Everything* is the image of God. That tree is the image of God. I've seen my dog Eloise disappear—she disappeared, and in her place I saw the... *God*—I saw the universe. I saw in the form of Eloise the entire universe. I saw Eloise as God. Dogs are just as much the image of God as people are.

DON: Back to my questions. How would you say you're using your talent now?

ELWOOD: By counseling people in great distress. I try not to lead them but to be a teacher and give them guidelines to the balance of life. Another way is getting into past lifetimes by life readings. Understanding your past lives gives you a grip on your present life. Why you've come back, why you've jumped from the karmic wheel—the law of cause and effect—to the wheel of total creativity.

DON: You go from cause and effect to creativity?

ELWOOD: Yes. Thirdly, for about a year Edgar Cayce has been coming in and giving diagnostic treatment to people and helping them out in their chemistry. [*Edgar Cayce, America's best-known psychic healer, prescribed while in trance, usually for distant people he had never met. He died in 1945 at age 68. In 1993, Babbitt will write and publish* Perfect Health: Accept No Substitutes.]

IRENE: You mean Edgar Cayce was coming to you?

ELWOOD: Yes. He's since returned from the school that he's been in. He came in here one time. I approached it in a very cautious way and found it to be true and Fisher says *Use it*. We've had some very remarkable success with some of the prescriptions he's given. [*Charles had Elwood bring in Cayce. Charles tells about Cayce having foreseen Charles's heart trouble. Charles often springs odd spirits on Elwood in his trance and such choices tell us as much about Charles as about Elwood.*]

DON: You're getting prescriptions from Edgar Cayce?

ELWOOD: That's right. But I don't prescribe. I say, *This is an opinion*. I am not a doctor and it's not me doing it. I'm in trance, so if they want to bring Cayce in, there's nothing I can say.

CHARLES: Keep in mind that Elwood does not remember anything.

IRENE: What is *déjà vu* to you, Elwood?

ELWOOD: Well, it's going to a certain place in the earth where you've lived before and recalling all the circumstances, details, and even conversations.

IRENE: *Ohhh!*

DON: It's sometimes called memory of the present. A neural lapse—it happens when people are tired.

ELWOOD: No, it's memory from a past life.

DON: Do you think Rockefeller will be president?

ELWOOD: No. I think the man who will be president of the United States in our next election and who will come to the fore will be a man from Arkansas called Bumpers.

IRENE: Dale Bumpers? Do you think that's a good solution?

ELWOOD: No. Because until they agree to feminize the democratic process by the opposite pole of energy and the woman vibration is intermingled from the president right down to the page in the White House, we will not have success.

IRENE: What is it women will bring?

ELWOOD: They are the creative force in the world. They're intuitive. They're sensitive. And they give balance to the positive force of man. It's needed in the *I AM* process of life.

DON: In *Voices of Spirit*, Benjamin Franklin asks, Where are my glasses?

ELWOOD: That was Bishop Pike. *Tilt!*

DON: All right, Bishop Pike lost his glasses. [*Bishop Pike was a radical Christian cleric who got lost and died alone in the desert near the Dead Sea.*] Franklin never appears?

CHARLES: Because *I'm Benjamin Franklin!* Back in the body. [*Elwood nods.*] And someone back in the body can't be called by Elwood.

DON: Well, how can Bishop Pike lose his glasses in the astral world?

ELWOOD: Because that was his last thought-form when he fell dead in the Holy Land and left the earth.

CHARLES: So he thought he still needed his glasses though he didn't?

ELWOOD: You want to see a cry for help? Like Pike needing his glasses? Those drawers are full. [*He opens two tall file cabinets, and points to the floor and a bushel basket that overflows with unopened letters.*] I haven't had the time! I have to answer them all by myself. People crying for an answer from spirit.

CHARLES: He needs a good court stenographer. A goddamn good typist. That's what he needs.

DON: In the geometrical growth of the birth rate on the planet is each baby a reincarnated being?

ELWOOD: Absolutely.

DON: That means there's had to be a death for everyone alive.

ELWOOD: I wouldn't say *death*. We live in a universe of life. I say transition.

DON: Do you see Dr. Fisher?

ELWOOD: I see him all the time.

IRENE: Do you see someone like JFK, or just get vibrations?

ELWOOD: No, *I* don't see him. That's what we call a complete trance. My unique gift is that I'm completely sucked out of the body—all of my cells at once—and there's a balance that has to click right. And Fisher sweeps in and takes complete control of me. Now if another energy like Kennedy wants to come in, it has to be taught how to do it. Dr. Fisher manipulates the energy of the cells—so that they balance exactly right in order for that energy to come into me. That's *dead* trance. At that point Fisher doesn't talk, Kennedy does. But Fisher is around so that I don't blow out.

DON: Do you do readings where relatives of the sitter come in from spirit?

ELWOOD: No. I do not encourage the Spiritualistic movement. We've proven immortality.

DON: Do you or Charles ever think of bringing back the spirit of Helen Keller? Deaf, dumb, blind—but tremendous inner being.

ELWOOD: I don't know. I don't get into it. That's up to Charles. I do my part and just forget it. I see it all the time and really I get sick of it. But I don't because I know it's helping people. As long as I can be of service with the gift, I'll use it. But I was talking with a friend of mine, a teacher for the Guild for the Blind. We were talking about the new approach where we can turn the blind on by opening the Third Eye and they can pierce the material world. The reason I do *dead* trance is because I'm out of it completely. I usually go up into the temple of the disciples and rap with some master. I'm completely out of the body and I know the entity using it uses *his* energy from where his dimension is, and what is coming through is true and factual and not colored by me.

DON: I've noticed that the spirit voices explain what is going on better than you do in person. Ha ha.

ELWOOD: Well, they're more capable. I couldn't pass a third-grade math test to save my life.

IRENE: Neither could I.

DON: Did you ever hear of the Spiritualist community in Lilydale? The town I grew up in—Jamestown, New York—is about twenty miles from there.

ELWOOD: Yep. I went down and we worked the camp down there for a couple of weeks—me and Ted Russell. He was billed as America's Premiere Psychic of the World—he was a mentalist. Beautiful mental medium—he could prove immortality without question.

IRENE: Elwood, you were saying that you didn't believe in evil, just error. But you've suggested that traveling in the astral plane is dangerous and that you wouldn't encourage it. You gave an example of Edgar Cayce—that he traveled this white line and felt he was being grabbed and pulled down by these suffering souls. All is not good! Who are these suffering people?

DON: These hands coming up?

ELWOOD: The suffering is not physical. It's the spiritual anguish of people who have been trained in a materialistic attitude on earth. The astral is identical to this world.

DON: The strength of our earthly impressions sticks with us when we wake up?

ELWOOD: Right. I've been in the astral and I can see people—and it amuses me—who still pick up their lunch pail, kiss their wife at the door, and go to work in a factory when the whistle blows. People will not let go of the world, even *there*, because fear is the killer—the mind-killer.

IRENE: What changes them there? Is this purgatory?

ELWOOD: They change by finally obeying the urge within to see the karmic picture of their life and review it. And reenter the earth again to overcome fear. But they will not always understand why they progressed back into the earth. As for the astral, when the silver cord is severed from the body, you become very light. You feel enlightened, you feel free. And then you get to see other people around you—people you know have died—and they tell you that you have made the transition—which some refuse to believe. It's the same there as it is here. Identically. Except you have no body. You communicate with thought-forms. Telepathy. You get to see other people around you—people you know have died—and they tell you that you have made the transition—which some refuse to believe. It's the same there as it is here. Identically. Except you have no body. You communicate with thought-forms. Telepathy. You grow according to what you accept, same as this world. Then you illuminate yourself by listening to some teacher or guru or swami or what we have on earth. You go to his temple and listen. Now, if you agree with it and like it, you learn from it. Then you let go of the astral and go into the next frequency. And so on up the ladder until you reach an understanding in the karmic wheel. Or because of the injustice that you caused in the world, you will volunteer to return and balance that karma, so that after a while you flow in a total compassion of life. *Grief*, though, will shut off any psychic manifestation. Balance is everything.

  DON: Well, could we go on with the reading now?

  ELWOOD: I'm ready when you are. You start the tape when Fisher comes in. Now, it's like in the heavens a cosmic vacuum cleaner is turned on and I suddenly start moving out of my body—the cells, the energy. I shoot flowing away. And as I flow away, Fisher will come in over it, into my body to sustain it to keep the cells moving and the atoms going—and while he is in it he'll be possessing it and he'll be talking directly to you from what he sees in the outer dimensions concerning your life. He'll take you apart—spirit, soul and body—and put you back together in truth. But then it's up to you to play your tape until you can bring yourself into the truth, which is pretty hard to do in this lifetime. He may sound far out but truth's truth, and people do not want it. All right?

Elwood sits back, his head drops. Breathes deeply, eyes closed, lips pursed and whisking. Something surprises about his fast drop into dead trance, deathly stillness as his body prepares to receive Dr. Fisher. I close my eyes to help. Five-minute silence. Then his lips purse and frisk, his cheeks sink utterly. Dr. Fisher enters. Elwood sits forward, cheeks plunged into bone as thumb and forefinger clasp his jaw. Elbow on desk, he speaks, vibrant and friendly and serious, in high phrases of a mid-nineteenth-century British medical man. The voice speaks each word from Elwood's voice box to its last clear syllable, every t crossed, each final -ed hit hard. My blood lifts and shimmers. Irene entranced goes glassy.

DR. FISHER: This is Dr. Fisher assuming control of the medium! *As we enter your vibrational force*, I wish to address my remarks at the present time to the energy of the young lady present.

Here we find looking at your *cellular* body a definite *slow rate of metabolism*. It also shows that in a previous vibrational force of your life, there has been a questionable *sickness* and nearness to spirit that occurred in a younger part of your life. [*Both Fisher and Elwood sometimes mean "life" to include a series of incarnations. Whether Fisher here speaks of Irene's present incarnation or an earlier one isn't clear.*] Furthermore, you are now entering a new vibrational force that will give you a totally new picture of health. I say this—for every seven years you undergo a new cellular *experience*—to give you the opportunity, along with the balanced mind of force, to enter a full compassionate *Idea* of the life and the understanding which you seek. [*I take Irene's hand as the strong, pleasant, high-minded voice speaks on.*]

As we enter the *soul*, or the sheath of the spirit, we open wide the Valley of the Yesterdays. And as we look in upon you, we find you in Egypt. Here you lived in the palace. I see you in gauze gowns of very thin material. You had about the same flesh-body you now wear except your hair reached your hips. You were most loving, sensitive, expressive and did not lean toward the romanticism of life—though you were *intrigued* by the prophets that came to the palace to speak to your father of the various *thoughts* wherein the philosophy of life had its full containment. [*Irene gasps—her father is a retired well-known candy maker in Boston who dabbles in spiritual matters.*]

Here, as you move through *this* lifetime you become highly perceptive of *outward forces*, and here your tutor teaches you many things about metaphysics.

Again in the change of energy—we find you entering Rome. Here you would have known the young man with you. You at that time were *again* a member of the palace—and yet you were not content with your lot at being part of the aristocracy of that time. Your father at that time was known as *Tiberius*, the ruler. [*Roman historians Tacitus and Suetonius record that Emperor Tiberius had a son—and an astrologer—but no daughter.*] And here, knowing the young man as a captain of the Praetorian guard in the palace, the consent to marriage was given and this young man elevated to a *senatorship* within the Roman legislature.

Here, *you* were a brilliant lawyer, a well-educated man from all that you had learned from excellent *tutors* that you yourself had *employed* when you were but the captain of the guard and as a young man *thirsting* for a knowledge that lay dormant within you because you *could not* give it the expression needed for the future work or change of spirit that would be occurring with you. Here you were brilliant in your *oratory*, in your lawyership, and you were counseled by various wise men. You in your perceptions gave balance to the young lady present, so that in your marriage you *consummated* a full and good relationship.

[*I am finding all this hard to believe—even from Dr. Fisher! It is not Elwood but Dr. Fisher we hear—a voice whose admirable dignity and high-flown but faulty grammar are as distinct as possible from Elwood's down-home speech. Irene grips my hand and her adult womanly glance lifts my disbelief onto her strong Armenian shoulders and one atom of me gives in to Dr. Fisher.*]

However, the yearning within your heart is *not* from your wishing to know more of the spiritual part of life. It stems from your two children who were killed before your eyes under chariot wheels at one of the great arena fights and caused a great sadness of spirit in both of you. Thus in your tie today there is a *nostalgia* that creeps within your hearts because of *not understanding* this loss that occurred to you so many earth years ago.

We find you circulating again in your present life. Once more a new wave approaches and carries each of you to a fuller experience. Your spiritual eyes open to the new way that now rises throughout your world. You will witness in your time many of the considerations from the rule of *Tiberius*. You will witness the wars. You will witness revolution. You will see famine, and pestilence—because of the downtrodding forces of man that *refute* the spiritual simplicity of life. And you will see that you will become teachers among those that search for the final truth which is the victory of all life.

[*I find Dr. Fisher's ghostly grammar throwing me—or rather drawing me in as his dizzying dips into history thrill me. Tiberius! What does Elwood know of gloomy Tiberius?*]

I see you changing and moving, and coming into more of a *compatibility* with your spirit. Yet this only occurs after you both enter a very strong perception, or clairvoyance, that is now very marked—for each has a *nearness* to spirit. You *feel* strongly. More than at other times when you are busy in the mundane. Here we see there is *almost* the seeing of spirit, yet the elusiveness comes from the turning of the brain to an analysis of what is actually happening within your spirit. You want to analyze, not let the spirit lead.

These two lifetimes in Egypt and Rome [*Irene sighs*] are the counterbalance to your present life on earth. And they reflect the endeavor throughout the years to enter the balance of life and to perceive the full meaning and intention of where you contribute to the wheel of life. Here you see yourselves move in various changes of energy, and you find greater *effect* as you enter into fuller awareness of self, which needs only to be honed a little more to give you a total clairvoyant picture of your other lifetimes and such interchange of karmic balances. Your other lives are not important—you, young man, for example, were a doctor—you, young lady, were a nurse—both living within the Civil War period. Here you have moved through various healing forces, for there is a strong sensitivity to the *judgments of mankind*, and you wish to serve with a greater sensitivity. [*The big collie barks outside the locked door.*]

As I gaze at your spirit, it is bright within the aura colors of *blue*, young lady, denoting your harmony of purpose, your sensitivity, your great yearning and *compassion*, not only [*the collie barks*] for the animal and plant kingdoms but for the *whole robe of Mother Nature* spread before you. It fills you with a *beauty* that you feel alone within your spirit, and brings you a calm that you do not find in other states of your world. We find this to be true also with your color green, young man, which shows a very strong healing force in your spirit hand. Here you have capability of regenerating the weak by the touch of your hand or by your thought. [*Intense satisfaction fills Irene's dark eyes, and her spell plucks at my sympathies: she thinks of my work with alcoholics as her spark from Dr. Fisher reaches out to include me.*]

To you, young man, there is also *the red, strong, positive color*, denoting your very outspoken wish to be more fully in tune with the organizational forces of self. Also, from your period as a doctor you move into a more positive attitude and are not afraid to announce *what is truth* as you see it, the truth you know and understand.

Now your souls are *old* because of the various transitions, but the depths of the Egyptian and Roman times indelibly mark your spirits.

As you *react* to that constant thought-force driving through you, you will find an *awareness* of clairvoyance that will give you a rich picture that reveals *completeness* in your life. You will strive to become a part of a new society which shall form throughout your planet. Here I see you moving and changing always in the mainstream of spirit rather than in the material-mindedness of so many around you. So your life, as spirit, if it is so wished by your free will, is to become spiritual teachers in the New Age.

How...may...I...serve...you?

DON: *Ohh! Dr. Fisher!* It's very good to meet you. Uh, I would like to know who is my spirit guide.

DR. FISHER: You have a spirit guide and he comes from India. His name would be *Tooma*. He is more of a master than what you would term an *ordinary* guide of the astral plane or of the other dimensions. You will witness him revealed by the deep-seated feelings that you have. And by your desire to enter the depth of power that surges through you and that you do not understand at the present time. It gives you a feeling of inspiration. Remind yourself—as you begin an *oratory* of the *future*—that your guide *Tooma* is the one you want to follow.

To the young lady, I speak of an Indian guide already most closely attached to you because of your sensitivity, your enjoyment of Mother Nature in all her *beauty*, your *soft harmony* which flows through you and affects your tenderness toward all living things. Here he stands in all his robes and splendor. He is an Indian chief of the Seminole tribe, and as he stands here would be named *Bald Eagle. Call upon him!* Witness his beautiful feathers, and his stance and power, his courage and humility. You will see him at moments when you are least aware that he hovers around you.

IRENE [*whispers*]: Thank you!

[*Both of us sit thunderstruck—I am myself part Iroquois.*]

DR. FISHER: Now here you have much to absorb! And as you play your *machine tape*, I shall be near, not forcing you into any circumstance beyond what your free will accepts. But know that as you play it, the energy force will be working with you. And from it shall come a newer *vibrational force* that will give you the greater contentment and satisfaction that you have sought throughout the ages. Let this be your road, your way. Till we met again [*dog barking*], my peace profound.

[*As Dr. Fisher leaves Elwood, the dog on the door sill barks and barks and whimpers. Minutes pass and then Elwood awakes coughing and the dog barks.*]

DON: Thank you very much.

ELWOOD [*his voice raspy and countrified as before*]: Not at all.

DON: I'm very happy to have heard from Dr. Fisher.

IRENE: That was very moving. Very beautiful. Absolutely astonishing.

ELWOOD: You come back, we'll take up where we left off. It's like you weren't interrupted.

IRENE: Overwhelming and very beautiful. Thank you. I know what I wanted to ask you. You said that we *choose* the families we enter. You choose your parents?

ELWOOD: According to your karma, even though you might be born into very trying circumstances—your family might break up or fight or one might be a drunkard. You might go through hell while growing up—it's all part of learning things—for them and for you.

IRENE: Do you see your life before you join your family?

ELWOOD: You see the whole thing. You know your whole life

before you take the body.

IRENE: *Ohh!*

DON: Then you may as well accept the idea that your body is worth entering and living?

ELWOOD: That's right. But then we put a cap on the spirit so we don't see it. We flounder in a world of industry.

IRENE: Then the concern of free will in spirit is free will to choose your own karma?

ELWOOD: You have that free will in spirit to choose which one you want to balance.

IRENE: But you don't have that free will in your own lifetime?

ELWOOD: You're always cleaning karma, yes. Every day you're cleaning some little incidental karma. Where maybe back five thousand years ago you called somebody a sonofabitch or stabbed him in the back or something. You're constantly balancing all these little things that we do. And the greatest error is to judge—put a judgment on something or someone—that is the worst karma you can incur. That's why judges never live too long.

IRENE: That's *astonishing*, isn't it! Donald and I have known each other through the ages.

ELWOOD: Are you asking? I don't know, I didn't hear it.

DON: We want to stay together—even in the next life. Do us a favor, will you, Elwood, and take our picture? Stamp our vibrations on this emulsion.

ELWOOD: Watch the pretty birdie now, and say cheese. *Cheese.*

IRENE: Ha ha! Thank you very much.

She is doe-eyed Egyptian.

Epilogue

As I put *Trumpet Rhapsodies* together, I respect the spirit—the rhapsody!—in which I wrote each piece and so have not been quite as skeptical as I should be of Dr. Fisher's reach into Rome and Egypt. Elwood and the late Hapgood are delightful, homespun people with deep belief in Elwood's gifts—well, Elwood has no choice—and I'm not one to abuse their hospitality—or that of Elwood's dogs. As it happens, Dr. Fisher speaks in spiritual generalities much like those of the spiritualists Elwood says he does not support. When Elwood takes on the vibes of Mark Twain, Jesus, Einstein, Vishnu, John F. Kennedy, or Charles's friend Erle Stanley Gardner or other famed figures, the message itself comes across in generalities and bears few personal quirks or thoughts specific to Twain or Einstein and like folk. Yet figures like Kennedy or Abraham Lincoln or even Queen Elizabeth the First rise to high tones, fine grammar, and they even at times in Miltonic inversions speak. Most of the dead have little personality in Babbitt's readings. They are vibrational forces, not social or earthly beings. Kennedy explains his assassination in finger-pointing that would please Oliver Stone. In part these figures share a hardship in using Elwood's voice box and often respond in much the same way to their new lives in spirit, to earth-memories fading, to far views of earth's bumpy future, and to foolish materialists striving in the material world. The temple of the masters and the teachers leading newcomers to higher planes are commonplaces of spiritualism.

For a while I thought it too bad we wound up with Dr. Fisher, Elwood's speaker, who was most focused on breathing life into us at the expense of speaking about, oh, I don't know—Henry James? I might have enjoyed a chat with Tolstoy or Dostoevsky or Kafka. How would Joyce speak of the life vibrational? What will Dante say about finding his scheme for *The Divine Comedy* revamped into vibes and thought-forces? Foreign tongues, by the way, from Socrates to Vishnu, all come over in English. Even Satchmo Armstrong abandons jive talk when he asks to enter Elwood. *Voices of Spirit* being published in 1975, I'd like to know how Louis can bring his wife Lucille's vibes along with him some eight or ten years before she died in 1983? But I'm sure Elwood can answer that. *Voices of Spirit* is somewhat more mind-altering for skeptics than I am here, while Ian Stevenson's *Twenty Cases Suggestive of Reincarnation* has been revised, updated and expanded since my reading it. It is, as I recall—now forty years later—a deep and well-balanced dig into the spirit world. My own views on spirit are metabiological and can be found in my memoir *Helen's Ass Strikes Homer Blind!*—currently available as a Kindle ebook from Amazon.

The Beast in the Strand Book Store
New York Magazine, Vol. 10, No. 31, August 1, 1977

An addiction to books can be for life. Or it may happen, as in my apartment, that enough is enough. It's a disease, says Fred Bass, the manager of that secondhand empire at 12th and Broadway—the scene of my illness in flower—the Strand Book Store.

I get an attack, something like a panic, of book-buying, he says. I simply *must* keep fresh used books flowing over my shelves. And every day the clerks weed out the unsalable stuff from the shelves and bins and we throw it out. And *I* bought 'em! But I just have to make room for fresh stock to keep the shelves lively.

Too lively shelves, I say. You want to beat your compulsive buying habit in the Strand? Know the exact book on the exact shelf before you walk in. Then hit it, pay, get out in three minutes. For me, otherwise, the mind bursts with a dozen titles I've forgotten. I go into an amoeboid swim through aisles—books on shelves waver on high and call me up a Strand ladder—and I'm lost. I find that a visit to the Strand can be baffling and fearful. The brain *deranges* and I turn from superhuman novelist into an ill-tempered creature who scrambles up to top shelves—without a ladder!—or digs down dark aisles into shadowy bottom shelves and then hugs his treasures—Kafka's *Metamorphosis!*—Mary Shelley's *Frankenstein!*—Meyrink's *The Golem!*—Wilde's *The Picture of Dorian Gray!*—I gloat, I gloat. Something comes over me. My fingers twist and nails grow. I must get out of here before the full change into Hyde takes me over.

Some years ago, not many—when I'd not yet published a book and the first paperback explosion had lifted to madness and buried the hard cover—I was sickened to step into the late Eighth Street Book Shop and see new paperback titles massed face-front to ceilings—strong titles I'd known brilliant in hard cover only days ago. A horror of the soul came over me. Giants—Joyce's *Ulysses*, Mann's *The Magic Mountain*, Dostoevsky's *The Brothers Karamazov*—novels burning with artistic labor—stood hidden among shabby paperback trivia and pipsqueaks. A shift in the American book market had shaken the first-class book stores—with the great novels racked with *I Am a Barbarian* and *Spaceship to Saturn*! Must the mystique of Eternal Life in Hardcover shrink to this paperback exit? The notion of emitting novel upon well-wrought novel from my birth canal to swell these racks left my brain soft and blood-soaked. My skin crawled. Hopelessness glistened in pepped up glossy graphics on these soft-bound horrors. Thank God for the Strand where the hardback reigned—though secondhand.

Limping homeward to Castle Despair, I'd sigh at the world's unreason. And yet I'd find my house—and myself—full of dead men's books. Even paperbacks, by steam pipes crumbling and dried yellow to a crisp. I'd walk through my valley of the shadow of books, and cry aloud at my own shelf bowed with unpublished manuscripts looking for publishers. *Can these books live? And, if so, why? To be paperbacks bound in cheesecloth?*

And my real obsession with books had not yet even begun!

Book-buying benders lay before me that would chain me to borderline poverty even to this day. I ask myself, Where will I lay my head when I die? What pauper's grave will claim me? Wouldn't it be wonderful, I whispered to myself, if the Strand Book Store had a catacombs, a subbasement where Fred Bass allows the bones of penniless city writers to be placed in perpetuity so that we need

not lie out in the rain through eternity but might, in fact, lie under the wondrous world-mulch of books in the five floors of the Strand above us and feel the radiance of our beloved writers drain down over our bones? This would be, of course, a private arrangement. Manhattan burial laws are not as lax as those at Pére-Lachaise cemetery in Paris, where artists are more or less just tossed in. Fred's Fellowship of the Strand would work, as they say, under the rose—which means that as the last day approaches, one need only carry a hard copy of *Bleak House* or *Journey to the End of the Night* into the Strand and pass it to Fred with a pressed rose peeking out of the pages. No word need be said. The rose would say all.

About seven years ago I found myself collecting secondhand books *that I absolutely needed* faster than I could read their jackets—if they had jackets. I'd moved into some kind of spiritual recovery from my life in the Sixties and—swept free of poisons—my mind had gone nova. I found myself magnetized to writers of deep livingness, to poets and novelists I'd once ignored, and to books about a state you might call "cosmic consciousness." Only later did I notice that nearly everything ever published—from the Vedic hymns to *Through the Looking Glass*—fits into cosmic consciousness. I already had a complete 19-volume hardcover set of Jung over my bed, plus lighter Jung memoirs and picture books. Time for Joseph Campbell's four-volume *The Masks of God* to bring it all together. Blast me off to the Buddhic plane.

You're not unique, I tell Fred Bass. I know how you feel. I've been there with books, the sense of mental disorder—but I've had somewhat less capital than you. Tell me, how did the illness start? Just creep up on you?

Fred does not sit still for this interview. He whisks about and talks as he moves, forever gripping a clipboard, an inventory, a list of requested books, crying out to one of his 65 painter-poet-writer-actor clerks, who at his bidding speed without rest to empty out book bags being brought in or to refresh a shelf. This haste must be kept up, for Fred and his father, Ben Bass, own the greatest usedbook store on the northern continent and it's still just an oversized babe in arms, its greater stock still unshelved. This pulped forest of one-and-a-half million books takes up eight miles of shelf space [18 miles in 2008]. There are three full floors of stock the public can browse. And other floors we'll tell you about.

You couldn't read all the titles, Fred says. You might get through one wall of ten or twenty thousand, but customers would be ahead of and behind you and the clerks behind them rolling up trucks of new stock. And you know what it's like in here on Friday afternoons and Saturdays. We're so deep in customers, maybe 500 at a time, that we actually lose our more select business. I mean browsers who come in with a $200 list of books they want and then can't get at the shelves because of the herd. Well, happily there's no place else to go. We've got the books.

Ben Bass the founder looks about in awe. I started all this fifty years ago! With a thousand books! He waves. It was 1928 and I was no good at anything. So I opened the Pelican Book Shop on Eighth Street and got dispossessed in 1929—the Depression, y'know? Then I scraped up $600 and started the Strand. Say I was an impatient failure.

I see Maurice Sendak the children's-book author/illustrator slip like the White Rabbit through the doorway to the basement art books. At my hand lies a used copy of *Priestess of the Occult*, a life of the cosmic Madame Blavatsky—out of print, six bucks. I want it! But I have only seven, and resist.

Come on, I'll show you the rare books, Fred says. We just added two new rooms.

A man with a twirled white British mustache and tweed hat mutters, Where is the section for espionage?

It overlaps the war and crime sections, Fred says.

Do you read, I ask Fred.

I wake up five every morning and read for an hour. Just finished David Markson's novel *Springer's Progress*. Mysteries for roughage. Now I'm into McNeill's *Plagues and People*. His brown eyes dart, reluctant to leave the main floor. Trimly bearded, he is a tanned, spirited bust of Shakespeare in full tide of managing the Globe Theater. My barber is a frustrated Elizabethan scholar, Fred tells me.

Fred wears a diamond stickpin on a yellow shirt and blue or brown box plaid (I dress schematically, he says), while half-lens glasses on a black cord hang from his neck even when he lunches out or walks the street.

It's incredible! he tells me. The excitement of miscellaneous buying. People drive up in cars and trucks. Sometimes thousands of books come in over the counter. Maybe a very fine first edition of Boswell's *Life of Johnson*—just like that! We paid in excess of $1,500 for it. You never know what you'll find in a private library. But no matter how much money or how many books we take in, we have to rush out and buy more books. It's a lotta fun—like a treasure hunt. I'm at it ten hours a day in here. It's stimulating—I wouldn't *be* in any other business. We're in the elevator to the rare-books rooms. Of course—some days—after lunch—I get depressed. But then there's England! I go there. I go out West. Wherever there are libraries, fresh stock—*ahh*.

Before we go into the rare-books rooms he takes me on a tour of the backup stock waiting to go down to the main floor and basement. It is hair-raising. The huge floor is a Great Plains of books, like Charles Foster Kane's cellar, far shelves vanishing into alcoves, waves of marked books bought from private collectors, a Thames or Mississippi of human spirit transfigured into printer's ink. The heart stiffens simply to take it all in.

Fred winks. I ain't foolin' around here. Don't forget, we have a tremendous mail-order business from independent buyers and libraries all over the world. I've forgotten what's in half these boxes we haven't unpacked yet.

A colossal Acme safe with its doors ajar rules the three-room rare-books room.

We bought it for $50 from the former tenants. It would have cost them hundreds to move it. A few weeks after we got this floor, two gunmen came in. "*Where's the stuff?*" I guess they thought we kept rare books in the safe.

I look into its depths. Only one book; I pull it closer. *Manhattan Telephone Directory 1976–77.*

They left it?

Oh, we have a much more sophisticated security system for the real stuff. My God, I've got a buyer waiting for me. *I'm late, I'm late!* He introduces me to Bill Stone. See you downstairs. Every time I'm up here I see 10 million items that have to be rearranged. Well, a *million* maybe.

Stone, a lanky, intense blond, slumps over a typewriter. He prepares Strand mail-order catalogues, which carry his own little tickles and fillips:

> WRIGHT, L.—Clockwork Man.
> Prof. illus. Not a technical history
> of horology but about everyday life
> of which the calendar and the clock
> have taken undue control. Packed
> with all manner of facts & figures,
> i.e. Time that Henry the VIII
> dined; Big Ben chimed 37 times at
> 1 A.M. on April Fool's Day, 1861, etc., etc.

I ask Bill Stone, Just between us, what do you hear about the subbasement?

The subbasement? We don't have a subbasement. But we have a basement.

I smile and show I know all about the subbasement. I look about. We're alone. The catacombs, I whisper.

I can't talk about that—even if we had a subbasement.

Okay, okay.

I move on to Chris Coover who runs the room, a cap sideways over his big schoolboy glasses. He shows me Boswell's *Life of Johnson* (first edition, 1791).

These are the original boards, he says. Only 1,750 sets were made. Nice. But I like this better. He opens a handsome blue box holding a stack of small magazines. These are the original nineteen illustrated 32-page installments of the Dickens *Bleak House* serial. It runs from March 1852 to September 1853. The last one is a double. Of course, this is first draft—he rewrote it for hardcover.

Bleak House, huh? Do you plan to sell this or just keep it?

Why should we just keep it?

Fred has a soft heart for *Bleak House*.

A soft heart? Fred?

Some people think he's a saint. You might say, the Saint of the Penniless Manhattan Writer. You know—a copy of *Bleak House* with a rose inside?

I don't follow you. You mean because secondhand books are relatively cheap and low-income writers can buy them, Fred is a saint? Fred charges what he can get, whether secondhand or rarity. He doesn't give books away.

I'll put it another way. Have you ever been to the subbasement?

We don't have a subbasement.

I think Bill Stone let the cat out of the bag. About *Bleak House* and the roses.

The roses?

I whisper, The catacombs!

Chris Coover sits back. The catacombs are in Rome, he says.

And in Paris, I say. And, uh, even Manhattan.

I've never heard of one in Manhattan. Would you like to see any more rare books?

This is the one I want, I say and lay my hand on the old Houghton Mifflin giant Andrew Wyeth book.

That's $300.

I'll wait. Do you have any rare books on cosmic consciousness?

They'd all be downstairs. There are no rare books on cosmic consciousness—not rare in any sense we recognize. You could go to Weiser's Occult Book Store, that's where they'd wind up. Now here is our first edition of Pepys *Memoirs and Correspondence* (1823), one of twelve copies he had made up on special heavy paper for presentation to friends and patrons. It's only $600.

It weighs it.

He shows me a two-volume Gutenberg Bible facsimile. There are only 47 originals surviving, Chris says, and 300 facsimiles—so Gutenbergs are scarce. Every big library wants one. It's $3,000—but I don't get much out of it. Here's what I like. The nine volumes [1759–67] of *Tristram Shandy*, handled by Sterne himself. The first three volumes are signed—$1,250.

Terrific. You have to love a writer to part with that kind of money. I've tried to read this many times but I get bored. It takes a special kind of preciousness to love this.

Joyce drew on it for *Ulysses*, Chris says. And Virginia Woolf and Thomas Pynchon. Sterne is the father of the modern novel.

Hm. *Tristram Shandy* is like reading a book and seeing the world upside down. I get topsy-turvy and nauseous. Have you read it?

Oh, sure. And *A Sentimental Journey*.

Then you love Sterne. That's what I say. You have to love a writer, to keep on reading him if he's doing something original, like *Ulysses* or *To the Lighthouse*. I find Pynchon is a little less than lovable. Original to the hilt—but not lovable. Of course, he doesn't want to be loved. He doesn't even want to be seen.

Right. Nobody knows what he looks like.

Well, his wife. And maybe his mother. My advice to young writers like myself would be to avoid originality at all costs—if you want to be published. Look about this room, the *crème de la crème*. These writers have risen to the top. Time cannot curdle their page. But downstairs, on the main floor, it's a jungle down there. It's tooth and claw. If we don't make it down there—and look at the odds!—Fred cries *Fresh stock, fresh stock!*—and bags us and heaves us into the sanitation trucks.

Chris says, But writers don't make any money off of secondhand sales at the Strand.

I'm not talking about money. I'm talking about cosmic consciousness. Becoming an archetype in the collective unconscious—a bright figure floating there in the mind of man—a radiant little touchstone we turn to for excellence, or even for flourishes against the darkness. Like that great Irish writer Terry Molloy says, I'm talking about being a contender. Of being somebody.

You should talk to Burt Britton about that. Down in the basement. He buys review copies and knows everybody who's anybody. All the contenders.

I'll do that. What's this?

This is a Picasso *Lysistrata* with his signature for $1,200.

Oh, don't give me that. Picasso reading *Lysistrata*? Yeah, and I'm sure he keeps Plato on his nightstand. Look at these illustrations. Scribbles! Took him thirty minutes at best.

I pull down the first American edition of *Ulysses* (1934) in cream-colored cloth. Hey! Ex Libris Carl Van Vechten. I'll bet he hated to part with this.

Fifty dollars.

Ohh! That would be nice. But I don't have it on me.

Fred will take a check.

I fondle the book but resist. That would not be a good idea, I say. And I already have one, though not a first. It's got a cream cover and—

The cream cover's an American first. How about these? He shows me an ancient book with carved, solid-silver covers; then an illuminated incunabulum from 1473 ($2,000); and a book from 1629 with a thick red, blue, green, yellow, and white embroidered binding on red velvet with gold and silver wire and small sequins.

Not for me, I say.

How about Froissart's *Chronicles* [1523–25]? Only $2,500?

But I'm looking through Jack Kerouac's first editions. Then my head floats *Big Table* number one [1959]. My gosh, this *Big Table* has a short novel by Kerouac, *Old Angel Midnight*, that's never been printed in hard covers or reprinted anywhere.

It hasn't? Chris says.

My blood sings. Excerpts from *The Naked Lunch*. Two excerpts from Edward Dahlberg. He just died. Hm! How much?

It says . . . $6.

No, *Hyde, don't*. I'll take it!

And, reader, I did.

Fred Bass whisks by. You don't need me to show you the basement.

Indeed not. I thank Chris and go down three flights to the basement with its many odd areas and tucked away corners. Here Burt Britton handles and buys reviewers copies. He may know more living writers than any man on earth. He published a book of writers' self-portraits, called *Self-Portraits*, and its publication party was held at the Strand. This party may have been the greatest gathering of writing genius ever seen in one place. Had Tolstoy, Dostoevsky, and Chekhov ever shared tea one afternoon *that* would have been the greatest. Proust and Joyce once attended a dinner together—but never hit it off. Britton's party—for sheer density of genius—eclipses all American literary social events I've ever heard of—and befitted the Strand. I'm sure the bones down below felt warmed by it.

And it befit Britton, whose personal book collection, not only astounds but quite likely—in its riches—is worth the entire stock on the store's three active floors, including the rare book rooms. This makes Britton, as a book obsessive, the Hyde of Hydes and the Napoleon of Strand bibliomaniacs.

It's a disease, Burt tells me, echoing Fred. His eyes and beard have a Rasputin gleam as he lights a cigarillo.

Why do you hate biographies?

They tell me lies! You couldn't write about your own dead grandmother with any authority—not her *mind*, man—so how you gonna write about a *genius's* mind? Lemme put it this way. Faulkner sits down and reads Blotner's biography of him, not that he *would*, mind you—to Faulkner that would be an act of self-loathing in the extreme—but just for argument, say he does read Blotner (although I can't even imagine it except for punishment, say in hell)—do you think he would recognize himself? *No, no, no!* he'd cry about every page. *That's not me!* I'm not saying anything about Blotner's writing itself, you see, just about the page's content. It's absolutely impossible for a guy sixty years later to write a page about what you were thinking *half a century ago! It's ridiculous!* That's why I only read the stuff itself, not the commentaries. I don't care what others think; I want what the writer thinks. For me the rest is waste. Now, how may I help you?

How do you feel when you trudge out of these lower depths of the Strand with your two bags of books—or rather your two haunches of beef—and ride homeward in the subway undergloom—and your wife greets you coming down the hall with your two sacks like Willy Loman about to have his cheese sandwich—how do you feel?

You put it very well. But wouldn't you rather know how she feels?

I believe I know.

Doesn't take a genius.

Moving along. Do you, uh, have any books on cosmic consciousness?

Well, yes and no. He looks about. Come with me, I have my own little corner and desk back here.

My eye sharp for a doorway to the subbasement, I follow him into a mossy corner where ferns spring from a bank of earth.

In this dark corner he points to a large cardboard box. Help me lift this.

Together we strain and lift the big box onto Britton's desk. He pulls an extra chair over. Stand on this chair, he says as he steps onto his desk. He stands over the box and lifts the lid.

What's this? I ask.

Let me tell you something. When the traveler is ready, the guide will appear. Are you with me on that? You dig cosmic consciousness, right? I nod as he points into the box. I see a big five-foot-square photo of stars in clusters.

It unfolds, Burt says. The whole box unfolds. It's one big photograph in this box. I couldn't unfold it down here if I wanted to, it's too big.

Bigger than the basement?

Bigger than the Strand. There's not enough floor space in this whole building to unfold this picture. What you're looking at, right there, that's a corner of Andromeda.

I thought it looked familiar.

This is a picture of the universe. Seriously. I realize there are certain logical anomalies, such as where would you stand to take a picture of the whole universe? Where would you set the tripod? Put all that behind you. The universe itself is too big to explain, right? It's like the mind of God, the Big Writer in the Sky—if you believed in God—and all this in this box is His book. *The Book.* Now cosmic consciousness. This little pinprick down in the left corner? This is our universe, the Milky Way. This pinprick. Now, you ask about cosmic consciousness and I ask, For how far out? Does it take in this whole box, or just the Milky Way? Maybe out here, where I'm pointing, or way down in the box, cosmic consciousness doesn't reach, right? Why should it? There aren't any humans deep in the box, or even in Andromeda. What do you think?

My brain feels displaced. I seem to be thinking through my testicles, where thought is born. Where did you get this?

I'd rather not say. The guy who gave it to me—a Manhattan writer of no great means or income—is getting ready to jump into the box. This box. He's leaving us, in a manner of speaking, although he'll always be close to the Strand. We care for our own. And I can say no more about that.

He wants to store this with you?

It's a gift outright. He won't need it any longer. I'm taking it home.

You have a truck?

That's not the problem. The problem is, I have no room for another book. Not one this size. But it is, as I say, more or less the mind of God. How can I resist it?

And why should you, Burt? Oh, who published it?

I know what you're thinking. I'm ahead of you on this. But there's only one copy.

Does Fred know about this?

Have I asked you any personal questions? I'm not breaking any laws. My real problem is my wife.

I wouldn't want to ask any personal question, Burt. But how

will she feel about this new trophy?
    It will be very hard on the both of us.
    How do you mean?
    I see no other way.
    Other than what?
    I'll have to move her out.

According to Esquire, *Donald Newlove is one of the most underrated writers in America. The Strand remainders his books.*

Rhapsody for Drunkspeare

Pieces from *Those Drinking Days: Myself and Other Writers*, 1981

The Golden Age wound down and *Esquire* lost its glow. On first looking back and gathering the articles for this book, I found only first drafts ripped out of my typewriter and sent off to one magazine or another and published. It has given me deep pleasure to give them swing arrangements here and bring out feelings lost in haste. I polished those first versions as well as I could, given the hustle of magazine work and the limits of typing. [That very sentence you just read went through seven or eight revisions on my laptop—revisions maddening on my old Underwood when correcting fluffed phrases and idiot sentence structure and typos.] Now those published drafts offer me themes for joyful inventions and variations like those of Alberto Pestalozza for his cornet masterworks "Ciribiribin" and "The Carnival of Venice," pieces made rapturous by the trumpet of Harry James—who during his own golden age created fiery swing arrangements of Pestalozza classics but never blew them the same way twice. By 1980 I'd published four novels and at fifty-two had little income other than from book-reviewing at bottom dollar. But I'd found the new world of sobriety and so chose to write up my drinking story. In writing *Those Drinking Days: Myself and Other Writers* (1981) it became clear that my whole life—even before birth!—swam in alcohol. I was born in alcohol, raised in alcohol, and thought its glow life at its most wonderful. As it may have been, here and there. But it caught up with me, as I tell in the few pages that follow. In my incarnation as

Drunkspeare, I'm just burying my father at a country graveyard and drop some lyrics onto his casket as the box goes down—verses I think Tolstoyan with self-analysis:

So my father dies and I shoosh down sherry and drain the last elbow of brandy and set flight to my death-lyrics to him. Or croakings. But, now sober and looking back, why be so hard on that young mist-swimmer, my other self? Well, because his ghost still lives, I get hard whiffs of those old feelings, the amber moments in sherry, the allure of release like woodsmoke in my veins. My Drunkspeare stops me on the street, his fixed grin saying, One last drink, Don, one last one. Remember the lift that made your knees weak? And then the ghost of chemical ego offers some gigantic destiny in the clouds which I deserve but have been denied. He will bring down the wild goose of the perfect four-liner and hand it to me on the west wind. I am the April drunk, I bubble with old moods—under gray skies the first roses droop and burn. My eyes mist. A drink, to lock into this mood, stay fixed. My mouth pools, greedy for chemical hope, the old tastes of malt and hops, the popped cork and sniff that pierces. My Drunkspeare wants his body back to smell and taste with. And say some tidal frustration, a really baffling defeat, pricks on exactly the right nerve and hairpins into a drink? With the first breath of bourbon, Drunkspeare rushes up my nose and is home. That unholy ghost is back, ready to spur me to brilliance. No squawking, he tells me, this will be good for you. And I agree. It's so good. Why fight? Let go and enjoy yourself. And after a few ounces, the old tunes wake up, that grandeur of jingling anguish, the lick and shimmer of language, the heartbreak at the core of things. I breathe with purpose and well with clear energies. Aerial, I settle down, ready for the hard joys of writing, the kick down the playing field. Follow the ball, Don, I warn myself, let's not be excessive. But within two sentences my spirit sways and aches, and I am borne downriver on buoyancy and pain. I strive to breathe each phrase. Each syllable has its germ of light. Sentences eddy with insights, then swerve dangerously—but I follow the sunsparks. What a rhythm I'm into! Let it build, don't look back. A paragraph swells. I burst with bliss and yet am all nerves that it won't come out right. I keep at it but the stream bends. Where did that thought go I was following? Is it lost? I try to force it back with a cheek slap and pinch my nose. As I head for the cold water tap for a facial, I turn to stone, the thought leaps into my mouth and I rush to my desk. The keys jam. But I get it down and sit back. Does it really follow the sentence before? The day darkens. A right verb dies, flattened by a moved comma. Some filigree melts. A cadence falls short of the beat. Now I write despite fading buoyancy, turn on the lamps, study the page-glare. Look back. My lift drains. Here is a cold Latin root I want Englished, always rewarding dictionary work—but I'm tired. Still looking back, I go stale. This is it, I'm stuck at retightening unstrung sentences if I want this paragraph tuned fit as a Rolls. Something chokes and suddenly I'm all over the page fighting breakdowns. Heartfelt words turn sticky. I go to clipboard and move to my rocker. Soon, false starts entwine the margins, inserts bear inserts, words crawl everywhere and curl upside-down over the top margin, phrases hang from spidery lines leading up and down into smudge. And I sense massive gaps ahead. Time for a refill, Don! Refreshed, I dump and scrape out phrases but racing thoughts spurt uncurbed, the page smears, similes mismatch, the big spark dulls. I loll in my chair, shout at myself for strength. Sit back for the big overview of a hairline crack leading to a meddlesome speck so stupid I'm breathless. The work it means! But I sit at my desk once more, typing myself dry, wringing my spirit stiff, and even after that go on—fibers parched, brain glaring, gambling in ingenuity, ghost-weaving into the night.

My trunk is stuffed to the lid with dead novels in manuscript, wine dreams that became forced marches, each more painful to write than the last—or more chemically joyous. A mania for originality grips me and the cost is clear before I begin each book: it will be unpublishable. This is still possible in the Fifties and Sixties, even necessary—to keep style sacred. Avoid the gray grist of the undead, the genre moneymakers at their grinding. A breakthrough will come. But I need strength to keep originality alive. Much sacrifice, too. Nothing and no one can become so dear that I waver and sell out. I need a very rich voice for my flights.

O bird of the bitter bright grey golden dawn!

I need a heavy mist of originality to veil my shortcomings. Let each sentence gleam deep as amber, glow green as a horsefly, shine like nicked lead. Wash grandly with Shakespearean bliss—over big clumps of large and meaningful pauses—toward Promethean periods. World conquerors must be fearless. And genius helps. My worst flaw: I have no genius, or the guided rapture of genius, no gift for ideas, only golden uplift or grimness and a need to give my life meaning through the glory of words alone. Even worse for a writer, I have no power to invent stories—just desire and heartache—and strain to boost endings hovering on a cat smile. Boy, I admire Keats and Thomas Wolfe, I mean urgently. Their burnings and overflowings help me hide my dumb endings. I feel stupid, never on top of my story, driven to blinding originality and making speech do the work of plot. So I sip beer and work at my flower arrangements out of Keats and Wolfe, not knowing my stories lack spine and focus. I trust in heartbreak.

All my set-pieces are Turner sunsets. I believe in divine sensibilities. Let readers say, He writes like an angel!

* * *

I am now almost two-hundred-and-fifty pounds, red-faced, losing my hair, given to cankers and bleeding gums, pissing so often I use the kitchen sink instead of the toilet down the hall. I find my teeth and nails loosening, am a victim of boils, my eyes are pink, tired, dry and scratchy and the lids stick together with sandy infection when I sleep. My ears ring and are supersensitive to any scrape or screech. My pores give off a staleness no soap can stanch, my crotch and privates are forever raw and cracked. I've lost the hair off my shins and pubis, my bellybutton stinks and I shave my armpits to no avail. My nose enlarges and capillaries split, the insides of my ears are raw from flaking, my taste buds wear smooth at the rear and grow apart up front so that I oversalt everything and can awaken before breakfast only with a tablespoon of salty red-hot pepper sauce. My skin erodes in the creases and rubs off in balls, I have a relentless belch for years from an ulcer, a liver that tries to flip out of me and die somewhere. Wine gas eats a hole in my bathrobe and leaves shitty shorts, I have breath that even I can't stand, sweaty cold soles and shoes I hide under the bed or into a closet if I have a girl overnight. I gasp during any kind of work and cannot get a full breath even while typing. I begin waking up nights on the floor having convulsed off of my floor mattress, wine trots are common and many hours spent near tears trying to wring out my bowels on the toilet, my pulse clogs and dribbles, false angina in my upper left chest comes and goes, someone is going to shoot me in my rocker so I move it away from the front window, but I have a waking dream for ten years of my brain exploding on impact. I lie unable to wake up but not asleep while strange men move about my kitchen and living room—they aren't there. I cannot sit comfortably in any position, I smell of stale semen between my weekly or biweekly baths, my gut bubbles day and night and I try to overfeed it to sleep. I have a two-year sinus cold and flu attacks that lay me out near death, I am hoarse and keep grenadine and lime syrups and pastilles for my hack, my memory self-destructs on the phone and I hang up wondering whom I've talked with or what arrangements we've made. I often cry out "I'm coming!" when no one has knocked and I answer or hear the phone ring when it is long gone for nonpayment. I feel fungoid and sexually impotent for two years, I sleep poorly and keep a pot by my bed in case I can't make the sink. I hear people laughing while I try to read, and ring with metallic sounds that echo, my over-swollen brain rolls liquidly in my skull. I get dizzy rising from chairs or picking up a handful of spilled coins—must I mention mere headaches and hangovers, my bloody morning shaves with safety razors, the mental fog that has me leaning on the table trying to remember my middle name, my age, or where I just laid down my glasses—my rage over a dropped spoon or lost paper lying before me on my desk or the endless drinking glasses snapping to pieces in the sink—my poor handling of kitchen knives—and the strange yellow bruises that wander up and down my arms and biceps, my harsh nerves and weird fugue states on paralyzing gruesome images of loved ones, the living dead people standing around my bed for hours on end—they're worth two mentions—and just normal things everybody has like wanting to sob all the time, especially intense over the sunset beaches and bathers in vodka ads, divorced wife and kid—any lost piece of cake or life or unearned joy as a pretext for just letting go with a thirty-minute screamer on the couch—and such clinical loneliness that my cat talks to me. When this happens one morning I think I've had a breakthrough on the language of animals and can't wait to test my powers on a dog. Loneliness? I sprayed my icebox firetruck red and pasted it solid with a collage of breasts. When I filled it tight with big green sweating quarts of ale I'd embrace it in a sex act. I had eleven cats and kittens and they all died in a two-week plague. I tried to hammer the last suffering big one to death on my roof ledge but its head was solid bone and so I threw it still alive six flights down into an empty lot where it squirmed with a broken back until dead—an image never to leave me. Music corkscrewed from my bedroom wall—music I seemed to have written. Until my middle thirties I'd detested fantasy and lying to myself, then one night I gave in and was lost, allowing myself any sweet dream under my roving finger palps. During better times I took two hundred acid trips, stocked hash, grass, speed, peyote, psilocybin, and kept a moon of opium like ground figs in my icebox. Barren of drugs, I'd grind up morning-glory seeds from the hardware store, down them hulls and all with wine—they were hallucinogenic in those days (no longer)—then sit for hours in night winds under a hard bright moon and loony as a June poet watch blue clouds unshadow Tompkins Square Park. And much, much more. I was a universe of unrecognized symptoms, fighting down wine, throwing up through my nose. Why go on? Let's get to my real life—although I don't deny I had some time in heaven as a drunk, even after the booze got to me, which was fairly early, fifteen or so—or maybe I should date it from a blackout under a bridge at seventeen and coming to under traffic with more traffic passing below me—no idea how I got there. Oh, the date doesn't matter. I denied it all the way.

The example of a fellow drunk, whom I thought the greatest living poet and who had joined a fellowship of recovering drunks, got me into the same fellowship. It took five years of slips for me at last to sober up. In part it came about the day I returned a ten-year harvest of stolen books and records to the Donnell Library, paid my fine, and then tried to turn to a nameless Higher Power.

That night in bed I faced my last embarrassment with prayer. My trouble had always been that I felt like a fake when praying, and had been too self-aware for a natural flow of thoughts. I'd no sooner get on my knees than I'd blush at the dumbness of what I was doing. I prided myself on my brains, detested sentimentality, was a badger for logic, a perfectionist about everything—you may have noticed that—and these attitudes stiffened as I'd try to speak simply to a Higher Being I sensed was guiding me. I could not escape *me*. So I got into bed, having said the Lord's Prayer, and tossed about in my failure. My sponsor's face rose before me and I said Bless Emery. Another face from the fellowship table arose. I said Bless Tom. Then another, Bless Jeff. Bless Helene. Bless Jack. Bless Euell. And I went around the table, naming and blessing each member into his face. Then I blessed my dead friends. My mother and sister and each family member, all the members of my wives' families. Like mushrooms more faces popped up demanding blessing, and I was soon into members at many fellowship meetings. The faces were backing up, but I named each one in a blessing. At least a half hour went by of intense blessing, an endless rosary of faces, and I was nowhere near exhausted of drunks on the mend and other friends. I've got to stop this and get to sleep, I gotta get up in the morning! But the faces poured in unstoppably and I was too fearful to leave anyone out who asked. And yet the very plenitude of faces kept me so gladdened at the sight of each rounded, smiling head with its eyes looking into mine that I lay tearstained with openhearted prayer, no mask, no personality, only a direct pipeline of blessings from my Higher Power to my friends in the Marines and Air Force, Paul and his wife Marian, my childhood friends, my old fellow reporters on the Jamestown *Sun*, my friends in publishing and reviewing, on and on and on—you can't withhold a blessing if someone smiles at you in a dream of prayer.

Acknowledgments

Thanks to the following for their generous financial support which helped to defray some of this publication's production costs:

Thomas Young Barmore Jr, Matthew Michael Barry,
Brad Bigelow (NeglectedBooks.com), Matthew Boe,
Brian R. Boisvert, Scott Chiddister, Eric L. Collette,
Christopher Ty Cooper, Joshua Cooper,
Malcolm & Parker Curtis, Pier Filippo d'Acquarone,
Curtis B. Edmundson, Aaron Finch, E Gaustad,
GMarkC, Damian Gordon, Everett Haagsma,
Aric Herzog, Tom Hochman, Dave Holets,
Fred W Johnson, Jacob H Joseph, Mark Lamb,
David Leiman, Nick Long, Elizabeth Lynch, Jim McElroy,
Donald McGowan, Jack Mearns, William Messing,
Scott Murphy, Michael O'Shaughnessy, Takisha Parks,
Andrew Pearson, Travis Pelkie, Judith Redding,
David W. Sanderson, K. Seifried, Bill Shute,
Yvonne Solomon, Ethan Stahl, David Streitfeld,
Threemoons, Elisa Townshend, Tim Tucker, Ed Vosik,
Elizabeth Weitzman, Isaiah Whisner, Charles Wilkins,
Nancy Y, The Zemenides Family, and Anonymous

www.ingramcontent.com/pod-product-compliance
Lightning Source LLC
LaVergne TN
LVHW031605060526
838201LV00063B/4740